INTERNATIONAL COLLABORATION IN WEAPONS AND EQUIPMENT DEVELOPMENT AND PRODUCTION BY THE NATO ALLIES: TEN YEARS LATER — AND BEYOND

ATLANTIC SERIES

A collection of studies related to the North Atlantic Treaty Organization

No. 11

International Collaboration in Weapons and Equipment Development and Production by the NATO Allies: Ten Years Later — and Beyond

ALEXANDER H. CORNELL

NATO Fellow, 1979-80

March 6th, 1982

For Frederick H. Hartmann,
Professor, Scholar, Author,
Naval Officer and Authority
on Global Strategy and Politics.
A true professional whom I am
proud to have as teacher, colleague
and friend, With appreciation,
Alexander H. Cornell

1981

MARTINUS NIJHOFF PUBLISHERS

THE HAGUE/BOSTON/LONDON

Distributors:

for the United States and Canada

Kluwer Boston, Inc.
190 Old Derby Street
Hingham, MA 02043
USA

for all other countries

Kluwer Academic Publishers Group
Distribution Center
P.O. Box 322
3300 AH Dordrecht
The Netherlands

Library of Congress Catalog Card Number: 81-51953

ISBN 90-247-2564-X (this volume)
ISBN 90-247-3001-5 (series)

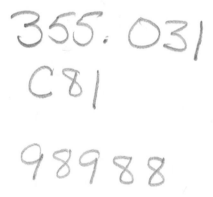

PRINTED IN THE NETHERLANDS

Contents

Preface

This study of perhaps the single most important issue facing the North Atlantic Treaty Organization in its thirtieth year — international military standardization in weapons, equipment and doctrine — was begun in 1968 because of the author's deep concern over the fate of the greatest alliance ever attempted and its effects on the future of the free world and individual freedom and dignity.

An initial analysis of the situation was made in 1969, which contained hypotheses and some predictions based on past successes believed appropriate to the next decade. The decade ending in 1979 bore them out and further proved the feasibility, capability and viability of collaborative standardization programmes and projects.

Again in the 1969-1979 period, distinct, workable, highly intricate, difficult, but *successful* endeavors were accomplished, and improved methods of collaboration were exhibited. Nevertheless, even with a wealth of hard-earned successes in weapons, equipment and doctrinal programmes and projects as examples, the entire programme or thrust toward IMS (International Military Standardization) remained a series of ad hoc efforts which kept the programme going but at about "dead-center." That seems to have changed in 1979.

Some new, exciting and visionary plans and actions are emerging now as NATO's fourth decade begins, fanned by a relentless, increasingly powerful common threat, that could result in the 1980s being the real turning point during which the goal of armaments superiority in kind, quality and numbers can be realized by the Alliance.

If this condensed, organized record of what has happened and what is possible can contribute in some measure to a clarification of the total effort, it will serve its intended purpose.

Acknowledgements

This study lays no claim to invention of any kind but rather is an analysis, a sorting-out and clarification of some monumental collaborative efforts and some achievable goals, plans, and actions which have been codified and generalized upon from expert sources.

My principal acknowledgements are to those dedicated and able members of NATO, both those who join and must leave as ordered and especially to those permanent members of Headquarters. These have been men and women who were and are unique members of a special kind of truly international-minded officials whose contributions will one day receive the recognition so richly deserved from those who inherit a free world.

There are dozens of individuals deserving of such recognition here and now, but this compact study permits mentioning but a few (in alphabetical order and without reference to position). The names of these friends and experts remain indelible in my mind: Mr. David Facey, Mr. Donald Floyd, Gen. H. F. Zeiner Gundersen (NA), Muriel Howells, Mr. Peter Jenner, Mr. P. Longé, Sec. Gen. Joseph M. A. H. Luns, Col. Daniel Malone (U.S.A.), Dr. A. Tyler Port, B. Gen. P. Kavendish (BA), Gen. William K. Knowlton (U.S.A.), Mr. John Stone, Dr. John B. Walsh, Dr. Fernand Welter, and Mr. P. Woirin.

The list of those outside NATO, in the U.S. and member countries would require pages. The outstanding advice and assistance received from secretarial/ministerial/senatorial levels, civilian and military programme and project manager levels, professors and other experts on the subject has been acknowledged to each individually.

For all of you, a salute and lasting admiration for being the real contributors to mankind's progress toward freedom and peaceful coexistence. You are proving that the cooperative, permissive, consultative give-and-take of free but allied sovereign nations is not only possible but achievable. Thanks too, to my daughter, Mrs. Alexandra D. Burlingham, for a superb job of typing and editing. It is fateful that her mother, Elizabeth, now deceased, performed the same tasks for my first publication on the subject.

This analysis was the direct result of a grant made possible by a NATO fellowship award, and as a recipient, I can only hope it is worthy of the trust and choice of the greatest successful organization yet conceived to perpetuate a free world and the dignity and worth of mankind.

Chapter 1

Introduction

The Approach

This analysis is one made ten years after an original one of 1969 by the author and attempts a composite, orderly, succinct yet thorough review of the record of international military weapons and equipment standardization by the NATO Allies. It addresses the crucial problem of where collaboration must lead if the Alliance is to persevere.

It commences with a chapter on authoritative-based observations, summarizing some basic facts and the status of the threat to NATO, the place of strategic nuclear and SALT agreements, and the prospects of a defenseless Europe and North America. The severity of the situation dictates the actions dealt with later.

Next, a brief reexamination of the original 1969 analysis, hypotheses, and predictions drawn from that in-depth study of three distinct examples, the Atlantique long-range maritime patrol aircraft, the F-104 G Starfighter aircraft, and the HAWK missile, will introduce organizational and managerial lessons learned from them.

This will be followed by a chapter on the 1979 analysis which again highlights three major distinct weapons systems and their similar organizational and managerial approaches — namely, the Roland ground-to-air missile, the F-16 NATO combat fighter aircraft, and the NATO Airborne Early Warning and Control System (AWACS).

Next will follow a chapter containing a concise examination and summary of thirty years of collaboration successes and failures, sorted out into two somewhat artificial but, hopefully, more useful major categories for both experts and other readers; (1)

1

Projects, Programmes and Weapons Consortia, and (2) Organizational/Membership/Institutional Structures, and Concepts and Modes of Collaboration.

The extent and range of both areas is quite considerable and should serve to reinforce the recommendation for a total, coordinated effort. Being explicit about them and clarifying the often-overlooked range, depth, and sheer number of ad hoc, as well as the more institutionalized, accomplishments should assist in clarifying similarities, objectives, results, and also reveal duplication of efforts. NATO-sponsored or "mantled" organizations will be clearly delineated to highlight such successes, as will NATO's present sponsorship role, the benefits and achievements of consultative and flexible approaches, and yet a certain lack of sufficient authority (and some structure) to bring about earlier total collaboration.

A fourth chapter will examine and argue the realities of some myths, half-truths, and real, imagined or "deliberate" arguments for and against collaboration, stemming from national, economic, industrial, business, political, military, "authoritative," and other sources.

The fifth chapter will be an assessment and forecast of the entire collaborative effort, posing and answering key questions, among them those posed in Tom Callaghan's penetrating study of "NATO's management orphans" and giving other answers to problems of greater collaboration. It will address the key question of collaboration between and among *unequals*, some reasons for a stronger NATO, and the fate of the Atlantic Community as determined by the degree of present and future military collaboration. Cost-effectiveness and comparable advantage, "creeds" which we have pursued as economists and analysts, will be put in their proper place when compared to the possibilities of growth, strength, and *survival.*

The seventh chapter will attempt to compile and coordinate those parts of the most feasible plans put forth to date in order to provide a balanced, attainable, combined blueprint for decision and action now and in the immediate future. The chapter will challenge all free-world member nations and others who still believe in the value of the individual to adopt the changes and modifications required now as part of their philosophy, policies, agreements, "common sense," modes, institutions, structures, requirements, and managerial practices. In the final chapter, the observation is made that the initiatives and structures, I believe, *could* be attained using existing treaty and organizational structures, *if* agreed to in principle, practice, or if only in spirit. Or they could spring from another foundation — a new treaty which recognizes the enormous and complex factors involved and incorporates them into a compact which may well require relinquishing some small measure of "sovereignty." The alternatives could be a drift toward national anarchy, a complete and disastrous change in the world balance of power, "blackmail," defeat, or perhaps its unacceptable equal, "preemptive surrender. " It is time to decide.

A set of seven important appendices is also included which afford, among other basic information, the latest achievements in structures and major planning programmes now underway, as described and reported on by those directly involved.

The Dilemma

After a year of intense research on the subject of international military standardization and collaboration by NATO, I am pleased to report that only two of over two hundred authoritative sources and recognized experts are opposed to the goals of weapons standardization, and even those two are *for* interoperability. All the others, with varying degrees of concern, strongly urge as much commonality as possible. With such overwhelming support, it is somewhat incredible that their recommendations have only been partially realized. The reasons for limited progress are well-known and range from outright "national sovereignty" on through to "common sense" as unsolvable obstructions. While good common sense *is* common sense, perhaps it would be better in our predicament if it yielded to more philosophy and some *uncommon* sense if the Alliance is to persevere.

To add to the sum of commonly held philosophy in the dozens of interviews, seminars, and other personal contacts made during the research, not a single individual or group was found who did not agree that freedom and individual human dignity were worth fighting for by the last of the free societies. Yet, right now, on the eve of their impending loss, we still *act* differently as individuals,

3

groups and nations and cling to beliefs in crippling national sovereignty (at best an illusion), senseless competition, wasteful duplication, old-fashioned economic and business arguments, political jealousies, pride, and a retreat into inaction because "common sense" precludes any new efforts for a real alliance, because our own man-made obstacles are "insurmountable."

While I know now that intelligent people need no further convincing of the case for collaboration and standardization and that it has been proven as perhaps the most important single, immediate need for Alliance success, this analysis and its generalizations attempt to bring the problem into correct focus and further to bring the total record and the present danger to the citizenry. I fear that those of us already convinced of what must be done have been guilty of preaching that conviction mostly to ourselves — i.e., "preaching to the choir."

Let me begin by stating that nowhere have I found a better way to bring about a reversal of undesirable characteristics we evidence as groups and nations and to move immediately toward an *interdependent security* than in the area of common, less-costly weaponry and equipment. Ten years ago, commonality projects were placed in the hands of ad hoc groups and committees. Today, they are the main event, the most important segment of the total effort, and deserve the agreement, structures and authority to be done right and be done right now.

Economically, growth-wise, population-wise, technology-wise, production-wise, politically, culturally — in all these and many more assets — the NATO Alliance surpasses the Soviet bloc by very healthy percentages. Why, then, have we failed to do so in so critical an area of modern weaponry and men-under-arms as Europe? Are we automatically doomed as democracies to failure when faced with more efficient totalitarianism? Can it be that, all other reasons acknowledged, we lack the will power to carry out a goal of survival in a free world when we have the means to do so? Are we unable to plan and act as an entity? Let us hope not. It is exactly because of all our available resources in a specialized field such as weaponry, that nothing is impossible; everything is possible. It is clearly an issue of making up our democratic-socialistic-capitalistic minds and hearts to do so. Many of those who lament about the problem gravitate to the argument of

4

inequalities among coalitions or member nations as the root cause. If so, why hasn't it impeded weapons superiority in the Soviet bloc as well? The quite obvious answer is, of course, that inequalities, if dictated to, can easily be overcome. Why can they not also be overcome by people of intelligence who wish to stay within democratic means? One answer to our inequalities problem is to admit they exist and recognize reality, and to insure that the unequals get their fair share of benefits and burden and are brought up to levels of equality as far as is possible. The best way to reach real "equality" here and now is simply to trust in one another and to accept the fact of proportional *sharing*, both in benefits and responsibilities.

Some Basic Facts

Among dozens of others that could be examined, let us just consider four basic facts. First fact: The Soviet bloc threat has *intensified*. Many experts believe it will overtake NATO nations' weapons technology by 1983 or 1984, just as it has surpassed NATO in quantitative weaponry and men-under-arms. Or, one may believe General Zeiner Gundersen, Chairman of NATO's Military Committee, who stated flatly in the October 1979 *NATO Reivew* that it is not merely Soviet *growth* versus a struggling West trying to maintain its *status quo* — an alarming situation in itself — but that:

> the most serious aspect is the rapid increase in the proportion of new and modern equipment in the Soviet inventory as old equipment is phased out. In Alliance forces the average age is increasing. Thus, the Soviets are implementing improvements in technology at a comparably faster rate, and from the technological point of view, may have to be considered as having achieved parity with the West.

Another recognized top expert, Dr. Malcom R. Currie, at the time head of the U.S. Department of Defense Research, Development, Test and Evaluation, offered this civilian estimate in February 1976:

> given an extrapolation of current trends, and without appropriate action on our part, it is my judgement that, on balance, and including a combination of quality and quantity, the Soviet Union can achieve dominance in deployed military technology in the 1980s.

Thus while one may choose yesterday, today, tomorrow, or the next few years, it is upon us. The Warsaw Pact has the most powerful armed force ever seen in peacetime in Europe.

Here are just one week's headlines and feature reports chosen at random from the local United States newspapers and periodicals during June 1979:

"CIA Challenged on Soviet Arms — CIA Analysts Testified Thursday That Soviet Military Expenditure Are Running 50 Percent Higher Than U.S. Outlays to Continue at Least Through 1985" (UPI).

"Private Analyst Disputes CIA Statistics, Claims They Were at Least 50 Percent *Too Low*" (AP).

"The Agency (CIA) Is Forced to Admit a Previous Miscalculation in 1970 Soviet Defense Estimates" (AP).

"British Admiral of the Fleet Sees Soviet Threat to NATO's Resupply" (AP).

"Soviet Navy Too Big for Defense, Is Claim" (UPI).

"Soviet SS20 Missile Terrifies all Europe" (UPI).

"Russia Catches Up With 4.4 Millions Under Arms, Military Budget of $162 Million, 1,477 ICBM's and 1,015 Submarine Launched Missiles, 45,000 Tanks . . ." (*Newsweek*).

When wishful thinkers rely on technological superiority, they should look too toward that quiet, almost unspeakable race for superiority in "space warfare," which could make strategic missiles and SALT agreements merely academic subjects, and reinforce soviet weapons of political power, military power, and blackmail. While it may not be necessary to match the Soviets man for man, weapon for weapon, the Alliance must have the physical ability "to make the ultimate consequences of aggression incalculable," as General Zeiner Gundersen said in an address at Rhode Island College on April 23, 1980. It appears, from what has been released to date, that the Soviets are enjoying several years headstart in satellite, laser, and other powerbeam weaponry. The West's technological lead has been eroded.

Second fact: NATO has persisted until now in relying on nuclear deterrence and has considered conventional forces more of a "demonstration of common commitment." Our forces are the proof, and even that "demonstrable strength" has suffered from lack of numbers, commonality, standardization or even interoperability. If we are to catch up after too many years of delay, more real money must be spent, uncontrolled duplication must cease, and a new approach of families of plans, families of weapons, common doctrine, and increased national sacrifices must be commenced *now*. We have lost twenty-five compounded years of headway by the loss of an average of $10 billion a year through duplication. Latest estimates are $14 billion a year lost to NATO strength by the same duplication. The best authority on this, in the absence of more concrete data and accounts is Thomas Callaghan, the dedicated scholar of NATO, whose landmark monograph in 1976 observed, "the past quarter century has witnessed an incalculable waste of tens of billions of dollars of American and European defense resources — manpower, money, energy, material, and structure. NATO has *not* provided the maximum defense possible for the resources available or the resources expended."[1]

Third fact: Secretary General Luns proclaimed this one as clearly as anyone ever has in his address to the Air League in London in October 1974. "There is no member country in the NATO Alliance which relies primarily on its own strength for its national security." European members of NATO know this without question. Speaking for the United States alone, it takes little expertise to see that the "ocean barrier" which has been relied on in the past has become merely another weapons platform. There is no doubt in this amateur historian's mind that the threat does *not* stop at the Rhine, the English Channel or the Atlantic Ocean. The United States, overpowered or immobilized by any means, is the ultimate prize for the Soviets, just as it was in Hitler's master plan.

Fourth fact: That which was considered a side issue ten and more years ago — namely, that cooperative weapons projects, standardization, and interchangeability could be given to ad hoc committees and groups to accomplish — has now become the main event. This has come about not only because of the first three facts alone, but by the realization that to overtake the

1. Callaghan, Thomas A., Jr. *U.S./European Economic Cooperation in Military and Civil Technology*. The Center for Strategic and International Studies, Georgetown University, Sept. 1975, p. 7.

Soviet bloc in weaponry and related capabilities, a *macro*-economic, *macro*-technological, all-out cooperative *military, industrial* and *political* coordinated effort is imperative, starting *now.*

Full treatment of the facts could add a dozen more imperatives. More experts can be added and quoted on the same theme and facts. For example, General Alexander Haig concluded upon the end of his command as SACEUR (Supreme Allied Commander, Europe), "the challenge . . . is clearly within the *capabilities* of the West . . . The key question in this new strategic environment is whether the West will *recognize* the new era of Atlantic interdependence and establish the necessary priorities to achieve the essential concert of effort and resources." Gardner L. Tucker, while Assistant Secretary General for Defense Suppport, was equally cognizant of the new era when, in 1975, he prophesied that ". . . it will, however, be necessary that throughout the next decade a sustained firm commitment to be effective, NATO standardization *permeate* national defense establishments if progress is to be commensurate with the *gravity* of the *need."* (Italics mine). His present successor, John B. Walsh, has underscored the same commitment and added during a recent interview the apt perception that, ". . . the personal touch and trust between and among those who *believe,* and the need to arrive at *procedures* which will permit *all* people to work within them, is mandatory." These statements are a suitable springboard to move ahead to the lessons of organization, management, and selfless cooperation and equity which must be heeded in order to reverse our present condition of inadequacy of forces in Europe. These statements focus on the need for real progress in what are called by many the "pivotal years".

The Purpose

United States Senator Sam Nunn, well-versed in the military status of the U.S. and NATO, has stated flatly that we must insure the defense of *Europe* without "reliance upon the nuclear crutch." That crutch is in jeopardy now amd most certainly will be in the future after SALT II's fate. He was making the case for redressing the need for conventional forces. For if the "crutch" is removed, stalemated, lowered, or whatever, a new political threshold, backed by theatre nuclear and conventional arms, will be added to the decision-making arena. Can it possibly be that the NATO nations and the United States wish *not* to be defended? Can it be that we subconsciously are ready to be blackmailed or defeated because the counter-effort is unthinkable? Are arms still vital to foreign policy or do we feel this phase of our policy can be allowed to atrophy and that a benevolent superpower can be trusted in the world of tomorrow? I think not. But if so, it is time to review the lessons of history and the meaning of power.

So much for the hortatory warnings, problem identifications, and grim facts. They have been far more completely documented elsewhere than in this brief overview. It is time to turn to what has been learned that may guide us to some immediate solutions.

The lessons learned certainly are not entirely the author's discoveries, and several solutions have been offered by experts from every quarter, but they need to be sorted out, to be made clear enough to eliminate confusion, agreements, and be convincing enough to stimulate action. There are *no* insurmountable obstacles. Let it be flatly stated at this point that both ten-year analyses, plus recent initiatives, indicate that NATO is *off* the dead-center position of ten years ago and is making headway. It is toward attaining more complete momentum that this analysis is directed.

Chapter 2

The 1969 Analysis of Collaboration —
A Starting Point

A comparison of the decade ending about 1969 and the decade ending 1979 has revealed some startling similarities between the two insofar as collaboration in weaponry is concerned. Even the individual projects and programmes themselves are impressive in their relationships as members of families of weapons and in their organizational and managerial success. But going beyond those similarities, which some interpret as a lack of real progress or as remaining of "dead-centre," one can discern a definite ground-swell, a perceptable trend and growing momentum toward more and better collaboration. The creation and goals of but one initiative, the Long-Term Defense Programme (LTDP) and all it embraces, is a splendid sign of forward movement. It is treated in the text and in Appendix D.

Hypotheses and Findings

As stated earlier, in 1969 the author selected three significant weapons programmes for analysis: the Breguet Atlantique Long-Range Maritime Patrol Aircraft; the HAWK Ground-to-Air Missile System; and the F-104 G Starfighter aircraft. At the time, Bullpup, NADGE, Sidewinder, and Mark 44 torpedo could also have served as fine examples of successful codevelopment and coproduction projects. But the three selected revealed significant organizational and managerial experiences to be typical of all kinds. The three comparative organizations of 1969 are shown in Figure 2.1.

In 1979 the selection of AWACS, Airborne Early Warning Aircraft; Roland, Ground-to-Air Missile weapon; and the F-16 All-purpose Combat Aircraft, were in most aspects direct follow-ons and complements to those chosen to be analyzed in the

10

previous decade. One might be tempted to conclude that little progress had been made apart from updating previous projects, but such was not the case.

The hypotheses and prophesies made in 1969 happily were borne out by the accomplishments of the next decade. In both studies, the issue function was limited to codevelopment and coproduction, within the broader system of international logistics. The hypotheses and findings arrived at in 1969 were as follows:

1. *First Hypothesis*: International weapons codevelopment and coproduction is a viable concept of organization and management for supporting international logistics programmes and accomplishing international military standardization.

Findings: All three programmes contributed successfully to cooperative procurement of badly needed weapons and proved the efficiency and effectiveness of multinational consortia to do so. The record proved that collaborative organizations could be created and managed of a size and complexity comparable to or exceeding any unilateral one. On both the governmental and industrial sides of the endeavors, new joint policy-making bodies, top-executive units and operational, manufacturing structures were created which proved to be as workable as any massive industrial or national combinations of other than a weapons systems nature. Figure 2.1 affords an overview of the structure and similarities of policy and executive levels in the organizations, both in the national and industrial areas, even though the specific names of components differ.

Production time, economy of resources, and quality of product equalled or surpassed many national or single industry programmes and there were no cost overruns. The results were acquisitions of important, quality, costly weapons by participating members *which they would not otherwise have been able to procure alone*.

2. *Second Hypothesis*: The common and particular patterns, institutions, agreements, structures, units, experimentations and managerial techniques can be clearly identified, recorded, analyzed, and generalized about to assist further collaborative efforts.

Findings: Figure 2.1 shows the commonalities among structural levels and the authoritative positions that operational groups enjoyed, subject only to broad agreement on policy from above. What Figure 2.1 does not reveal is the remarkable record of dozens

11

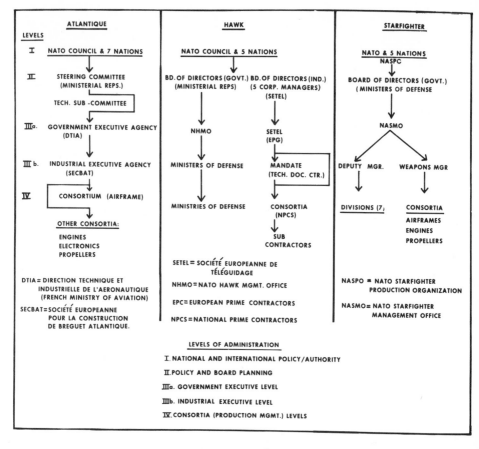

Figure 2.1. A comparative chart of programme organizations — 1969.

of obstacles surmounted such as tariffs, trade barriers, accounting differences, customs, work modes, taxes, self-interests, technical data and transmission of data, languages, as well as economic strengthening, jobs, expansion of industrial technology and reduction of the weapons technology gap, among other benefits and initiatives.

Atlantique showed uniqueness in the relative simplicity and effectiveness of its organization by the use of a going institution, the French Ministry of Aeronautics; while one of HAWK's contributions was the successful management of exceptionally complex problems inherent in a sophisticated weapons consortium. F-104 G proved that a multibillion dollar, tremendously complex and technically advanced weapons system was capable of efficient coproduction.

Some Additional Organizational and Managerial Conclusions – 1969

Without the complete study, which is not possible in a brief article, no figure can reveal other notable results of the programs.[1] Here are a few results in highly condensed form:

—The outstanding people, accomplishments, and exceptional spirit of cooperation which took place. In every case a unique understanding resulted in flexibility, tact, understanding, superb leadership, and coordination seldom found in most unilateral endeavors. The personal equation, the give-and-take of common regard for the ideas of everyone from executives to grass-roots workers, and the prevailing goodwill of men of goodwill united in a common challenge is documented in the analysis. One cannot measure such things, but intelligent people can recognize their existence as nonquantifiable ingredients of success. There proved to be a surprising amount of loyalty to mutually approved international programs.

—Another example of a specific laudatory practice was that of each nation and/or industry naming only *one* responsible person to represent them at the top policy making and executive levels. Moreover, these leaders were, for the most part, given commensurate authority by their sponsors.

—With the exception of the four other projects mentioned above during the period ending 1969, and perhaps one of the least known coproduction successes, the French 75 field gun of World War I, it was apparent that nothing like deliberate, planned coproduction

1. The 1969 analysis was released to the public, distribution unlimited, by the U.S. Department of Commerce, National Technical Information Service, Springfield, Virginia, 22161, U.S.A. It is available for purchase at cost from that source in either microfilm or printed copy, Title No. AD 727 105, Vol. 18, 1971, entitled *An Analysis of International Collaboration in the Organization and Management of Weapons Coproduction*, by Alexander H. Cornell.

13

programmes had been attempted earlier. Indeed, in retrospect, there was no real concern in the early years for commonality because of the Marshall Plan which provided most weapons for all; moreover, nuclear superiority and conventional weapons equality contributed to this as well. But times and enemies change, dictating more collaborative effort, and after a slow start, there were some marked successful cooperation efforts in the decade 1959-1969.

—To return to Figure 2.1, the organizational level similarities already have been mentioned. While differing in some degree of authority and, of course, nomenclature, there evolved a pattern of national/ industrial acceptance and guidance, followed by allowing a free-hand to the operating consortia. At the apex could be found the top policy-making boards of single member representatives, and beneath that a governmental executive agency, paralleled by an industrial executive agency. Beneath the industrial agency were typical functional components, usually organized by major producers of components of the weapon system. Where necessary, additional organizations were wisely set up to meet particular needs, such as more liaison for more intricate weapons, language and translation bodies, and document control units, to mention a few. Subcontractors fell into place beneath the major component industries and assembly organizations strategically and equitably set up.

—The common use of "groups of experts" when needed was another keystone of success.

—Both "permissive" or (outside NATO-initiated) and "institutional" (NATO-sponsored programmes) succeeded equally well. In fact and in retrospect, the permissive, encouraging, consultative approach appears to have worked very well.

—Some significant trends and principles emerged from the decade which augured well for more, but perhaps smaller, more informal, fewer-member projects begun outside of NATO. This indicated that the permissive, national-initiated projects would endure, and they did. But even then, the goal of NATO was to strive for larger, multiple-nation, big pay-off projects which could be planned sufficiently in advance to preclude the usual last-minute, ad hoc attempts. Bilateral and trilateral projects seemed to be assured of taking place and would contribute to the cause of transnational business.

14

—The 1969 study revealed NATO's role as follows:

1. NATO's role remained one of infrequent instigator and co-ordinator and also sponsor after the initiation of some projects. The fact that NATO was *there* provided the forum in which nations met, consulted, and agreed to collaborate was really its most effective contribution to standardization. Both NATO-initiated projects were successes.

2. NATO's flexibility and permissive, helpful approach was the key to bringing together nations not yet convinced that total collaboration was necessary and encouraging them to do "weapons business" with one another.

3. NATO's sponsorship, when utilized, was a meaningful, useful technique, never offensive, always discreet, contributing greatly to a successful cooperative effort.

4. NATO's dedicated and expert staff provided structural guidelines which were acceptable to industry. The staff became a permanent, increasingly expert source of information and guidance.

5. NATO's staff learned that ad hoc approaches, so often lamented by many, is still a useful learning technique. It is only wasteful if the lessons are not recorded, analyzed, and used by those who follow.

6. NATO realized it was not yet time to attempt to force any collaborative efforts, and that planning, scheduling, and institutional, structure, and doctrinal agreements were sorely needed to move forward.

7. NATO realized that as many programmes as possible should be announced, planned for, and take place under the NATO aegis in order to obtain wider participation and proper cycling of weapons systems. It was hoped to avoid unilateral efforts being carried so far that nations were reluctant to stop them, even though a combined effort would have gone much farther toward standardization, at less cost to each nation.

—There were beginning to emerge some proven managerial principles equally applicable to transnational businesses:

1. *Coordination*: As it ranks as number one, along with decision-making in private business, so too, the success of the programmes were due to excellent coordination as they developed, and also contributed to a larger, more coordinated production base in Europe. Success often leads to success and the projects set the stage for even more joint projects.

15

2. *Standardization and Economics of Scale*: Standardization should be a principle and goal for multinational, common-purpose weapons, perhaps even more so than it is for any single industry. Successful industries know that fewer models, interchangeable components and increased production mean greater profits. The HAWK success is concrete proof of the economies of scale as production steadily increased toward the agreed number of units. Standardization should be of even more concern to the military, especially where the war to be fought would be in central Europe. Economies of scale are of equal concern to participating industries and national economies, especially where a common goal and limited resources are concerned.

3. *Cooperation in Production*: The early efforts made it clear that *if* "families of weapons" could be agreed on, and the most important weapon(s) within a family were to be pursued, bigger savings and larger pay-offs would follow. The F-104 G is an example of the key weapon in the family of air-to-air combat weapons, and its follow-ons of three such light, high-performance aircraft (F-16, Jaguar, Tornado) are continuations of that approach. The principle of a family approach is sound, equitable, feasible, and inevitable if total collaboration is the goal. The term, "families of weapons," now deemed an integral part of the Long-Term Defense Programme, was used in the 1969 analysis.

4. *Common Logistical Support*: The common support which was developed to support HAWK and F-104 G became excellent examples of standardization and economies of scale of another kind — logistics. The organizations which evolved, especially for HAWK, served as models for future collaboration in the vital logistics follow-on phase of all weaponry.

Chapter 3

The 1979 Analysis of Collaboration —
The Pivotal Point

Again in 1979, as in 1969, there are excellent examples that might have been used which bore similarities to each other in organization, management, and in their acknowledged success. Among them are NICS, Sea-Gnat, Sea Sparrow, Jaguar, Tornado and Alpha Jet, each of which will be described later. NICS became a follow-on to NADGE and Jaguar and Tornado to the F-104 G. However, the three selected for in-depth study were AWACS, Roland, and the F-16.

NATO Airborne Early Warning and Control System (AWACS): A NATO Project

Choosing AWACS to analyze at this time may be a case of an amateur rushing in where even politicians fear to tread. However, in view of its importance as a turning point in "two-way street" procurements, its unique mangement structure, and its important affect on other collaborative decisions, it is considered a key example of collaboration and must be included.

Background

As early as 1974 it was learned that Warsaw Pact forces would have the capability to penetrate NATO air defenses by using low-level tactics. NATO studies since showed that an Airborne Early Warning System would be the most effective solution if radar improvements could be developed to "look down" into sea and ground clutter and isolate moving targets.

The capability to do so was demonstrated in October 1974, by the United States E-3A aircraft and led to the U.S. decision to go ahead with production.

17

In August 1975, a NATO statement of Requirements (SOR) was signed which outlined additional enhancements to incorporate into the NATO operational concept. After a review of the SOR, NATO defense ministers initiated planning efforts for a NATO AEW&C program in July 1976. There followed a Multinational Memorandum of Understanding (MMOU) on the NATO E-3A Cooperative Programme, signed on 6 December 1978. A charter of the new organization, and an Acquisition Agreement between the United States Government and the NATO AEW&C Program Management Organization (NAPMO) was in effect by May 1979, and was closely followed by a Memorandum of Agreement between the new U.S. Government Agent USAF/RDP and NATO AEW&C Programme Management Agency (NAPMA). Twelve NATO countries agreed to share aircraft acquisition and ground environment costs.

Purpose

The specific purpose of the agreements was to provide direction for the development and production of a force of 18 E-3A aircraft and associated equipment and services for NATO. In addition to the force of 18 aircraft, one E-3A main operating base and several forward operating bases, plus 11 Nimrod aircraft (British surveillance aircraft) and up to 52 ground environment interfaces were provided. The purpose, as was indicated earlier, was to provide improved warning and tracking information for battle management by NATO forces, especially low-level attacks from aircraft and missiles which could evade the ground-based NADGE system.

Costs

The number, 18, might appear somewhat misleading, but the unit cost is that of an extremely expensive, extremely sophisticated airborne surveillance platform, now estimated at $70 million each or a total of approximately $1.8 billion in 1977 dollars. Because the E-3A had been basically researched, developed, and prototyped by the U.S., an agreement on financial procedures was set up in which the U.S. share of total acquisition was $769 million in 1977 and $400 million in support costs through 1985. NATO itself would provide the remainder. The programme represents one of the largest single, commonly funded programmes ever undertaken by the Allies. It is without any doubt, a weapon the cost of which could *not* be borne by any one NATO nation.

The System

Basically, it is an E-3A (Boeing 707 airframe) aircraft like those used by the U.S. Air Force, with an advanced-pulse Doppler radar mounted to track a higher number of targets, together with data processing, communications, and other mission-related equipment. It can cover an area hundreds of miles from its position and is considered superior to the Soviet air surveillance system, now in use called Moss. The AWACS is planned to be operational in NATO in the early 1980s.

Organization and Management

Figure 3.1 summarizes the unique organization for AWACS and clearly shows NATO as the multinational head of the programme on a par with the initiating government. Further study of the organization reveals the same four basic levels found in the three 1969 models, and a carefully structured industrial complex with clear lines of communication between NATO's NAPMA and the USAF and contractors on a frequent, even day-to-day basis. The United States industries, Boeing and Westinghouse, are the prime contractors for the frame and radar; Pratt and Whitney for the engines; and Germany and Canada for the electronics (Dornier).

The two key programme direction agencies are the U.S. Air Force and NATO's NAPMA. The owners of the aircraft will be NATO; it will be manned by *all* nations under three commands — SACEUR, SACLANT, and CHINCHAN.

Problems and Offsets

It goes without saying that the cost is staggering, especially when one looks back to Atlantique at $7 million a copy and then ahead to one of possibly $70 million each. This had caused some members to be alarmed, yet they are convinced it must be mutually

19

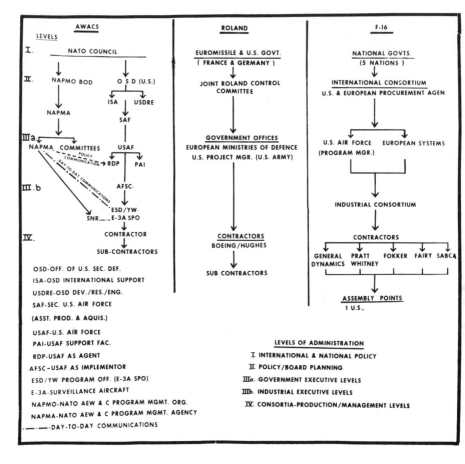

Figure 3.1. A comparative chart of programme organizations – 1979.

accomplished. But it is that very point, *necessary costs for necessary weapons*, which should serve as a primary impetus toward the goal of more collaboration, individual savings, and offsets where appropriate. The weapon, another "first" for NATO, as was Atlantique, is visible evidence of the determination and ability of the Allies to cooperate in the most complex, sophisticated, costly areas. Competition with Nimrod was a problem, as will be the offsets the U.S. has agreed to, especially with Germany, to help equalize the cost of European acceptance of another U.S.

weapon. Bad timing for introduction of the E-3A was admittedly a problem, but until NATO has the power and structure to plan ahead and schedule weapons families, etc., it was inevitable that one of the already developed weapons had to be chosen. Nevertheless, it showed the need to get away from such de facto weapons choices which by definition rule out long-range planning, scheduling, development, and controlled competition.

One who is extremely knowledgeable of AWACS, Mr. David Facey, Director of Air Defense Systems at NATO, felt that the major hurdle to overcome was the introduction of a common programme of such magnitude with far too little planning time.[1] Additionally, the ball is presently in the U.S. court to prove its pledges involving the FRG and Canada. The FRG's share of the total cost is 30.7 percent, and it has been agreed that Germany will be given $265 million in direct offsets, which still leaves $250 million to be made by U.S. procurements of German telephones and non-tactical equipment.

Summary and Postscript

Despite the poor timing (a necessity), the costs, the "choice" of a *fait-accompli* weapon system, the lack of long-range planning, the late point of entry for NATO, and the lack of other industry inputs, it is clear that these are the things which better planning and organization, better scheduling, a better treaty perhaps, but above all, better structure and authority could provide. It is significant that what one expert called a "major lost standardization opportunity" in 1977 has *not* been lost. Again, NATO's *being* there and providing the arena reveals its nonquantifiable worth. AWACS should go down in the history of collaboration as being a primary impetus for the new Long-Range Defense Programme, and hopefully, for a more authoritative role for the Alliance in the future. Both Atlantique and AWACS are the real NATO "first-borns" for each decade. Both are airborne platforms, both were selected by NATO, and both are the best for their

---

1. From an interview with Mr. David Facey, Director of Air Defense Systems, Defense Support Division, IS, NATO, on 12 October 1979.

missions. One sincerely hopes that AWACS does not suffer the sales fate of Atlantique, or that current Roland agreements and related offsets are not lived up to by the United States.

To date, the Germans have purchased over $4.5 billion worth of weapons and equipment from the United States. AWACS is very vulnerable to the attitude of Germany. For example, a member of the Bundestag recently put the offset matter squarely in place when he told the Military Committee of NATO that the U.S. military and U.S. Congress must realize that the Bundestag will not vote for Pershing II and PATRIOT as they did for AWACS *unless* there is complimentary buying of German products. Among them is Germany's insistence on U.S. adoption of the 120 mm. tank gun, German equipment and labor for installation of a new U.S./European telephone system, and the purchase of German non-tactical vehicles. Unfortunately, at this writing, the U.S. House of Representatives seems to have seen "political pressure" behind this and takes a narrow view of the two-way street — i.e., to be *only* used for standardization.

Roland — An Integrated Surface-to-Air Defense Missile: A Tri-National Project

The NATO nations, and especially the United States, have been well-aware for some time of the necessity to provide armoured units with an integrated air defense element to protect against a rapidly growing Soviet air threat. Such a weapon already existed in three nations, and it was the choice of the United States to procure and produce the Franco-German Roland weapon system. This milestone represented a "first" for the United States — the purchase of a weapon developed by its Allies. It represented, at last, the opening of the two-way street *both* ways.

Background and Participants

In Roland the U.S. Army found an acceptable weapon system, badly needed and already researched, developed, and produced by the Franco-German consortium. It was estimated that $800 million could be saved by adopting Roland. The U.S. Congress was sold on the idea of such savings in development, to say nothing of about ten years of valuable time. Unfortunately, the "Americanization" of Roland has reportedly wasted half the savings, but the adoption marks a significant milestone in the two-way street policy. The U.S. bought a weapon made in Europe. The alternative of not using Roland now could cost an amount equal to that required to develop another (Rapier?), and a loss of valuable time. To remain with the Roland can *save* ten years. At this writing, the appropriation to proceed with Roland has been extended one year by the U.S. Congress.

Roland was developed by a consortium of SNI Aerospatiale of France and Germany's Messerschmitt-Boelkow-Blohm combine (Euromissile). They are the prime contractors in Europe and owners of the weapon. They have been joined by the United States through sale of the technology and research, and now Hughes and Boeing are contractors in the U.S. Curiously enough, the records reveal that the purchase was really prompted by *need* and the whole idea of interoperability or interchangeability seems to have followed. Today, it is interoperability that is the keynote of the project and one which the European members hope will not be jeopardized by U.S. modifications to a weapon which is adequate for NATO use. The United States has reaffirmed the interoperability/interchangeability of components.

Purpose

Roland is a perfect example of advance planning and time as key elements of weaponry. Its beginnings were in 1964, and after fifteen years of concept verification, prototype development, and testing, is now ready for engineering production. It bears out David Facey's insistence that it is necessary to begin planning for important weapons at least *fifteen years in advance*.[2] In the case of Roland, it suited U.S. purposes beautifully, as that country was reportedly ten years behind in its own efforts.

2. Interview with Mr. David Facey, 12 October 1979.

Costs and Offsets

The figure of $800 million has been quoted as the cost of developing such a weapon. The Euromissile version, if retained would have saved the U.S. that amount. However, what is done is done, and the improvement in capability, while still retaining interchangeability of components, should not be written off without due acknowledgement. Two major improvements account for most of the cost:

1. A track radar change to provide higher countermeasure capability and a boost in transmitter power by a factor of four.
2. The missile itself was upgraded for handling and safety-level purposes.

The ultimate cost of Roland can only be calculated by the number of vehicles the U.S. Army decides upon, and based on roughly 3,000 at this time, the cost could exceed $3 billion.

While AWACS was sold to NATO by the U.S. on an offset/coproduction basis, the Roland agreement calls for offsets; which were agreed to by the Germans; to be paid by U.S. industries. These should consist of equitable sums paid to the industries of Germany and France to reimburse them in part for drawings, specifications, licenses, and experience – i.e., the costly technology which went into Roland. Offsetting these costs for the U.S. are the prospects of earlier production work and profits for industry than would have occurred if the U.S. started from its own concept ten to fifteen years after France and Germany.

The System

Roland surface-to-air missile is a system for short-range defense against low-level attack. It is an all-weather, day or night system, the key component being a turret which acquires targets automatically, identifies friend or foe and can fire by radar at night or in bad weather, or visually. A computer provides tracking update information to the launched missile. This has been described as "flying it up a tunnel." It is mounted on a tracked vehicle.

Organization and Management

As has been stated, the tri-partite project is the result of an agreement between France, Germany, and the United States. Using a Memorandum of Understanding (MOU) as in the F-16 case, Roland production in the U.S. is now in motion. The U.S. Army was given complete control over further development and procurement for the United States. All three participants have made changes, but none as sweeping as those of the U.S. Fortunately, it is assured that interchangeability is still intact. The broad organization is depicted in Figure 3.1, which shows that the same major levels of policy making and management obtain as in other projects.

Summary and Postscript

The benefits of Roland are quite significant:

1. $800 millions or more of Research and Development (R&D) funds were saved by the U.S. for something else.

2. The U.S. capability to fill a vital air defense gap has been attained ten years sooner.

3. Industry work and profits can start ten years sooner.

4. The "two-way street" operates *both* ways.

5. Research, experience, and technology gains are made by all concerned, and European technology now flows *to* the U.S.

6. Agreed optional levels of standardization and interoperability insure that a common configuration will be adhered to, to the maximum extent.

7. Logistics and support capabilities for the weapon are enhanced.

8. National credibility and prestige are gained by the French and Germans. The project should lead to leverage for other sales.

At this writing, the U.S. Congress (House of Representatives) has agreed to a one-year trial by the U.S. Army to prove its case for modifications and for ultimate savings because it feels that changes have equalled what the U.S. would have paid to start itself. The ten years seem to be overlooked. One can only hope the facts will bear on their decision. It is noteworthy that a great many dedicated people in the U.S. and Europe went all-out for national and industrial compromises to encourage adoption of

Roland. Once again, the indispensable personal touch showed itself in collaborative efforts. It is to be hoped that Walter LaBerge's observation will prevail, when as Assistant Secretary General for Defence Support, in the June 1977 *NATO Review*, he stated that it was "because of this European/U.S. negotiation that the U.S., using entirely its own industrial base, is well on its way to the introduction of its own Roland system."

As the first attempt to transfer European technology of a major foreign-developed weapon system and build it in the U.S.A., Roland is truly a key to future developments. Among the consequences of Roland's cancellation could be the delay or cancellation of other NATO cooperative programmes of U.S. design, notably AWACS and its excellent cost-sharing agreement. It would be a shame if false or post-mortem "cost-effectiveness" arguments, or a "not-invented-here" syndrome leading to a purely U.S. weapon were to affect Roland, a weapon designed for NATO. American industry feels the same if this quote from John H. Richardson, Executive Vice President of Hughes Aircraft Company, is taken as the U.S. contractors' attitude: "The magnitude of the problems encountered is relatively modest compared to the large savings in money and time that will be realized when Roland becomes operational ... I do, however, regret having been a contributor to a cost-growth problem for all of us. The hope is that by sharing experiences as we learn those who follow will be wiser."[3] In other words, the complex management problems and *means* are far less in importance than are the *ends* — standardization, interdependence and survival. Again, it is an example that intelligent people can overcome any problem, if they are motivated.

F-16 — A High-Performance Fighter Aircraft: NATO's Newest Military/Industrial/Economic Project

The organizational and managerial significance of the F-16 lies in its comparability in most respects to the F-104 G Starfighter of the previous generation of lightweight, high-performance combat aricraft.

3. Richardson, John H. "Roland, A Technology Transfer Program," *Defense Systems Management Review*, Summer, 1977, p. 17.

Background

The F-16 was the result of a United States decision to develop a lightweight fighter technology to prove that a lower-cost, high-performance aircraft could be built to complement a very superior and more expensive fighter such as the F-15. It was needed to round out a modern tactical air force. Begun in 1972, by the time it reached prototype stage, it was clearly a leader among air superiority mission aircraft because of its combat radius, acceleration, and maneuverability. The F-104 G, used by several NATO nations, was reaching the end of its life cycle and required replacement in the coming years.

Purpose and Participants

The purpose for which the United States built the aircraft was first accepted. The next purpose was to place it in competition with other nations' lightweight high-performance fighters as a candidate for adoption by these countries in which the F-104 G had to be replaced. Jaguar and Tornado had already been developed by Germany and Italy for essentially the same purpose of air superiority. After close competition with the French Mirage and Swedish Viggen, the governments of Belgium, Denmark, the Netherlands, and Norway selected the F-16.

A formal Memorandum of Understanding (MOU) for procurement and production was agreed to by the five participants. The objective was to form a consortium programme as a partnership in the truest sense of the tern — namely, equal participation based on requirements and benefits. Just as with F-104 G, there was again born an agreement between nations to purchase a U.S.-developed aircraft and also to share in its production. It has been perhaps the case involving the largest transfer of advanced technology, broadened industrial base, and increased standardization ever to be achieved by a single weapons system. It was indeed the "arms deal of the century" — thus far. Interestingly enough, its *economic* implications were looked upon as being as important as the military ones in strengthening the Alliance.

The agreement provided that the U.S. would procure about 1,000 (as of October 1978) F-16 aircraft, most of them to be based in Europe. The European nations would procure 348 additional aircraft for a total of over 1,300. The possible third-country sales, in which both the U.S. and its partners would share, were estimated to be 4,000 to 5,000 aircraft. That estimate was made prior to the Iranian situation of October 1979.

Since the United States funded the development programme, a significant portion of the research and development costs are to be recouped from the European Participating Governments (EPG's) upon delivery of aircraft. But the most interesting feature of the MOU is the provision for full industrial participation in the F-16 programme, which will provide a significant production opportunity for the EPG's just as was the case with the F-104 G. The initial 348 aircraft and all follow-on purchases will belong to the EPG's. The European partners also will produce components equal in dollar value to ten percent of the U.S. aircraft, forty percent of the European aircraft, and fifteen percent of future third-country sales. The forty percent will continue for all follow-on F-16 purchases by European members.

The initial total cost per aircraft was estimated at $6.08 million; however, costs have climbed because of agreed improvements and may eventually be about $8 million. This is still about half the cost of an F-15. The total programme was projected in October 1978, to be about $15 billion, extending through 1987, with the eventual total projected at $24 billion.

Organization and Management

The F-16 is a stellar example of a multi-national consortium set up to pursue selection and production of a replacement aircraft on a multi-national basis. It is a classic example of a member of a highly sophisticated weapons family, now in the follow-on replacement stage. It would have been an even better standardization leap forward if Jaguar and Tornado could have been scheduled at the same time, and perhaps one of the three selected for a broader, single use. However, in keeping with a precept of this analysis and the opinions of others, it is probably all right and *safer* to have two or three weapons of such major importance and nature. But certainly not 23!

As a joint business effort in the U.S. and Europe, the management task has been the most complex and successful to date. Aircraft engines manufactured in Europe will be made to U.S. specifications. The enormous transfer of drawings and data defies the imagination. Their conversion to the metric system, translations of data and information, factory papers, shop instructions, blueprints, process sheets, etc., is equally impressive.

Over thirty European industries are involved, the main ones being Fokker, Fairey, and Sabca. In the U.S., General Dynamics is the U.S. manufacturer, along with Pratt and Whitney for the engines. Fabrication and assembly of major structural components take place in the U.S. and at two European locations. Configuration management was brought under early control when it was evident that the impact of five nations needed a central control unit. Hence, a Multinational Configuration Control Board made up of all five was established to decide on the acceptability of all proposed changes. Figure 3.1 shows the present organization, now familiar to those who recall Starfighter and similar major collaborative organizations.

Problems

Once again in F-16 the old familiar, tough management problems arose in a complex multibillion-dollar programme. Agreements, structures, wages, currency exchange, vacations, production rates, schedules, capital, accounting, and numerous other problem areas were encountered, and it seemed to a reviewer that most of them were lessons learned fifteen years earlier, but not recorded or at least not well-remembered. Nevertheless, the necessary compromises were arrived at and this time the valuable lessons have been recorded much better and have been more widely spread and available to others. Documentation of the effort is excellent. As a student of management, the writer firmly believes that the exceptional management and records of both the F-16 programme and the Roland programme will provide answers to the most complex and intricate organizational and management problems requiring solutions that one can foresee in the most intricate, largest programmes of the future. .

Summary and Postscript

In addition to the real benefits of a standardized major weapon, at a cost to each nation which it could *not* afford on its own, and the tremendously successful complex managerial solutions born of the F-16, the programme demonstrates the many benefits to be enjoyed by all partners on both sides of the Atlantic. There has been an increase in jobs in the Fort Worth, Texas area for General Dynamics. There have also been an undeterminable number of related jobs created throughout the U.S. Estimates show that about 6,000 jobs have been created in Europe due to the programme. The interchange of technology and managerial expertise has been phenomenal, overriding in importance for admitted difficulties and work. The Americans have learned more down-to-earth knowledge about the European way of production and operations — as the Europeans have about the American way. The exchange of experts and management personnel has been without equal to date. This programme has "brought people together" and brought about fair compromises and changes of attitude that have been acknowledged by all concerned. The tendency to form national points of view has diminished and an "international view" increased as the big picture unfolded. Spirit and trust surely were in evidence. The *need* for the weapon was never in question; it was a matter of getting the most and best for the money. The military benefits are evident without further comment. Political ties have been strengthened. As Major General Abrahamson summed up in his article on the F-16 in the summer 1977 issue of *The Defense Systems Management Review*, F-16 can be described as "a major cornerstone expected to put teeth in the NATO Alliance and provide better defense for all. This then is the real value of the F-16."

Some Early Observations

The three programs — Roland, F-16, and, in a sense, AWACS — show a remarkable similarity in weapons chosen, competition,

30

codevelopment and coproduction arrangements to the previous decade's F-104 G, HAWK, and Atlantique. The similarity of the weapons which attracted cooperation bolsters the argument for the need of a "family of weapons" approach and all it implies, including a Long-Term Defense Planning Programme and common, coordinated scheduling. The element of competition, while it could have been better, with longer planning times, nevertheless was controlled essentially for such major weapons. The codevelopment and coproduction *arrangements* were all successes. The objectives of all the programmes directed at achieving standardization and improving combat effectiveness, and even cost-effectiveness for *each* participant vis-à-vis "going it alone," were achieved. They were excellent examples of big pay-off items, wherein the costs from research to obsolescence could be equitably divided among partners, and showed that unnecessary, duplicate research and development and prototype production could be avoided.

Thus far, the basic facts of Soviet arms intensification and technological advances have been set in proper context, as has the Allies' inability to rely on any one nation's strength, and the fact that standardization, in its broadest connotations, has become the macro-problem for the NATO members. The pivotal years are here. Again, all the hortatory statements and warnings now have been voiced and we need no more. The evidence, the threat, the challenge — all have been exposed.

The hypotheses developed in the first analysis regarding the feasibility and practicality of collaborative efforts were again proved in the 1979 analysis. The predictions that the second decade would be more of the same, even to more, but smaller, cooperative ventures came to pass. But now there is a difference. The whole Allied attitude, the exigencies of the threat and the frightening facts of armaments comparisons, plus wide, renewed interest in standardization — all these and more currents thrusts should take NATO *off* dead-center in the next few years and lead to some radical changes and agreements. A series of excellent models now exist for codevelopment and coproduction. Generalizations and concrete lessons are in hand. The outstanding achievements of brilliant NATO and national members and especially industrial/managerial executives of all nations are the best indi-

Breguet 1150 Atlantic prototype is shown during test flight. Aircraft has maintained schedule well, despite multi-national nature.

". . . from 1961 to 1971 U.S. weapons designs continued to dominate NATO inventories through licensed production in Europe of nearly 1000 F-104 G Starfight". . . Picture shows the F-104 G.

". . . from 1961-1971 also licensed production in Europe of more than 4000 HAWK air defense missiles . . .".

NATO needs a standardized airborne warning and control system to maintain effective defenses against low-flying aircraft and control of its air space. This is the U.S. Air Force's Airborne Warning and Control System aircraft.

An agreement between the United States and the European Participating Governments allows the European members to purchase more than 300 F-16 aircraft and to share in production.

Roland anti-aircraft missile system. The United States made the selection of this French-German system before expending large sums of money on a similar development.

cators that such men of goodwill and intelligence *do* exist and they can do the job.

NATO's present role of instigator, or coordinator, or sponsor; its record of flexibility, dedication, and intelligent handling has carried the goal of standardization about as far as it can without additional authority. To proceed now toward the common goal, NATO must be strengthened either within the present charter, or given limited supranational powers for weaponry and military doctrine under a new military/industrial/economic charter. These proposals will be covered later in detail. They are not to be construed as advocating expanding NATO's territorial responsibilities in any way.

In sum, the six transnational production successes showed the same basic principles of coordination, standardization, economies of scale, transfers of factors of production, the need for homogeneous families of product approach, and common logistics support, among others, that unilateral business has adopted. With national/NATO/industrial rededication, an enlarged role for NATO and a slight relinquishing of "sovereignty" *only* in the area of *weaponry* and related areas, the job ahead can be done. But time is running out.

Next, the total efforts of thirty years will be reviewed and the arguments for and against collaboration dealt with prior to offering some proposals for concrete actions now and in the immediate future.

34

Chapter 4

Thirty Years of Efforts

Thirty Years of Peace

That very interdependence on combined capability which Secretary General Luns clearly described in 1974 has built an alliance which, thus far, has deterred the Soviet bloc from any aggression in the West since the end of World War II. True, in the early years it was mostly Marshall Plan aid which provided the base, with large numbers of troops and weapons deployed plus economic aid. But soon after, the balance of forces became more equitable as the Soviets recovered and then forged ahead while NATO reached a plateau and depended more and more on the strategic nuclear umbrella. The NATO percentages of contribution to the whole effort now total about 35 percent European funds and 65 percent United States' funds. Full equitable status ought to be about the same as the Gross National Products of each — 44 percent for Europe and 56 percent for the U.S. The latest published figures indicate 40 percent for NATO Europe and 60 percent for North America. In addition to the billions of dollars spent for defense which have provided what strength NATO has, one of the real contributing factors has been a sometimes maligned but impressive record of standardization, interchangeability and interoperability in weapons, equipment, doctrine, and logistic support. The next two chapters will record that record.

Another major reason for thirty years of peace is simply that the *aims* of the Alliance have remained valid, and generally its actions have been in keeping with those aims.

Common defense and security have been the aims, together with an ability for adaptability and flexibility in national views and in NATO organization, all of which have enabled the Alliance

35

to persevere. Also, peace has existed simply because NATO *existed* and possessed sufficient nuclear and less sufficient conventional capabilities. Thus the Soviet bloc has chosen not to take any offensive to the West to date.

Still another reason for strength and peace may be in the nature of the adversaries. In the free and open societies of the West, as exemplified in NATO, there is a spiritual power which, while it may ebb and flow, stems continuously from a free people. The power of free people is well-understood by the Soviets: witness how it is kept under close hand in their society.

Some say that the attraction of communism is diminishing in Russia because there has been so little spiritual nourishment for the people. If so, and if that trend is combined with reported unsettled conditions there due to ethnic and population problems, resource scarcities, and popular unrest, the Soviets may find it *necessary* to make political and military moves to cover their problems and to remain in power. This disquieting projection is another compelling reason for the West to be ready as soon as possible in all respects.

If NATO initiatives are taken *now*, if a *broader* Alliance is born again of military/industrial/economic collaboration to create a coalition of military power second to none, we can look forward to another thirty years of peace, or at least be ready to meet the threat and to persevere.

Accomplishments and Potentials: Programmes and Projects

To lend credence to the above statements about the past thirty years of successful holding power, it is appropriate to review the total record. The number and importance of cooperative weapons and equipment programmes and projects becomes quite impressive when gathered and presented in one place. As described earlier, the two major areas of standardization efforts can be segregated into programmes and projects, and institutions/structures/modes and concepts. This chapter will cover programmes and projects. Because it is impossible to rank them in importance, they are simply listed in alphabetical sequence and identified by initiation times where available. There is no attempt to describe the weapons fully, as it is not the purpose of this overview; however, some words on their significance and their contribution to "the cause" of standardization, interchangeability of interoperability are included.

1. *AIM-9L — Sidewinder Air-to-Air Missile*: Now under dual production by the United States and Germany through a consortium, this latest member of the Sidewinder family has four major components: guidance and control, rocket motors, target detector, and a warhead, which lend themselves to component production by the partners and which are interchangeable. A potent, proven weapon, it marks a significant milestone in equal, dual-production and a significant savings in developmental costs.

2. *Alphajet — Ground Attack Trainer*: This is an outstanding example of a NATO-endorsed consortium of Germany and France to produce an excellent military ground attack trainer having possibilities for widespread use in all NATO forces. The accomplishment of *early*, deliberate *planning* for this collaborative programme is significant.

3. *AS-30 — Missile*: A successful pioneering achievement of 1962, this tripartite programme by the United Kingdom, France, and the Federal Republic of Germany produced nearly 2,000 missiles by 1966. Its significance lies not only in having been a very successful industrial accomplishment but also in its excellent use of a Steering Committee and now, continued common follow-on logistics support.

4. *Bullpup — Air-toSurface Missile*: Another early success for NATO was the adoption of the U.S. Bullpup missile in the 1960-70 time frame. Bullpup and the first Sidewinder air-to-air missile share the honor of being among the earliest multi-nation coproduction programmes.

5. *CL-89 (AN/USD-501) — Reconnaissance Drone*: This was a British and German collaborative success which was introduced into both services in 1971. Significant for its codevelopment as well as coproduction.

6. *CVR-(T) — Armoured Fighting Vehicle*: A European partnership of Belgium and Great Britain featured codevelopment and coproduction of a standard vehicle.

7. *European Transonic Wind Tunnel.*

8. *EXOCET — Naval Surface-to-Surface Missile*: This was an early successful French development of a surface-to-surface

missile of about a 20-mile radius, similar to Germany's Kormoran air-to-sea missile of the same period. The two nations cooperated and Germany's MBB and France's Aerospatiale were later joined by Manufacteurer Aero-Electronique Dassault, TRT, and Belgian Aerospace as component manufacturers. Significant in that it shows that consortiums can grow if successful, from the original partners and from single-country development.

9. *F-104 G — Starfighter Combat Aircraft*: One of the subjects of the 1969 analysis, the F-104 G represented, at that time, the largest, most costly and perhaps most complex coproduction program of the 1960-1970 decade. Five nations combined in this monumental effort, and the technological, organizational, production, and management lessons learned from it have been of lasting value and example to the Alliance.

10. *F.H. 70/S.P. 70RS80 — Towed and Self-Propelled Howitzers and Free Flight Rocket*: The British and Germans agreed to collaborate on these formidable anti-tank weapons and have been joined since by Italy. It is an example of multi-national action outside the NATO mantle to pool technology and save costs for a heavy 155 mm gun and associated ammunition. A self-propelled version is under development.

11. *F-16 — Air Combat Fighter Aircraft*: Described in the first article and chosen for analysis because of its massive coproduction and standardization example, its significance lies in the size of the program, its potential and the added, recorded lessons of massive coalition programmes involving tremendous transfer of technology and data. It is also significant because of its recognition of the need for offsets and equitable agreements necessary with each member country.

12. *G-91 — Tactical Reconnaissance Aircraft*: An early *ab initio* project, a "first-born" of NATO, the G-91 was begun in 1954 as a tripartite project which eventually was carried out by two members, Italy and Germany. Its significance lies in its pioneering success, impressive numbers (600), and the fact that components and parts were procured from all the members — Italy, Great Britain, France, Germany and the Netherlands — for its construction. It is also famous for being a "first" for NATO.

13. *General Support Rocket/Missile System*: More of a systems concept at present, plans are underway to standardize on a general

support system in order to eliminate most of the excessive number of types and models now in use in the areas of rockets and missiles for general support.

14. *Harpoon — Anti-Ship Missile*: Developed and produced by the United States, this naval-launched missile is about ready for replacement and has been listed as a suitable candidate for the family-of-weapons approach as an international ASSM.

15. *HOT — Anti-Tank Missile*: An anti-tank wire-guided missile evaluated and dually produced by both France and Germany, this vehicle-launched missile commenced coproduction in 1974.

16. *Interoperable Helicopter Force*: The same partners who produced the ground trainer and Alphajet are negotiating at present to collaborate on an International Helicopter Force. Prototypes of three specialized-use helicopters are being included in the evaluations.

17. *Jaguar — Ground Attack Aircraft*: A lightweight, multi-purpose strike-fighter developed by Panavia Aircraft GmbH, a consortium of Great Britain, Germany, and Italy, this superb fighter reportedly has saved one-third the cost to each member by such collaboration. Significant in that a special agency, the NATO Multi-Role Combat Aircraft and Production Management Organization (NAMMO) was created for this major programme as well as the use of a special NATO Jaguar Steering Committee. Jaguar has become the third replacement for the ageing F-104 G for three countries, Tornado and the F-16 being generally considered of the same air combat family.

18. *Kormoran — Air-to-Ship Missile*: Dual development of this long-range air-to-ship missile began in 1974 between Airospatiale of France and MBB of Germany. Now in production for German forces, the French contractor has assumed the status of sub-contractor.

19. *Lance — Tactical Ballistics Missile*: An early missile of its kind with a 75-mile range for tactical land purposes. Lance is an American-made weapon which has been purchased by several NATO nations, thereby avoiding research and development costs to a large extent.

20. *MARK-20-RH 202 — Rapid Fire Gun.*

21. *Martel — Air-to-surface Anti-Radar and TV-Guided Missile*: As its name implies, this guided missile has a dual purpose and is

being built by an Anglo-French consortium. Its development goes back to 1964, a prime example of the need for long planning-long lead time of at least fifteen years for most major weapons. A ship-launched version was announced in 1970 as a private offshoot venture.

22. *MBT-2 — Battle Tank*: One of the most ambitious dual development/production efforts to date was the aborted Main Battle Tank project of the United States and Germany. However, agreement has been reached on a common caliber gun, and most experts feel that two main battle tanks in the NATO inventory is not objectionable and still in phase with optimum standardization.

23. *M72 — Light Anti-Tank Weapon*: An example of the effective use of a NATO Steering Committee to assist in multiple coproduction, the M72 was adopted by Canada, the Netherlands, Norway, as well as its developer, the U.S.

24. *Milan — Anti-Tank Wire-Guided Missile*: A very high-speed weapon for tank defense purposes, this dual project by France and Germany was begun in 1965 and deliveries commenced in 1973. Also, a man-portable Milan is now in service.

25. *Mutual Logistics Cooperative Programmes*: There have been several successful international cooperative logistical support programmes and agencies in the past twenty-five years, the most notable being the agencies for HAWK, oil products, NAMSO which supports twelve weapons such as NIKE, Honest John, F-104 G, Sidewinder, M37 and 44 Torpedoes, and for communications/electronics support. The significance lies in their great success and proof that common logistics support works.

26. *NATO Acoustics Communication With Submarines*: Another NATO-sponsored project which has standardized acoustics communication with NATO-assigned submarines.

27. *NATO — ACPS*: Little known but extremely important agreements, the ACPS or Allied Communications Publications on Common Doctrine are as important as weapons, as these and other tactical agreements get to the heart of the commonality of doctrine matter and provide for future equipment and operational collaboration.

28. *NATO — ATPS*: Like the ACPS, these Allied Technical Publications on Common Doctrine agreements cover an even

broader field and thus have even more potential for doctrine and weapons standardization.

29. *NATO Fixed Accoustics Range in the Azores (AFAR)*: This has been a NATO-sponsored project in which the partners collectively established a Fixed Accoustic Range in the Azores. An example of the versatility of common efforts and the standardization of heretofore separate, standard, and often unavailable service and testing facilities.

30. *NATO Air Defense Ground Environment — (NADGE)*: One of the largest, most complex early cooperative efforts by all NATO nations under NATO sponsorship, NADGE produced and operates the highly effective Air Defense Ground Environment system of communications as part of a modern complex system of air defense. The NADGE is still undergoing modifications and is in the hands of a mutual follow-up agency.

31. *NATO Common Infrastructure*: Still another, often overlooked, major accomplishment of NATO collaborative efforts are the 220 airfields in NATO countries, 31,000 miles of communications, and 6,300 miles of pipeline. Common infrastructure such as these are as important as common armaments.

32. *NATO Atlantique — Maritime Patrol Aircraft*: NATO's "first-born" programme, Atlantique's superb development and production programme, following careful, deliberate planning and competition for this important airborne surveillance system, is best known for several "firsts". The aircraft was built well, on time, and within budgeting projections. Eighty-seven have now been delivered to five member nations.

33. *NATO AWACS — NATO Airborne Early Warning and Control System*: Described earlier as a key programme, AWACS is a prime example of total NATO adoption of a major weapons system which was already in production by the United States. Part of its costs to NATO will be offset by mutual arrangements. It was called the "arms sale of the century" thus far, and it is estimated that from its beginning to final obsolescence it may involve costs of as much as $24 million for the NATO nations. It also stands as a lesson in *late recognition of a critical requirement*, hence the need to make direct procurement from one member without long-range planning, competition, and more participation.

34. *NATO Frigate*: This is a unique ship which is being built

under German and Dutch leadership, acting as a kind of supranational body for all the participating members. The NATO standard Frigate will be significant as a ship having the best competitive components of participating countries. The long lead time programme, calls for 12 to be begun through 1985 for Germany and the Netherlands. Its adoption by others is under study. A new type frigate is under consideration calling for wider production and an emphasis on modularity and exchange of standard components.

35. *NATO HAWK — Surface-to-Air Defense Missile System*: Described in the 1969 analysis and reviewed in this study, HAWK is a classic model of a major weapons system coproduction programme. Highly successful, it is still the backbone of tactical air defense and is now in its follow-on generation through the HELIP organization. HAWK's complexity, technological exchange and excellent organization, including common logistics support, all have been significant contributions to the common cause.

36. *NATO HAWK European Improvement Programme*: A unique example of follow-on to a highly successful major weapons coproduction programme, the European HAWK partners have formed their own improvement programme. It is significant that the standardization resulting from the first generation will now continue in the second as it has in common logistical support.

37. *NATO Long-Term Defense Programme (LTDP)*: While this epoch-making milestone in collaboration is listed and described more fully in the section on organization/structure/modes and concepts, it is included here as the most important single step forward in weapons planning to take place in NATO since its beginning. Together with the family-of-weapons approach and new cooperative measures and structures, LTDP is the "centerpiece" for future NATO weapons collaboration and standardization. The plan includes 38 major areas for equipment planning, both mid-term and long-term.

38. *NATO Lynx, Puma, and Gazelle Helicopters*: This has been a NATO programme for cooperative development and coproduction of a trio of specialized military helicopters through a Memorandum of Understanding between Britain and France. It is significant in that each agreed to buy offsetting aircraft from the other.

39. *NATO Mark 44 and 46 Torpedoes*: The Mark 44 was another early success in collaboration under NATO sponsorship, whereby a U.S. advanced-type torpedo was coproduced by three nations. Several hundred are now in use. The Mark 46 which followed, has been adopted by the Netherlands, Belgium, and the United Kingdom. One of the several excellent managerial techniques attributable to the early program was the use of a group of experts to ensure full interchange of technology.

40. *NATO Naval Forces Sensor and Weapons Accuracy Check Sites (FORACS)*: Similar in purpose to the acoustics range, NATO's joint establishment of common sites for naval forces to check sensors and weapons has contributed to a solution of the earlier problems concerned with individual nation and ad hoc sites, which had a record of contributing to lost time as well as dissimilar testing conditions.

41. *NATO Integrated Communication System (NICS)*: NATO's newest and largest integrated communication system is now in place and operating in all member countries. The benefits of standardized or compatible equipment, improved communications, command and control are new capabilities second to none. Follow-on improvements already are underway.

42. *NATO Patrol Craft Hydrofoil Missile (PHM)*: Another example of the range of potential standardization is the NATO-sponsored hydrofoil craft in use by several navies as patrol vessels.

43. *NATO Seagnat — Ship Defense System.*

44. *NATO Seasparrow — Ship-to-Ship Missile*: A new point-defense ship-launched missile developed by Canada for surface-to-surface defense, the Seasparrow is a very successful example of *codevelopment* and *coproduction* and has been procured by other nations. A surface-to-air version is also now under production in Canada and the Netherlands.

45. *NATO STANAGS — Standardization Agreements*: Nearly 100 standardization Agreements were prepared by NATO with Military Committee leadership, covering a very large range of weapons and equipment goals. A few have been carried out, but the potential input now of these agreements for the Long-Term Defense Programme should prove invaluable.

46. *OTO MELARA — 76 mm Compact Gun.*

47. *Patriot — Air-Defense Missile System*: This most recent air-

defense missile has been evaluated as a superior forward step in air defense. Developed by the U.S., it is now under consideration by NATO for adoption. Its high cost is an important factor for those with limited budgets. Some offset agreements will no doubt be necessary for NATO nations to take advantage of this acknowledged advanced weapon.

48. *Sea King Helicopter*: A British-made helicopter for use at sea, it is now in multiple use by Germany, Belgium, Norway, and other non-NATO countries.

49. *Scorpion — Reconnaissance Vehicle*: This tracked reconnaissance vehicle is produced jointly by the United Kingdom and Belgium.

50. *Terrier — Sea-to-Air Missile*: A U.S.-developed missile for ship defense of an early generation, Terrier is in use by some Allied navies and is being phased out by longer-range, more advanced systems.

51. *TOW — Anti-Tank Weapon*: A heavy anti-tank weapon system which has been in service since 1972, TOW was developed by Hughes Aircraft Company of the United States and has been procured by Belgium, Canada, Denmark, Germany, Greece, Italy, the Netherlands, Norway, and Sweden. Netherlands production is also underway. This is a prime example of developmental costs saved by Alliance members and the comparatively low cost resulting to economies of scale.

52. *Tornado — Multi-Role Combat Aircraft*: A companion programme to the Jaguar, Tornado is a multipurpose high-performance lightweight fighter aircraft built by the Panavia consortium. The programme includes common production of components by the partners. Great Britain, Germany, and Italy all have industrial participation in this third member of NATO's new high performance group of tactical aircraft.

53. *Transall C-160 — Medium-Range Military Transport*: Production of this versatile, medium-range military air transport was carried out by France, Germany, and Belgium and was completed in 1972. Transall is an example of successful tripartite development and production and featured equal shares in production.

This concludes the impressive record of project and programmes for weapons and equipment with perhaps the omission of one or two. Only two initiatives were not completed, the Mallard and the Main Battle Tank. Mallard was to be an innovative communications system but it failed to materialize; however, the Main Battle Tank had some beneficial spinoffs, such as guns and ammunition commonality. Over *fifty* weapons and systems — some huge some smaller, but all important — were successfully undertaken by NATO nation consortia, at least half with NATO sponsorship, and the other half by member nations themselves, which is indeed a record of considerable collaboration.

Next, a look ahead at some other programmes and projects now pending and other initiatives being considered as standardization gains momentum. These will be listed and only briefly described to reveal the range, depth, and direction of present and future commonality endeavors.

Pending Programmes and Projects in Electronic Warfare (EW)

Already agreed to as part of the LTDP, these ten initiatives in the important field of electronic warfare were launched in 1978-79:

1. EW Units in Support of Assigned Corps and Divisions.
2. Basic EW Self-protection Capability for Army Aircraft, Combat Vehicles, and Troops.
3. Self-protection Suit for Tactical Aircraft.
4. Chaff and Decoys and a Dispensing System for All Ships.
5. Shipboard Threat Alert Receivers.
6. Jamming Equipment for Major Combatants.
7. Expendable Jammers in Support of Corps and Divisions.
8. EW Direct Support of Combat Operations.
9. NATO-Assigned Expendable Drone Force.
10. NATO EW Software Facility.
11. And three additional concept, organization, and staffing initiatives to improve NATO forces EW capability.

Other Major Initiatives Underway

1. *NATO Future Identification System (FIS)*: This initiative is an Alliance-wide effort to define the next generation Identification Friend or Foe (IFF) system for use by NATO. Five

nations had studies underway, and a coordinated proposal for a NATO FIS was to be presented by 1980.

2. *Joint Tactical Information Distribution System (JTIDS)*: In 1976, the U.S. offered the specifications and characteristics for European development of compatible and interoperable equipment for an ECM-resistant communications system. Germany undertook similar development. NATO nations generally have been supportive and the systems are undergoing performance tests at SHAPE Technical Center at this writing.

3. *NAVSTAR Global Positioning System (GPS)*: The SAMSO office is in charge of this GPS project and a U.S. MOU is in existence for direct participation by others in what has been described as a revolutionary system. A decision was to have been made by the CNAD in 1979.

4. *Mobile Accoustic Communications Study.*

5. *NATO Airborne Early Warning (AEW)*: Described earlier under the AWACS programme, it is still in the initiation stages, although approved by NATO. Hence, it is listed here under current ongoing programmes.

That brings to over seventy the number of accomplished programmes and projects, or those underway at this time. There follows a list of those currently in the discussion stage, which add ten more to the total.

Additional Programmes, Projects and Consortia Under Discussion — 1979

1. A Short-Range Air-Defense Weapon System.

2. Explosion Resistant Multi-Influence Sweep System for Mines (ERMISS).

3. Electro-Optical Devices.

4. NATO Anti-Surface Ship Missile (ASSM).

5. NATO Small Surface-to-Air Ship Defense System.

6. NATO Defense Research Programme.

7. Coordination of National Armaments Schedules.

8. Establishment of a NATO Small Arms Test and Evaluation Programme.

9. Integration of National Research and Development and Procurement of Weapons Into the Long-Term Defense Programme.

10. Establishment of a Permanent NATO Weapons Planning Programme.

Reduction/Standardization or Interoperability Potentials

There remains a vast area concerning same-purpose weapons yet to be initiated, standardized, integrated, made interoperable, and above all reduced in types and models. The potential reductions of duplications which lie ahead are as impressive and challenging as the accomplishments:

1. Reduce 100 different types of ships.
2. Reduce 50 different types of ammunition.
3. Reduce 23 different families of tactical combat aircraft.
4. Reduce 41 different types of naval guns (20 mm and up).
5. Reduce 8 different families of armoured personnel carriers.
6. Reduce 20 different calibers of weapons (30 mm and larger).
7. Reduce 6 different types of recoilless rifles.
8. Reduce 5 types of aircraft ordnance.
9. Reduce 31 different types of anti-tank weapons.
10. Reduce 7 different main battle tanks.
11. Reduce 36 different types of fire control radars.
12. Reduce 100 different types of tactical missiles.
13. Reduce 8 different SAM systems.
14. Reduce 6 different Napalm containers.
15. Reduce 6 different types of Anti-Surface Ship Missiles (ASSMS).
16. Reduce 16 different types of auxiliary full tanks.
17. Reduce at least 36 (exact number unknown) different full nozzles and 28 power units.
18. Establish a Common Data Link.
19. Implement all remaining Standardization Agreements (STANAGS).

Although numbers are not always meaningful in view of major differences and the relative importance of weapons without further analysis, they still are enlightening — *19* areas, types of weapons, or equipments with over *600* different kinds still in existence, in the aggregate.

In sum, it is now clear that a remarkable number of weapons have attained greater commonality. But while many duplication reductions have been realized, a great many remain. In addition, the increasing number of bilateral and trilateral cooperative weapons development and production projects to date have not really attacked the larger job at hand, that of optimum standardization rather than partial approaches. Perhaps the fault has been too much attention to the immediate need for a weapon, as experienced by two or three nations, or too many ad hoc procurements, rather than all the members seeing the need for determining long-term objectives and scheduling *first*, and then providing the *means* to achieve them. There obviously is need for requirements to be carried out through a more permanent, structured, general framework of mutually agreed organization and procedures. In short, it is clearer now that *structure* is needed first and now, and *equipment* and *weapons*, properly planned, should *follow*. Thus far the reverse procedure has not been too successful. Recommendations for an attainable framework will be offered in the final chapter.

Accomplishments and Potentials: Organizational/Institutional/ Structural Concepts and Modes of Collaboration

As mentioned in the beginning, a separation of projects and programmes from organizations, institutions, and concepts concerned with collaboration may be useful to the reader in sorting out the accomplishments and in obtaining a better overview of their relationships. An alphabetical listing follows, first of NATO-sponsored or affiliated agencies and structures, and then purely alphabetical for others. Organization charts showing the general position of most of the major components are included in Figures 4.1 and 4.2 and most of the others on charts in Appendix A and referred to as they are described below.

NATO Sponsored/Affiliated/Related Structures/Concepts and Modes

1. *Advisory Group for Aerospace, Research and Development (AGARD)*: Formed early in 1952 as the result of Aeronautical Research Directors collaborative actions from NATO countries, and then by agreement by the then Standing Group of NATO,

NATO ORGANIZATIONS

CONCERNED WITH COLLABORATIVE WEAPONS EFFORTS

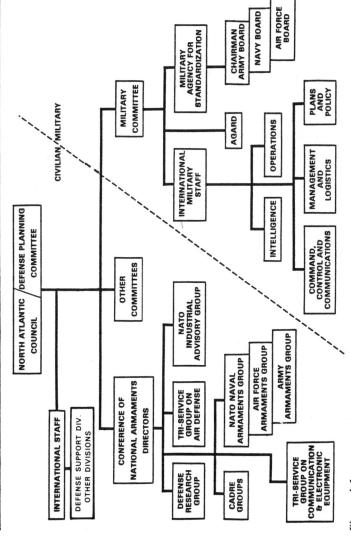

Figure 4.1.

NATIONAL ORGANIZATIONS
Concerned with Collaborative Efforts

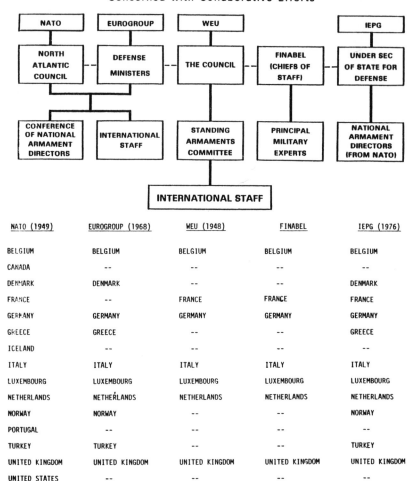

NATO (1949)	EUROGROUP (1968)	WEU (1948)	FINABEL	IEPG (1976)
BELGIUM	BELGIUM	BELGIUM	BELGIUM	BELGIUM
CANADA	--	--	--	--
DENMARK	DENMARK	--	--	DENMARK
FRANCE	--	FRANCE	FRANCE	FRANCE
GERMANY	GERMANY	GERMANY	GERMANY	GERMANY
GREECE	GREECE	--	--	GREECE
ICELAND	--	--	--	--
ITALY	ITALY	ITALY	ITALY	ITALY
LUXEMBOURG	LUXEMBOURG	LUXEMBOURG	LUXEMBOURG	LUXEMBOURG
NETHERLANDS	NETHERLANDS	NETHERLANDS	NETHERLANDS	NETHERLANDS
NORWAY	NORWAY	--	--	NORWAY
PORTUGAL	--	--	--	--
TURKEY	TURKEY	--	--	TURKEY
UNITED KINGDOM	UNITED KINGDOM	UNITED KINGDOM	UNITED KINGDOM	UNITED KINGDOM
UNITED STATES	--	--	--	--

Figure 4.2.

AGARD has been a NATO agency from the beginning. It has since come directly under the Military Committee. AGARD brings together leading experts from NATO nations who are recognized in science and technology related to aerospace, for the regular exchange of information and to stimulate advances and improve cooperation toward the common defense. AGARD is composed of top-flight groups of dedicated scientists. There are now nine permanent panels with over 350 members:

Aerospace Medical Panel	Avionics Panel
Electromagnetic Wave Propagation Panel	Flight Mechanics Panel
	Fluid Dynamics Panel
Guidance and Control Panel	Propulsion & Energetics Panel
Structures and Materials Panel	Technical Information Panel

AGARD's position in the NATO structure is shown on Organization Chart 1, Appendix A, and on Figure 4.1.

2. *NATO Early Warning and Control System Programme Management Organization*: This is the newly-formed NATO programme to carry out the Early Warning and Control System (AWACS) described earlier.

3. *NATO Conference of National Armaments Directors (CNAD)*: The CNAD is the highest level body on the civil side of NATO which was established by the Council to encourage and assist the countries to join together in equipment and research projects, provide a means of exchanging information on operational concepts, on national programmes, and on technical and logistics matters where such cooperation can benefit NATO. Together with the Military Agency for Standardization (MAS) and AGARD, the CNAD provides a very strong and powerful input by recommending and advising on collaborative and standardization programmes and projects. Among recent programmes due largely to their efforts are NATO Jaguar and MRCA, Seasparrow, the Azores Fixed Acoustics Range, FH-70 Self-Propelled Howitzer, FH-70 Towed Howitzer, Puma, Gazelle, Lynx, Reconnaissance Combat Vehicle, the MH20 RH203 Rapid Fire Gun, Milan, FORAC, the NATO Frigate and the Hydrofoil Patrol Boat.

NATO and its members are taking ever-increasing advantage of this outstanding collaborative organization, and it will play a key role in the new LTDP and RSI programmes. It is working more closely than ever with military authorities to insure a *combined* input of industry and military ideas. It is an excellent way for NATO nation industries, through their expertise and country's representatives to serve in their important role toward the common cause.

The CNAD now has six major suborganizations covering each armed service and related matters: (1) NATO Army Armaments Group (NAAG); (2) NATO Navy Armaments Group (NNAG); (3) NATO Air Forces Armaments Group (NAFAG); (4) NATO Industrial Advisory Group (NIAG); (5) Defense Research Group (DRG); and (6) Tri-Service Group on Air Defense. (The CNAD's position in NATO's structure is shown on Charts 1 and 2, Appendix A and on Figure 4.1.)

4. *NATO Common Infrastructure Programme*: This is the generic term given to a vast number of common facilities and systems, such as 220 airfields, 31,000 miles of signals and communications, 6,300 miles of pipeline feeders, NADGE, and War Headquarters. As an indication of its magnitude, the total expended for all "slices" of the Infrastructure has been $2,359 billion to date.

5. *NATO International Staff (IS)*: A highly capable coordinative staff of dedicated, appointed Under-Secretaries and career NATO staff members, the IS is situated immediately beneath the Secretary General as a permanent group of assistants and experts in their fields who are also involved in coordination of the military and civil sides of NATO. The IS provides constant, yet discreet impetus to the common cause of standardization in its broadest connotations. Its six major divisions reveal the breadth and importance of their responsibilities: the Political Division; the Division of Defense Planning and Policy; the Division of Defense Support; the Division of Scientific Affairs; and the Office of Council Operations and Communications, each under an Assistant Secretary General. Three of these are directly engaged in commonality as their major functions.

Its excellent record of service and stability as well as initiative in cooperative efforts has brought the International Staff to a position in the forefront of the entire collaborative effort. It will be a key component in any new or revised organization of NATO towards the goals of complete collaboration in weapons, equipment, and doctrine. The IS will be addressed more fully in the recommendations of the last article of this series. (The International Staff's position in NATO's structure is shown on Chart 1, Appendix A and on Figure 4.1. The organization of the Defense Support Division of the IS is shown on Chart 3, Appendix A.)

6. *NATO Long-Term Defense Programme (LTDP)*: Already referred to frequently because of its enveloping relationship to the future of all standardization efforts, the NATO LTDP is the product of top-level consultations and agreements throughout 1978, and is now in motion. An impressive programme and structure designed to be carried out generally *within* NATO's present organization, it has several noteworthy features. First, it calls for a mid-term *and* a long-term plan, something needed for a long time, which extends NATO defense planning into the future in nine major areas. The first five underway are obviously needed now: readiness, air defense, electronic warfare, maritime posture and communications, command and control. Three more will follow: reinforcement, reserve mobilization, and consumer logistics, all directed toward support for forces and weapons in being and to sustain combat. Finally, rationalization (described later) and a NATO Nuclear Planning Group are planned to develop into the ninth and tenth study groups. Second, the essence of the LTDP is the fact that it really breaks new ground for NATO goals and will challenge existing conventions. As examples, the tough tasks of identifying and costing the required national inputs, and exploiting standardization to the fullest are among its important aims. It has been called rightfully the "centerpiece" of NATO's entire thrust for the future. Its importance warrants a more detailed status report made in October 1979, by the North Atlantic Assembly, which is reproduced as Appendix D.

The North Atlantic Assembly is an independent parliamentary organization with no formal links to the North Atlantic Treaty Organization. It provides a forum where West Europeans and North American parliamentarians meet regularly to discuss and recommend on a wide range of problems facing the Alliance. Economic, military, political, scientific, technical and educational, cultural affairs, and information issues are debated and voted upon. The Assembly's excellent work and inputs to NATO thinking are nicely illustrated by Appendix D.

53

7. *NATO Military Agency for Standardization (MAS)*: One of NATO's oldest agencies dedicated to standardization, the MAS was organized in 1951 and is one of the principal means of maintaining military inputs into standardization in weapons projects and programmes, both through weapons review and through its position as the key *military* agency concerned in NATO. As an arm of the Military Committee, MAS injects military opinion and expertise on weapons requirements and is also an effective member of the three groups, CNAD, IS, and MAS, on coordinated proposals which go forward to the Council. Few are aware of its size and scope, but there are no less than eight major naval panels, fifteen Army panels and twenty-two Air panels within MAS, each responsible for a large, service-wide segment of total military operations and weaponry. (These panels are listed in Appendix B. The MAS position in the NATO structure is shown on Chart 1, Appendix A, and on Figure 4.1.)

8. *NATO Maintenance and Supply Organization (NAMSO)*: Another early major structure begun in 1958, NAMSO is the largest of a series of NATO Production and Logistics Organizations (NPLOS). It provides common supplies and spare parts for a number of weapons in the NATO arsenal. Set up as a NAMSA (agency) at a single location, two more units were set up, one to support the F-104 G in Germany and one to provide support to the southern flank. Headquarters and the largest facility is in Luxembourg. It stocks over 81,000 line items for support of NIKE, Honest John, Sidewinder, Bullpup, HAWK, Lance, TOW, F-104 G, NADGE, torpedoes, NAMFI and forward scatter and satellite communications. NAMSA is proof that common logistics support can work and that "national logistics," long a nightmare to commanders of combined forces, can be entrusted to common agencies and common support procedures. It is "national logistic support" responsibilities, until now narrowly construed, which have proved to be extremely difficult to maintain and operate during joint exercises. In turn, this had further repercussions and has contributed to *destandardization*. (NAMSA-supported systems are shown on Chart 4, Appendix A.)

9. *NATO Air Defense Ground Environment (NADGE)*: NADGE still stands as the largest single NATO defense project thus far, in terms of its size, scope, and importance. It is a vast ground net-

work of communications and signals to provide early warning of and response to hostile aircraft and missiles. When AWACS is in place, the two systems will provide unequalled surveillance and detection capability of air and ground movements and weapons. NADGE, operating in nine countries, is a classic example of international cooperation in a highly complex system.

10. *NATO Armaments Planning Review (NAPR)*: Tied in with the newly introduced Periodic Armaments Planning System (PAPS) under the CNAD, the new NAPR procedure is directed toward identifying military needs *prior* to the establishment of *national* programmes and also will provide feedback on NATO programmes for analysis and publication to all concerned. The NAPR is a new NATO publication to inform all nations and industries concerned of weapons replacement plans and opportunities to cooperate and also to point out potential divergencies. It is a practical and significant step toward attaining the first goal of providing a vital new service — the promulgation of information in a single, authoritative publication. (Appendix C contains a fuller, recent progress report on PAPS and NAPR.)

11. *NATO Basic Military Requirement (NBMR)*: Once a useful technique, now abolished, NBMR's were drawn up by SACEUR and served as another direct means of promulgating military requirements as seen by SACEUR into collaboration and standardization planning.

12. *NATO Central Europe Pipeline System*: This is a vital control system for management of the vast international pipeline system. See *NATO Pipeline System* for description.

13. *NATO Codification System*: A key factor in common logistical support, the cross-identification of components, parts and stocks is another NATO accomplishment which has resulted in common knowledge of common items and some very real reductions in inventories and management costs.

14. *NATO Force Planning and Exercises*: Not to be overlooked in any recital of NATO techniques leading to greater standardization is NATO Force Planning for exercises. These plans undergo tough evaluation in major exercises and the results have yielded many significant improvements to be made in weapons, operations, doctrine, tactics, and logistical support. Recently, the need for much broader, common logistical support during major exercises

has been clearly brought out. The fact that each nation is still attempting to use its own or the available support structure precludes real efficiency for any one of them and, above all, for NATO forces an an entity.

15. *NATO HAWK Management Organization (NHMO)*: This landmark success was covered in depth in the first analysis. To repeat just the primary lessons, NHMO's significant contribution to standardization, its size, organization, complexity, and number of nations involved testify to the remarkable success of one of the most intricate widespread programmes ever undertaken. Now in its second generation phase, HAWK remains a common effort through the new HAWK European Limited Improvement Program (HELIP), a prime example of follow-on collaboration and maintenance of a standardized weapon.

16. *NATO Industrial Advisory Group (NIAG)*: One of the CNAD's most important groups, the objectives of NIAG are to provide a forum for the free exchange of industrial views and aspects of NATO armaments. It fosters international involvement in research, development, and production and has the goal of closer industrial participation and cooperation. Its potential as a contributor to the new LTDP, Families of Weapons, and RSI should be significant, considering both the CNAD and NIAG can speak for groups of industries as well as large single ones. NIAG has dozens of subgroups all engaged in making prefeasibility studies of major weapons and equipment. (The position of NIAG in NATO organization is shown on Chart 1, Appendix A and on Figure 4.1.)

17. *NATO Integrated Communications System Management Organization (NICSMO)*: NATO's communications needs have grown with the Alliance. To keep up with that growth and to meet recent emphasis on consultation and crisis management during hostilities, NATO saw the need for an integrated military and political communications system for high-level consultation and improved command and control. The outstandingly successful NICS system is now a fact. It incorporates earlier NATO SATCOM Systems, ACE-High, and NATO-wide networks. A separate, ongoing management agency, NICSMA, has been created by NATO as an international policy-making body to head the system. NICSMA is significant both from the point of view of an operational success

and in bringing together senior military and civilian officers from participating countries.

18. *NATO Land Force Tactical Doctrine and Tactical Air Doctrine*: These operational agreements are excellent examples of NATO's ability to take on the hardest tasks of arriving at common doctrine, which lies at the foundation of weapons commonality. The doctrinal agreements number in the dozens in both areas.

19. *NATO Military Committee (MC)*: This highest military committee of NATO under the Council — as AGARD is for civil matters — is charged with several major responsibilities regarding standardization and operations. It represents the most influential *military* input group for NATO armaments decisions. It also is charged with recommending measures considered necessary for the common defense. As such, it heads the major NATO military commands, directs the Military Agency for Standardization, a newly formed Armaments and Interoperability Division, five Communications Agencies, the Advisory Group for Aerospace Research and Development and the NATO Defence College. All of these are involved in varying measures in international military force and its complete support. Also included is the SHAPE Technical Centre, which provides SHAPE and the NMC with scientific and technical advice and conducts research, studies, developmental projects, and testing. Still another arm of the NMC is the SACLANT ASW Research Center in Italy. The NMC is becoming more and more concerned about providing the necessary military requirements for advance planning, as well as requirements research, and about development and standardization of weapons for NATO forces. The MAS has recently been augmented by the new ASI organization under the Military Committee to concentrate on future weaponry.

The Military Committee's position in the NATO structure is shown on Chart 1, Appendix A and on Figure 4.1.

20. *NATO Production and Logistics Organization (NPLO's)*: In addition to the HAWK logistics support organization, NATO has established other significant production and logistics support programmes such as for Sidewinder, naval torpedoes, Starfighter, Bullpup, AS30 missile, M-72 light anti-tank gun and several others which have been listed elsewhere. Common weapons were often

followed by common logistic support and follow-on agencies. NAMSO is a major example. The NPLOs come direct under the Council. (NATO NPLOs are shown on Chart 5, Appendix A.)

21. *NATO Multiple Combat Aircraft Management Organization (NAMMO)*: As its name indicates, this organization has been planned to coordinate the efforts towards the successful cooperative multirole combat aircraft which have been described earlier, e.g., Tornado, Jaguar.

22. *NATO Pipeline System*: A major accomplishment for common support is the NATO Pipeline System with over 3,500 miles of pipeline in central Europe and other networks in Turkey, Greece, Italy, Denmark, and Norway. As part of the multibillion-dollar infrastructure to service NATO forces everywhere, the system is a civilian agency, responsible to a military Central Europe Pipeline Committee. A major step toward standardization, the Pipeline stands, together with the 220 NATO airfields, as one of NATO's most ambitious common infrastructure projects.

23. *NATO Technical Trade and Cooperation*: A long and successful NATO history of nonmilitary, yet contributing, programmes in political, economic, scientific, technical, and informational inputs to collaboration in general has been taking place since the inception of the Alliance. The "Committee of Three" (Italy, Norway, and Canada as members) did a masterful job in 1956 in paving the way for NATO recognition and resolution of many differences in the above related areas in their new classic report to the Alliance.

In addition, a 30-year history of summit meetings, military exercises, foreign affairs actions and reactions to military crises such as Cuba and Berlin, the creation of a truly mobile force, MBFR participation, cost-sharing agreements and many other united actions, has forged the Alliance into what it is today. All of these events, together with more than twenty successful major agencies and hundreds of affiliated subunits, afford some idea of the task of building the structure already in place and working in NATO. Next, a listing of non-NATO, but influential, international participative modes, structures, and concepts concerned with cooperative multinational progress toward weapons commonality are listed and described.

1. *Common Defense Market*: This name has been proposed for a new and greater NATO-wide, NATO-Europe, or even North American/European or North Atlantic Common Market for defense equipment and weapons which several experts have put forth as the necessary initial step toward the goal of optimum collaboration and strength. Some foresee that in the future years it even could become a *larger* North American/European Military/Industrial/Economic Common Market.

This proposal is so ambitious and important a part of the recommendations covered later that it deserves further description at this point. The name, North Atlantic Defense Market, and its requirements, were offered by Thomas A. Callaghan, Jr., in an address given in 1978 wherein he saw in it "the largest peacetime politico-economic cooperative effort ever undertaken by free people in their own defense."[1] It is included in the recommendation at the end of this study, but some broad requirements he outlined are repeated here in part. Among them are: (1) the United States should offer to match every defense dollar Europe spends in the U.S. with a dollar spent in Europe; (2) the U.S. should offer to match the cost of every system developed in Europe for NATO use by an American defense development, also for joint use, and commit itself not to duplicate.

In return, Europe should agree to: (1) offset fully America's balance of payments deficit on military account; (2) establish an institution (presumably IEPG) which would permit Europe to plan, finance and manage intercontinental, nonduplicative, multiannual, multiproduct defense research, development, production, and support programs with the U.S. and Canada; and (3) increase Europe's collective defense expenditures by at least 3 percent per year in real terms as long as there is an imbalance in American and European defense budgets, or on other levels if mutually agreed.

1. Thomas A. Callaghan, Jr., "The Conventional Force Balance Can Be Redressed." An address given at the American Institute of Aeronautics and Astronautics Conference on The International Aerospace Market Outlook, Los Angeles, California, 22 August 1978. The Center for Strategic and International Studies, Georgetown University, Washington, D.C., p. 6.

The proposal, which is now part of a larger, new North Atlantic Treaty plan, includes short-, mid-, and long-term goals spelled out in terms of inventories, standardization agreements, procurement, research development and logistics proposals, and timing.

2. *Common European Armaments Effort*: Similar to the Common Defense Market proposal, this would restrict the initial effort toward what is also called a European Common Defense Market (ECDM) as the more immediate need for a stronger European partner to the Alliance.

3. *Commonality*: In defense jargon, this term is applied to that quality of material or a system possessing *like* and *interchangeable* and *interoperable* characteristics. Commonality implies a capability of a weapon system or equipment to be operated and maintained by all personnel, anywhere, who have been trained in their operation or use. It also includes the concept of interchangeable components, parts, and consumables.

4. *Dual Production*: One of the important Triad of Initiatives introduced by the United States, dual production has been offered to all NATO nations and covers coproduction of an imposing list of weapons and equipment in the U.S. inventory. The concept extends between and among all members as well. This initiative, like GMOUs and Families of Weapons, should open the door to wider participation immediately.

Examples of the offerings for dual production, the specific terms and conditions of which are negotiable between the interested parties, are these candidates:
—AAH — Advanced Attack Helicopter
—Blackhawk — Utility Tactical Transport Aircraft System
—HARM — High Speed Anti-Radiation Air-to-Surface Missile
—Hellfire — Helicopter Borne Anti-Tank Missile With Laser Seeker
—IFV — Infantry Fighting Vehicle
—SOTAS — Light, Short-Range Unguided Anti-Tank Rocket
—AIM-9L — Air-to-Air Missile
—MODFLIR — Night Vision Equipment
—Patriot — Air Defense System
—Stinger — Man Portable Air Defense System
—JTIDS — Tactical Information Distribution System
—M735 — 105 mm APFSDS Tank Gun Ammunition
—Copperhead — 155 mm Cannon Launched Laser-Guided Munition

—M483A1 — 155 mm Artillery Round
—RAAM — 155 mm Remote Anti-Armour Mine
—ADAM — 155 mm Artillery Delivered Anti-Personnel Mine

The initiatives will not be realized without problems or issues, and is expected that requirements, competing systems, proprietary restrictions, third-country sales, reciprocity and cost-effective consortia, will all require substantial industry-to-industry and nation-to-nation involvement for success of these offers.

5. *European Defense Community (EDC)*: This is another term which describes the proposal for a strictly defense (armaments) counterpart to the present successful *European Economic Community (EEC)*. It has also been expanded by some to propose an *Atlantic Community for Defense.*

6. *European Defense Procurement Agency (EDPA)*: Seen by most as the first step towards a European Defense Community, the establishment of a single European procurement agency for defense acquisitions is viewed as a more reasonable beginning to a common market.

7. *European Integration*: This is another of the growing number of terms and concepts directed toward the integration of European arms industries which seek to provide larger, similar-product bases for more effective competition and efficient production.

8. *European Programme Group (EPG) and (IEPG)*: The EPG is a group of NATO nations, excepting France, which has the operational goal of a European arms programme on a united, shared, collective basis.

It has since been expanded in 1976 into a group named the Independent European Programme Group, which includes France. The IEPG appears to be *very* well underway and there have been several successful cooperative weapons programmes to date which the IEPG has formulated and encouraged.

The IEPG organization is shown on Chart 6, Appendix A, and on Figure 4.2.

9. *Eurogroup*: Almost identical with the EPG, but with broader objectives and actions, Eurogroup celebrated ten years of progress in 1978. With a recognized record of solid achievements in fostering European solidarity and cooperation, the broad composition of Eurogroup is shown on Chart 7, Appendix A. Its objective is to strengthen the *whole* Alliance by ensuring that the European

contribution to common defense is as cohesive and united as possible. In doing so, it has given impetus to a wide range of common equipments, improved quality, participated with the EDIP and is involved in the Long-Term Defense Programme. A very real and potent organization, it played an important role in major cooperative procurements such as the F-16, Tornado, the Belgian Leopard Tank, and others. It, too fosters maximum standardization and standardized follow-on projects and support. An impressive record of the work and contributions of Eurogroup is revealed in the "Eurogroup Communique" on pages 30-31 of the February 1980 issue of *NATO Review*. Its many appendages, interests, accomplishments, and active support for NATO strength is quite impressive and appreciated. Eurogroup should and will play a very important role in the recommended plans outlined at the end of this study.

Charts 8 and 9 of Appendix A show the members of NATO, EUROGROUP, WEU, FINABEL and the IEPG, and their relationships; Figure 4.2 combines them.

10. *Family of Weapons (FoW)*: The third leg of the Triad of Initiatives, but in use for some time in the vocabulary and plans of NATO, the FoW will be a major part of the Long-Term Defense Programme. The principle behind FoW is to obtain greater efficiency by reducing needless duplication in research, development, and especially production while fostering standardization. Once the "families" have been agreed on, the objective is to assign one or more of the family to one nation for R&D and possibly the same or others for production. For example, one member would be designated to develop a long-range air-to-air missile, while another a short-range version. At this time, these four major families, among others, are being actively explored: (1) Anti-Tank Guided Missiles; (2) Air-to-Surface Weapons; (3) Ship-to-Ship Missiles; and (4) Air-to-Air Missiles.

Other broad categories proposed are Navy Surface-to-Surface, Navy Surface-to-Air, Army Surface-to-Surface, Army Surface-to-Air, Air-to-Surface, Air-to-Ship and Air-to-Air weapons. Most of them can be subcategorized for assignment to a member for R&D and/or production. The possibilities of common, but specialized-production weapons by the most appropriate and equitable source, with attendant savings, is among the impressive goals for this concept.

62

The whole idea and thrust behind the FoW concept is essential to the goal of total IMS. It will lead to more data exchange agreements, system-wide general MOUs, as well as the benefits mentioned above. No doubt it will face obstacles of scheduling, fear of interdependency, requirements concepts, competition, possible domination by a few, and third-country sales, among others. Obviously, it will take careful planning to ensure that short-term assignments do not overlap with medium- or long-term assignments to different members. However, accentuating the positive side, its obvious place in the total effort, the interest and initiative being taken by the U.S. in proposing FoWs as a vital part of its Triad of Initiatives, and the early favorable reactions of members, all augur well for its future despite the problems.

11. *FINABEL*: This is the acronym for the multinational consortium of France, Italy, the Netherlands, Germany, Belgium, Luxembourg, and the United Kingdom, representing international cooperation and collaboration by these countries. It is illustrated on Charts 8 and 9 of Appendix A.

12. *General Memoranda of Understanding (GMOUs)*: While specific MOUs have been in use since the beginning of NATO's collaborative efforts, it is only fairly recently that *General* MOUs, covering a broad range of agreement areas, have been approved and are in effect. They can even be applied to Family-of-Weapons agreements. These GMOUs include dozens of minor and major areas which, heretofore, required separate agreements and now should provide exceptional assistance to early-planned and pre-agreed cooperative programmes, projects and dual (or more) production efforts. The U.S. has led the way with this forward step and has GMOUs with Canada, the U.K., Germany, France, Italy, the Netherlands, Norway, and Portugal, and has four more in negotiation with Greece, Turkey, Denmark, and Belgium at this writing.

Because the new General Memoranda of Understanding will be a major contributing factor in the future success of the entire IMS programme and will have significant affect on the success of the LTDP, Family of Weapons, and other collaborative and offset efforts, a complete example of a recent one between the United States and the Netherlands is included as Appendix E. This GMOU, completed in April 1979, is illustrative of the amount of work and

63

agreement which is included in the many significant areas designed to promote "standardized" collaboration.

The GMOU first exhibits a typical U.S. Memorandum of Promulgation to U.S. departments and agencies concerned which encourages the use of Netherlands sources. It is followed by a Preamble setting forth the goals of increased military capability and an improved economic position through standard and interoperable equipment. Annex I to the GMOU covers principles of cooperative effort, action, and "counting procedures" (types of joint enterprises and reimbursement). Appendices to Annex I list in detail the Indicative Products Lists for the Netherlands and applicable Research and Development organizations. Annex II covers the principles governing logistics support of common items. Finally, a statement on exceptions to the "Buy American Act" is included; and a notice regarding potential foreign source competition. A sample U.S. Department of Defense List of Restricted Defense Items Under MOUs for Reciprocal Defense Procurement has been added by this author to make the exhibit complete in Appendix E.

13. *Harmonization*: This is a general term used for the *process* or *results* of adjusting differences in qualitative basic military requirements. Its importance lies also in its insistence that operating procedures be brought into line to ensure standardization, the optimum use of resources, and compatibility.

14. *Interchangeability*: Part of the common jargon of commonality, interchangeability is that condition whereby two or more items possess characteristics that enable them to be *equivalent* in placement, use, performance and durability. They are, in fact, completely interchangeable with each other, except perhaps for minor adjustments. Its significance as a part of standardization is obvious, somewhat the same as interoperability which follows.

15. *Interoperability*: This refers to the ability of systems, units, or forces to provide and receive services from other systems, units, or forces and to use them interchangeably. One of the more achieveable goals of standardization, there are some units which may achieve interoperability with relative ease, while on the other hand they may be more difficult to standardize. Indeed, one school of thought on the standardization effort feels that interoperability of a few common items like beans, oil, and bullets, should be sufficient standardization! The writer and most experts

64

do not concur in these limited goals. Interoperability is the third part of NATO's thrust toward Rationalization, Standardization and Interoperability (RSI). Interoperability is considered as a *total* possibility by an overwhelming number of experts.

16. *International Military Standardization Council (IMSC)*: This proposal could really be literally substituted for, and include, "commonality, standardization, interoperability," etc. as used throughout this study. IMS has been the NATO goal since 1949 and is descriptive of the common objectives of standardization, military effectiveness, and cost savings. Likewise, it is the specific goal of NATO groups such as CNAD and MAS, European groups such as Eurogroup and FINABEL, and the goal of U.S. programs such as the Triad of Initiatives.

17. *NATO Long-Term Defence Programme (LTDP)*: Already referred to frequently because it is such a landmark of progress toward commonality, the LTDP's lofty goals and 38 areas for greater cooperation by sensible functional grouping and specialized, intergrated forward planning, are among the most ambitious objectives ever attempted under the present NATO structure. It should provide the first *comprehensive* set of building blocks toward achievement of the common cause. With medium-term as well as long-term plans, its scope includes just about everything the Alliance could desire, if properly followed through and effectuated.

The Long-Term Defence Programme is of such future importance that it deserves further detail at this point. During the 1979 meeting of the Military Committee's Subcommittee on Defense Cooperation, the programme was described as nothing less than the "centerpiece" of NATO's efforts to rationalize collective defense. The major part of the Subcommittee's deliberations and report focused primarily and in depth on the LTDP. That part is reproduced as Appendix D as a current, objective report on its status. It affords an excellent overview of the programme's scope, ramifications, and relationships with other major current projects and programmes, and emphasizes the requirements to translate it into the real "cutting edge" of agreements on enhanced fighting capability.

A second excellent reference regarding the LTDP, covering its relation to other continuing efforts to enhance NATO's capabilities, is the June 1978 issue of the *NATO Review*, which featured several articles on the programme. Commencing with Bill Mumford's "Foreword" (NATO's Assistant Secretary General for Defence Planning and Policy), on through Military Committee Chairman General H. F. Zeiner Gundersen's "Military Perspective" on the programme, and also Robert W. Komer's "Origins and Objectives" (Mr. Komer is Adviser for NATO Affairs to the U.S. Secretary of Defense), the series of articles affords an excellent and expert treatment of the LTDP and its wide-ranging effects.

18. *Offsets and Trade Liberalization*: "Offsets" is a broad term to describe any reciprocal procurements or payments made by one or more of the partners in a collaborative endeavor to one or more of the others. It can be applied to research, development, production, or licensing costs and is the method by which the procurement member may receive some *reciprocal* purchase or payment for the item or system procured from the originator. An *internal* offset can be based on direct participation in production, shared in proportion to the size and participation of the recipient. A *nonmilitary* offset can be based on trade liberalization and *may* tie in civil sector procurements as offsets for military buys. The goal behind offsets or trade liberalization is to strive for total, equitable, periodic, multiproject offsets rather than being bound by single, end-of-year or end-of-project settlements, as at present. In other words, fixed-calendar, fixed-project offsets are not in consonance with long-range plans and programmes. If the offset problem is solved, and admittedly it is a complex one, *more* willingness for *more* cooperative procurements will follow, if the parties involved know that equity will prevail at an agreeable time in the future.

19. *Parliament of Europe*: Already a reality, the *political* Parliament of Europe is providing a much-needed forum for the exchange of European national ideas. Some have suggested a similar parliament for *defense* which would reflect the public voice, or even to expand the present Parliament to consider defense matters. One expert, Robert Ritchie, infers that such a parliament is the only way to reach the electorate which is so necessary in peacetime efforts.[2]

2. Ritchie, Robert S., NATO, *The Economics of An Alliance*, The Ryerson Press, Toronto, 1956, passim.

20. *Periodic Armaments Planning System (PAPS)*: Ideally, any collaboration should begin at the most advanced planning stages where requirements are first defined. The record is testimony to the consequences of too-little, too-uncoordinated, and too-late planning. The CNAD has developed a Periodic Armaments Planning System which features two main areas. First, there are the procedures to assist in the identification of needs *prior* to national programmes being initiated. Second, feedback is planned for all programmes for all nations in an annual NATO Armaments Planning Review (NAPR). PAPS is definitely a constructive building block toward better definition or missions and weapons requirements, so vital to the LTDP. Its significance lies in the fact that it is to be a regular procedure and mechanism for NATO to define common military requirements and to publicize direction. Because PAPS and NAPR could become such important factors in the success of the LTDP, MOUs, RSI, and indeed toward the total goal of International Military Standardization, a progress report is included in Appendix C. This report was taken from the selected readings of the Multinational Program Management Course, now given by the U.S. Department of Defense Systems Management College at Fort Belvoir, Virginia.

21. *Rationalization*: The first part of the *Rationalization, Standardization, Interoperability Programme (RSI)*, rationalization is a brilliant concept and an equitable step toward the goal of commonality and total involvement in NATO by its members. It is simply *any* action that makes more efficient use of NATO resources and nations without changing total, planned defense funding. Rationalization requires adjustments of production, tasks, or any functions within national force structures or between and among nations to further the cause of common defense. Such adjustments are designed to increase the overall capabilities of NATO forces but not to reduced national defense efforts — admittedly a rather difficult path to follow. If carried out, rationalization means achieving the best collective capability at lowest cost and best individual member talents. It includes technological assignments, but *rationally* decided, and would permit each nation to concentrate on what it does best, so as not to upset national well-being. It means greater *interdependence,* and that could well mean the abandonment of any future pretext of "national defense" in favor of "Allied defense".

67

22. *Specialization*: Closely allied with rationalization, the term specialization is becoming more acceptable in its reliance on the most efficient use of limited resources and technology by assignments to best qualified sources.

23. *Standardization*: This is really the term of the ultimate objective. Standardization has much broader connotations today than it did twenty years ago. While it does strive for absolute likeness of weapons or systems, it is more of a total *process* and a goal by which all members deliberately attempt to achieve the closest collaboration and commonality in the pursuit of military effectiveness and efficiency. Research, development and production now are directed toward standardization and rationalization as well as the most efficient use of resources. It means the optimum attainment of military effectiveness through commonly used weapons, systems, facilities, and material. Four results are expected:
—Common or compatible tactical doctrine, operational, administrative and logistical procedures.
—Common, compatible, interchangeable and interoperable weapons, components, supplies and equipment.
—Common or compatible technical criteria and procedures.
—Common, compatible, interchangeable, and interoperable weapons, components, equipment and supplies.

Standardization *does* increase effectiveness, which in turn increases common logistics, which in turn increases common training potential (30 to 50 percent estimated), which in turn counters the costs of national defense and strengthens the credibility of NATO. Standardization even standardizes *military excellence*, as Dewey Bartlett concluded in his excellent article on NATO's survival.[3] One other meaning offered is that everything should be built to a "standard". However, standardization must *not* mean standardization of U.S. equipment. It must be an equitable goal in which all participate. Standardization embraces the whole spectrum of commonality, interoperability, interchangeability, implies controlled competition where feasible, economics of scale, multipurpose systems, common modularity

3. Bartlett, Dewey F., "Standardizing Military Excellence, The Key to NATO's Survival." *Air Defense Review*, 1977. passim.

and other subfunctions of the "common cause".

Standardization, together with rationalization and interoperability, is by no means a narrow issue, even though the technical nature of individual weapons projects and programmes tend to focus attention on the weapons rather than the broader benefits of IMS. They lie at the heart of the attempt to make NATO a genuine alliance; they permit more efficient and cost-effective use of resources in NATO countries; and above all, if achieved they *can* provide a credible military force for deterrence and defense.

24. *Triad of Initiatives*: A U.S. term, already discussed elsewhere in part, the Triad includes the initiatives of General MOUs, Dual Production, and Family of Weapons. The whole program is designed to increase total force effectiveness, attain more efficiency, foster controlled competition, promote direct industrial teaming, technology sharing, increase industrial bases, and solve the two-way street problem.

25. *Two-way Street*: This is now a popular phrase, attributable to Tom Callaghan, meaning the *necessity* that R&D, production and procurement of armaments be a *two-way proposition* and actuality between buyers and sellers of armaments. Procurements by one or more members from another member should be offset by reverse procurements at whatever time, items and methods which may be appropriate, and agreed to in advance. The European partners have fully accepted the concept and now look mostly to the United States for such reciprocal procurements.

There are more structural or conceptual arrangements and agreements which could be included in this overview, among them important consortia such as The Western European Union, Airbus Industrie, Euromissile, Heli-Europe, European Prime Contractors, Panavia, SECBAT, SETEL, SEPECAT, and many, many others. However, the chief significance of this recital has been to focus attention on more than *thirty* such important structures and concepts of cooperative armaments procurement that have been or are in being, and have brought NATO collaboration to the impressive point it has reached, without supra-national means, to date.

Summary

This has been a chapter devoted mainly to recording and highlighting over eighty significant projects and programs, and over thirty modes, structures and organizations, as well as dozens more under consideration. An imposing record — and yet the road ahead is still wide open for greater collaboration for the common defense. The next chapter will be devoted to illuminating important argumentation, pro and con, and then the study will offer some flexible, generally agreeable attainable recommendations for total success which many experts have offered as solutions.

Chapter 5

Argumentation For and Against Collaboration and Some Recent Initiatives

Before proceeding to the positive actions needed for total successful collaboration, it is appropriate to lay to rest, or to capitalize upon, some persuasive arguments which have come from different quarters. Like the record of accomplishments, these arguments also have been sorted-out and categorized to make them more homogeneous, identifiable, clear, and more useful to address in the recommendations.

National/Governmental Arguments

Nationalism

Perhaps the most lethal and persistant argument which has hindered total collaboration is the defeatist belief that "nationalism" can never be overcome. Oddly enough, it has been the more numerous single-member and few-member projects during the past twenty years that have contributed to an increase in the numbers of different weapons — i.e., destandardization.

John Stone made the observation that "one of the slightly curious aspects of the situation is that in recent years NATO has been progressively destandardizing."[1] He believes "the present proliferation of equipment types is, in a way, a tribute to the inventiveness and vitality of industry and technology in Alliance countries."[2] Elliot Goodman goes further and sees the existing pattern of a dozen European states producing military goods

1. Stone, John, "Equipment Standardization and Cooperation," *NATO Review*, No. 4, 1974, Vol. 22, p. 27.
2. *Ibid,* p. 28.

in small- and medium-sized markets that are highly protective and highly inefficient, and that they must organize on a multinational, European basis to compete with North American partners.[3] These statements clearly emphasize the basic "national" causes. David Fouquet sees the problem of an "Atlantic Arms Race,"[4] again with its roots in nationalism and economic fears. General Henry Miley, Jr., (U.S.A.) (Ret.) sees the need for a multinational body empowered to achieve standardization and that "requisite to the ultimate success is a surrender of national perrogatives to concensus determinations . . ."[5] "Nationalism" is not without critics.

Feudalism was overcome, as was tribalism in Europe and America. So too, one day, will nationalism, but not in our time. But for now, nationalism and sovereignty need only to be overcome insofar as collaboration in weapons and equipment are concerned. Only a *limited* amount of sovereignty and pride need be sacrificed for security. Flexible, consultative progress, albeit slow, is not to be cast aside.

Duplication is "Necessary"

Agreed, duplication is not only necessary but desirable, *up to a reasonable point.* For example, most will agree that an inventory of at least two main battle tanks or two tactical fighter aircraft are reasonable and desirable, but not what exists today. Duplication is the offspring of competition, which is also healthy, but only if *controlled* in military coalitions. It is the now well-recognized "nightmare of duplications" that is wasteful. To those few who argue for a plethora of types, models, and different weapons for a single purpose, one might ask the unanswerable question, "How much is enough?" One of the most ludicrous arguments has been that war would destroy *some* European producers, thus

3. Goodman, Elliot R., "The Puzzle of European Defense: The Issue of Arms Procurement," *The Atlantic Community Quarterly*, Winter 1976-77, p. 473.
4. Fouquet, David, "To Compete and/or Cooperate? The Atlantic Arms 'Race'," *Military Review*, April, 1977, pp. 37-42.
5. Miley, Gen. Henry, Jr., "Weapon Standardization," *National Defense*, Nov.-Dec., 1977, pp. 212-213.

NATO needs many sources of weapons, including many kinds of each. If this situation comes to pass, it will not be lack of weapons but members and forces that will be the deciding factors.

Custom/Pride/Not-Invented-Here

These three well-worn arguments are well-overdue to be dropped for reasons of both common sense and common philosophy. The record of over seventy successful projects and programmes surely has laid to rest the "custom" argument that nations and industry cannot change. Pride can be maintained and *enhanced* by successful multinational successes. Pride will follow the full acceptance and practice of the two-way street. As for the Not-Invented-Here (NIH) syndrome, it too should fall to changing customs, increased technological and productive capabilities of *all* due to cooperative initiatives, two-way procurements, and, of course, with the hope that some present military/industrial/governmental minds change their thinking and actions. The creation of a real NATO common identity, purpose, and increased capability is the best remedy. What is needed is the opportunity and capability to compete, where reasonable, and for each to be able to offer weapons for procurement by the other partners — weapons so superior they cannot be refused.

Independence vs. Interdependence

With nationalism usually comes a permanent bedfellow, the determination to become independent. New, Third World nations are continuing the habit Old World nations began. It is interesting to see one of the most independent-minded nations, the United States, coming around to realize its industrial dependency on the *wrong* nations! It is of vital importance that all NATO members not only accept interdependence but that they accept it as a way of business and the end to be achieved — if indeed it is to remain a coalition of free nations confronted with a totalitarian adversary. If not, the end will be to resign to alternatives that are not of our choosing.

A heartening case-in-point to demonstrate how more positive changes are coming about is that of the United States' recent actions and policies. Retreating from a strict policy of "Buying American" which was clear evidence of an attitude of independence, the U.S. has taken the following measures in 1979-1980, among others:

1. The Buy-American Act has, for all armaments purposes, been set aside by public law.

2. The U.S. has proclaimed publically its intention to follow a two-way street in procurements.

3. The U.S. has set in motion a Triad of Initiatives which includes General Memoranda of Understandings, Dual Production offerings, and leadership and support for the Families-of-Weapons concept.

4. The President and the Congress have gone on record for all-out support of RSI and the two-way street. The latest requirement by law is an annual report to the Congress on steps taken by the Executive to achieve collaboration with European members of NATO.

5. The Department of Defense has created new and active structures dealing only with weapons collaboration matters with NATO and NATO nations.

6. The Legislature and the public have approved increased military spending of a "real" 5 percent, and a 3 percent increase in strictly NATO armaments support, at a time when cuts are being made in other government departments and programmes.

7. United States Military War and Defense Colleges have set in motion entire courses to educate military and civilian leaders in coalition operations and procedures.

Additional moves and initiatives will be mentioned later. The point now is that "nationalism" *is* giving way to realities and the need to support the Alliance. Momentum *is* gaining in both the U.S. and in most NATO nations toward the "common cause". The recent agreement to place intermediate range missiles in Europe should be solid evidence that the Allies do *not* intend to fight only on Western European soil.

In varying degrees, some age-old arguments have persisted also in other NATO nations — arguments for "inevitable nationalism," unchangeable "differences," "customs," "pride" and the "NIH" factors. But the actual record of a large number of dual and multiple member consortia in the past ten years evidences their realization that they, too, *must* combine and overcome old traditions in the face of economic realities (which have always been there), and the increasing military threat. Experts see a U.S.-type "Culver-Nunn Amendment" to their laws as an impetus to standardization as an *imperative.*

Industrial Arguments

Industrial Size and Success

In these related industrial areas, one discerns a curious ambivalence. Being business-minded, smaller industries have strongly supported projects and programmes in which they are able to become partners. On the other hand, they have been slow to consolidate, merge or form some more lasting and larger structures necessary to compete in major weapons categories. As a result, many have lost out because of trepidation, bad timing, lack of planning time available to them, and domination by larger industries. There now is evidence the European members are tending toward stronger coalitions and fewer independent industries. The bad thing about trying for a weapon system development or production and losing, is the effect on national pride, patience, and economics — all of them easy to understand.

Robert Basil has addressed a common observation about industry in view of the lack of more support for both European and United States industries by their governments as well as the lack of more industrial alliances. He is one of the broad-gauge experts who sees clearly the impact of Standardization/Interoperability which cuts deeply across the entire national fabric: technological, economic, political, industrial, labor and employment, and even quality of life. As he concludes, "it involves the vital sectors of the Nation."[6]

Insofar as capabilities and industry inputs are concerned, most observations by industry experts lament the fact that the whole procurement cycle seems to remain *behind* the power curve — too uncoordinated and too late. They would be the first to agree to the new approach to long-term planning and scheduling by NATO.

Charles Wolf offers the idea of a whole new structural approach to trade liberalization and offsets by industries by enlarging them to include the civil sector, which he sees as possible and feasible. He agrees with most others that cost subsidization by governments may be needed, that the decisive advantages for American firms must be altered, and that "winner-take-all" competition cannot work in NATO procurements.[7]

The State-of-the-Art/Technology

One of the more covert and often smug arguments against more collaboration and cooperation has been the one that has been based on differences in the state-of-the-art in weapons technology between countries. The argument contends that projects and programmes cannot be spread more because of this unquantifiable quality difference. While it may have been true to an extent earlier, it is no longer a valid reason. European is as good or better than North American technology in many key areas, and the cross-fertilization and exchange of such know-how has been one of the great achievements of the entire effort to date. A good example is the F-16, a landmark in technological transfer. Roland is another. Again, the whole argument is passé if the concept of total capability and effort is espoused and when current plans for the LTDP, Multiple Production, General MOUs and the whole theory behind Families of Weapons now are unfolding. Certainly the Soviets made short work of the problem of technological capabilities when they decided *who* would make *what*, and such a problem

6. Basil, Robert A., "NATO Must Standardize," *National Defense*, Nov.-Dec., 1977, pp. 208-209.

7. Wolf, Charles Jr., *"Offsets," Standardization and Trade Liberalization in NATO*, Rand Corporation AS 36 R 28 No. 5779, Santa Monica, California, October, 1976, passim.

never arose. Instead, duplication, waste, and lost productivity were avoided.

To inject some expert opinion on technological differences, Bray and Moodie in a perceptive report have branded it as the generator and devisive force in NATO's defense posture. They, too, include nationalism as a deterrent and look to a reconciliation of national interest and technological requirements as necessary first steps to creating an Atlantic framework mind.[8]

Dr. Malcolm Currie sees the technological problem as being one which has resulted from a number of highly industrialized, technologically advanced nations, all responsible for equipping their own units and for which R&D on various projects started too early to permit coordination now.[9]

NATO Nation Armament Industries

Until recently, the European members have found it easier to enter into cooperative development and production programmes among themselves than with the United States. Not entirely, of course, but in general. The agreements were due to legitimate reasons ranging from size, force requirements, industrial bases to technological capabilities. However, if they continue to form more lasting and follow-on consortia as they have, this should no longer be the case. They could soon be in a position of greater equality with North America and therefore enjoy greater participation in the common cause.

In the opinion of Frederic Anderson and others who voice our mutual concern, continued ad hoc collaboration by industries gives the impression of a lack of common identity and purpose in Europe, and in turn affects the U.S. attitude.[10] The United States

8. Bray, Frank T. J. and Moodie, Michael, *Defense Technology and the Atlantic Alliance: Competition or Collaboration?* Foreign Policy Report, April, 1977. Institute for Foreign Policy Analysis, Inc., Cambridge, Massachusetts, p. v, and passim.

9. Currie, Malcolm R., *The Department of Defense; International Cooperative Research and Development.* Statement before the Research and Development Subcommittee, Armed Services Committee of the U.S. Senate, 21 April 1975, pp. 2-3.

10. Anderson, Frederic M., "Weapons Procurement Collaboration: A New Era for NATO?" *Orbis*, Winter, 1977, p. 968.

realizes this and has urged more European industrial combinations and has proclaimed a policy of open, dual production as well as a policy of strengthening both European and American industrial bases. Again, the Triad of Initiatives is working proof, as is the thrust toward the Family-of-Weapons concept and all it entails. The goal is an Alliance reliance on multi-industrial, interdependent R&D, and Production, backed by all governments. Concentration on high-leverage programmes and projects yielding big techno-logical and production pay-offs for fewer resources is also part of the new thrust.

NATO nation armament industries in Europe tend to be split into many more units than in the United States. We are prone in America to think of Europe as a whole, but the fact is that it *is* a group of independent nations. Hopefully, time will continue to change this. Meanwhile, most experts have advocated that the ideal structure for transnational European industries would be to group related ones in each major weapons area. For example, it is suggested that airframes and missiles would benefit from a combine of two groups, each consisting of one British, one French, and one German member. Aerospatiale, BAC, and MBB would thus become a powerful missile conglomerate; Dassault-Breguet, Hawker-Siddely, and VFW for airframes. Their size, capital, and technology would ensure greater European competition and growth, even though their production facilities may not become quite as cohesive as, say, Boeing in the U.S.

Gardiner Tucker has called attention to the fear among European industries that an Americanization of NATO armaments and an atrophy of European could result unless something is done. He questions whether it is the *objective* or the *mechanisms* that are at fault in developing more European capability. If the objective is a Europe increasingly independent in armaments matters (as a hedge against possible U.S. wavering in the future), then a European solution is correct. But if the objective is a more equal partnership between the U.S. and Europe, a whole new military/industrial complex may be the correct route.[11]

11. Tucker, Gardiner, *Towards Rationalizing Allied Weapons Production.* With the assistance of Fabio Basagni, The Atlantic Institute for International Affairs, Paris, p. 15 and 48.

Such merges will be very hard to bring about unless the governments exert a strong political will, a subject which is discussed later. The risk of failure (always present in industry) is more than offset by the opportunity to stand up to greater industries and participate in the action. At this writing, as mentioned, there are signs that some industrial partnerships are showing stability. Nevertheless, at the risk of being repetitious, the *political commitment* must be present; it is a vital key to almost every argument made in this study.

Research and Development; Production and Sales

Breaking down the state-of-the-art into its major segments pertaining to collaborative procurement, Research and Development should be further enhanced with the advent of Families of Weapons. A deliberate, sensible assignment based on capability and equity will go a long way toward replacing wasteful R&D duplication, now estimated at $14 billion a year. Production is under somewhat better control as it does not depend so much on that of the first phase, R&D, which now evolves from unplanned competition and "sunk costs" *not* being given up as they should. However, one can understand any nation's or industry's reluctance to do so. Production is generally as good or better by licensees as it is by the owner industry or country. New initiatives, new offers, new realities, together with increasing capabilities, are spreading production more and more.

As for sales, three main countries concerned have excellent records of competition with Third World nations, and sales are increasing. There is one drawback to this. So long as the major sellers continue to emphasize sales more than they do boosting their own spending, the Alliance will be the body to suffer. Some maintain that the U.S. wants to boost *spending* for armaments for NATO, while Europe is concerned more with sales.

As Europe has lacked a relatively large, homogeneous sales market as is the case in the United States, the trend for its industries has been toward selectively capturing a more limited market and also depending on export sales. Then too, through government ownership, some proliferation of weapons has been maintained, as has the "nationalization" of products. This all results in price considerations which differ across the Atlantic. Recent major programmes have led to recognition of the need to re-evaluate sales methods which can be equitable to both kinds of preponderantly private and heavily supported industries. The fear that some adjustments necessary for weapons collaboration will destroy the "free enterprise system" is ridiculous.

Finally, with regard to the related matter of economic regulation of industries, one can find a marked history of U.S. "disincentives to export" as compared to Europe. The balance of payments has caused the U.S. to take different steps. Unfortunately, in most argumentation, the balance of payments problem for weapons gets tangled up in the *total* imbalance.

On balance, it would appear that major changes are happening in the industrial area which, if aided by politicians and top executives, should promote more homogeneous ways of doing business in the Alliance. The time is ripe to consider all industrial and market imperatives to bring about fuller economic cooperation, to arrive at new agreements, and thereby to get a maximum return for the NATO military budget. World events can be depended upon to drive the West inexorably to new and stronger economic/industrial ties.

Scientific Cooperation – A Bright Area

It would be unfair if one did not include under Industrial and Technological matters the scientific progress of the past twenty-five years. The hundreds of scientists who have shared their knowledge, the NATO Science Committee Programmes, the exceptional technological transfer and diffusion, the future orientation of science, the selfless personal contributions of able professionals, the spread of new ways of thinking and education – all are a matter of record to the success of the scientific side of NATO. But the additional value of it all is that such efforts have direct transferability into modern weapons technology, resources management, and industrial advances. It is one of those "unquantifiables," which everyone knows exist. Examples are the adoption of modern forecasting and managerial techniques now in full exchange among weapons industries and the lowering of "security barriers."

Economic Arguments

Closely allied with National/Governmental arguments, but still a major sector by its own effects are economic agreements. Perhaps the most important relationship is that, if a country fails its people economically, the government fails with it. Economic pressures are more acute and unrelenting than ever before in every country. There is a simple, imperative requirement for weapons at a price *each* can afford.

Economic Nationalism

The number-one argument economics poses for collaboration is, of course, what affect does it have on the well-being of a nation and its people? If nothing new is ventured on the collaboration area, nothing should be lost. However, if a nation winds up on the purely buying-end of a weapons system, it has lost jobs and industrial growth, only to be replaced by armaments spending which must be met by its production gains in areas other than armaments. The economic value of collaborative efforts must be important to the members, otherwise it would not be the critical matter it now is in coalition agreements, *quid pro quos*, dual production, offsets, trade liberalization, and the like.

It is true that, until recently, because of technology, capital, size, productivity, and other reasons, many members could neither participate in development or production programmes, nor could they even be assured of a "just return" of fair share of other markets — and certainly not a profit on purchases. But the new Alliance agreements and those proposed in the study would prevent those detriments, and fairness and equitable assignments and returns would be a central part of the total rededication. But it is certain that to bring this about, to make work, to make jobs, to participate, *all* must apply themselves to the task and freely join in new, equitable, structural, controlled consortia. Protectionist policies and home procurement must change. The alternative is to "go it alone" and hope to get a monopoly on something. Curiously enough, monopolies of a *kind* will occur if the new concepts are brought, but they will be intelligently planned ones, agreeable to all, and in turn, will be offset by all members having a monopoly of certain weapons. It is certain to result in more interdependence.

Market "Imperatives"

It has been argued that the "imperatives of the market" can never change, just like cost-effectiveness. The old school holds to independence, comparable advantage, and profit, among others. If independence is standing in the way of mutual survival, it deserves a quick demise. *Interdependence* is the keynote now in times of scarcer resources and a growing threat. It must override all other economic considerations. That is, of course, unless one erroneously feels an economic threat outweighs a military one!

The question of whether to compete or to cooperate for markets has an intelligent answer — do both, but do them wisely. Enough energy and resources already have been expended wastefully in weapons competition. It is time to realize that "market imperatives" for coalition armaments procurements differ from the usual commercial world of competition and sales. Robert Basil's article invites our attention to the next section, which concerns the insistence of the economic purists who would pursue pure economic efficiency above all else. As one official even suggested, we should completely dismantle our present overproductive capacity and rebuild it to conform to standards set by hard-bitten efficiency experts.[12] It does not seem too feasible or likely at this date.

Cost-Effectiveness and Efficiency

These twin goals seem to have become so sacred in every-day business and industry that they have been applied as unquestionable arguments. First, as has been mentioned, a weapon *can* be cost-effective to *a partner* if it was obtained at a cost less than if the member had to go it alone, despite the fact that the total cost to *all* nations might exceed that which would have resulted from the biggest (or any other) one doing it alone. But the name of the game is survival and equity and a broader technological and economical base for *all* concerned. Second, a weapon is *very*

12. Basil, Robert, *op. cit.*, p. 209.

effective if it can be possessed by all who need it and could not have been acquired without cooperation and collaboration. There are some who say, without factual basis, that codevelopment and coproduction results in weapons that are only 80 percent to 90 percent "effective." Setting aside the matter of their judgment and assuming it is true, is it not better to *have* 80 or 90 percent-effective weapons yielding say, 96+ percent if *two* are used rather than *none* at all? Or, consider Lanchester's equation of $N^2 \times Q$ which indicates that measures of different quantities and different qualities when put together, yield something other than mere summations

As an economist, the writer is well aware of the case for normative cost-effectiveness. It is a proper goal – in its place. It should be applied – where applicable. But it is not entirely valid as a criterion for cooperative weapons efforts.

Economics and Alliance Goals

One very potent argument for more economic cooperation and even compromise is that it contributes in a very real way to the goal of making NATO something more than a military alliance. It can give substance to the promise in Article 2 of the Treaty of mutual help and support in the interests of economic stability and well-being. It would not be easy to bring about, as the "Three Wise Men" found in their difficulty in coming up with a solution. But it is apparent by now that a shared defense effort cannot be accomplished in isolation of other important factors – and certainly not holding together a *lasting* association which is affected by a complex network of factors. A military/industrial/economic/political broad approach will be discussed in later recommendations. It is apparent for one thing that if the economic threat could be allayed, military cooperation would follow more easily.

One last note on the economic dimensions of coalition security is in order. In the First Annual Report of SHAPE on 2 April 1956, these words were used: "We must be careful that we do not prove that free countries can only be defended at the cost of bankruptcy." This must not happen. Past methods *have* been wasteful of R&D and Production monies. Coalition security must rest on proper use of resources just as any other enterprise. Free nations must therefore act as one in building a proper defense force. It is imperative that waste be avoided by everyone through common goals and economically sound assignments directed at achieving those goals. It is a fact behind Soviet success, as compared to NATO's.

The impact is indeed an economic one as well as military and political where coalition security is at stake. It is essential that security be achieved with the least adverse economic impact. Compromise and agreement toward economic sharing is easier in war; it is a tough job in peace, when it is needed the most.

Objectives, Policies, Plans, Profits and Budgets

These five sacred business and economic areas are well-known and have been considered the backbone of good management. Objectives are indispensable. Plans must be made to reach them and policies arrived at to serve as a backdrop to such plans, (one of which is the policy or objective of making profit), and budgets are almost always the battle ground for the others to be exposed. Today, costs and scarce resources have catapulted the budget into first place — that is, it has become the overriding factor in deciding exactly how far the others may go. Weapons are no different. Building to a fixed cost, or cost-indicated weapons development has become a reality. The same budgeting constraints apply to coalitions. All the more reasons that each member should see that in *necessary* armaments, not just *desirable* ones, collective funding can provide *more* weapons capability than any one member could obtain. It is a way to reduce costs per member, while still experiencing growth, and leaving some additional funds for other important national objectives. In short, cooperative pooling, together with wise assignments, can result in savings for other badly needed investments. A concrete example is that of the hundreds of millions of dollars saved, for other opportunity costs, by the purchase of Roland's research and development by the United States.

Curiously enough, the same five sacred areas of objectives, plans, policies, profits, and budget often are used to plead inability to "change." Yet objectives do change, even though comparatively slowly; successful business plans do change daily; policies are reviewed and realized periodically; profits are adjusted to need for growth; and budgets immediately are adjusted to reflect the consequences. A "balanced budget" is almost a myth, especially in governments and in defense. It is time these same business arguments were brought in to effect changes in NATO's plans, policies, profits (effectiveness), and budget.

National Sales Attitudes

This economics-based argument, that sales attitudes and practices necessarily differ from country to country, is not one with which I would quarrel. It is accepted up to a point. If nations with limited internal markets and high specialization must sell outside the nation to exist, so be it. Let competition take its rightful place. But if production for *sales* becomes the objective over and beyond investment for one's fair share of defense, there is danger in the practice.

Sales are not evil. Third World nations and others will continue to buy from *someone*; why not a NATO nation? France and Britain emphasize sales. They do provide for greater economies of scale in production and they do provide more incentive to build up weapons industries. They do provide opportunities to sell to other member nations — again, for example, the F-16 and Roland. Although the sales picture is somewhat bleak at this writing, the multibillion-dollar business will persist.

Economics and the Two-Way Street

This economic argument has been saved until last as it is of utmost importance to Alliance economics. Now a familiar phrase to everyone, the two-way street *must* become a reality. As evidence of progress, the new Triad of Initiatives of the U.S. is an example, as is the sale of Roland (at last, a sale to the U.S.), and numerous sales between European members. The Family-of-Weapons concept can become one of the most practical ways of creating a *multi-way* street, fanning out (and back) research, production, and sales in many directions from every member to every member.

Political Arguments

Executives/Legislators and the Public

National arguments are given their voice and implementation by these three, and it is somewhat artificial to try to disassociate them from the national arguments themselves. However, the point to be made is that politicians *do* lead nations and do make up the corpus of legislatures, executive branches, and the judiciary. Basically, they are perhaps the most potent group, backed by their constituents, in any fundamental decision-making about the Alliance. An example of their potency is the renewed, aggressive interest in NATO sparked by the U.S. legislative bodies and the executive branch. All too often, political arguments are grounded in "equality" and "independence". They should be grounded in *equity* and *interdependence*. The lack of public knowledge of facts, perhaps also the public's lack of interest or ability to see beyond domestic problems, lie at the root of the argumentation. This is why dedicated politicians, scholars, military, and industrial people who know the threat must take up the task of educating the public. It really calls for an all-out NATO effort to plan and carry out an educational program enlisting every known means possible. Examples include the audiences given to dedicated NATO scholars like Tom Callaghan and the publicizing of his observations and recommendations and the visit early in 1980 of General Zeiner Gundersen to Canada and the United States and his offer to speak to as many groups and institutions as possible. From the initial response here in the author's New England area, it was obvious the people are ready to be included in the truth. A great deal more of this kind of exposure will help NATO's image and its affect on the public. One as knowledgeable as Roger Facer of the British Ministry of Defense clearly stated the importance of the political factor for all those who see it as perhaps the number one argument. "In the final analysis, however," he wrote, "it is the political argument which sustains the case for a new initiative to create a more effective system of European procurement — collaboration."[13]

13. Facer, Roger, *The Alliance and Europe: Part III Weapons Procurement in Europe — Capabilities and Choices.* Adelphi Paper Numbers One Hundred and Eight. The International Institute for Strategic Studies, London, 1975, p. 46.

Power and Inequalities

The arguments about the "realities" of power and inequalities among members are sensitive ones which need to be addressed. There is little purpose in arguing the fact that, in this world, we are all equal, but some are more equal than others! The real point is that provisions be made for unequals to share in proportion to their costs and benefits *equitably* and that a constant effort be made to bring the less equal members upwards toward total equality. If this may require some slight dimunition of power which is inherent in "sovereignty" by granting limited supra-national power and responsibility to NATO to move forward towards more equality in the field of common armaments, it is not the same as giving up one's basic sovereignty. As mentioned before, the Soviets are not faced with such a problem. They have decided for the bloc without concern for equality — hence, witness their armaments success.

The Political Argument for a North Atlantic Political Community

Although this will be included in the plans which come later, it has a place here under the political caption. We have an Atlantic military community. We are moving toward an Atlantic industrial community. We are thinking of an Atlantic economic community; why not help all three and try for a political community, restricted, of course, to parliamentary (popular) support for the whole area of military coalition and armaments collaboration? There could be no better way to publicize the cause and to educate people than through such a popular body.

Military/Strategic/Doctrinal Arguments

Military Dependence vs. Independence

In this, one strikes a vital area. Having spent thirty-two years in the military, particularly in logistics and weaponry, the writer is keenly aware of the demand by commanders for their own weapons and support and the reluctance (refusal at times) to rely upon any others but their own. It is permeated and promoted national interservice rivalry, and it is a real factor which is present in NATO as well, especially on the part of the larger members. Military doctrine has suffered from the same parochialism. But times and habits are changing. One can sense it in interviews and see it in current accomplishments and plans. Total change will not be easy, for it is the kind of thing that is beneath the surface (sometimes open) where weapons decisions are concerned. It is not something of which to be ashamed. Anything taught and ingrained early in a life-long, dedicated career, is a fact of life and humanity. It must be modified, and can be, if it is acknowledged that sheer economic necessity and survival are the stakes. So, while the "military mind" may be the result of training, so too, must an "open mind" be the result of retraining, Common requirements must be agreed upon and made the objective. It may be, as one appropriately observed, that some remaining individuals in high places may have to die first. As for military backing of common standardization, John Stone has firmly asserted to the author that, after more years of experience than most NATO experts, compatibility can only be based on common requirements.

The Military Need for More Voice in New Weapons

After having castigated the military somewhat above, it is only fair to follow with an argument the military appears to be correct about — namely, that military leaders do *not* have the sufficient amount of input into the choice of future weapons (even standardized ones), that is required. The impetus of science, the dictations of technology, the persuasiveness of governments and industries, the economic dictates of the people, public opinion, and the political will of politicians — all are felt to have more affect on such important choices and directions. An illustration is the United States' long-proposed B-1 Bomber, now seen by many as a necessary weapon to counter the threat. The U.S. Air Force made its strongest attempt for the weapon starting well over 15 years ago. It became the target of political and personal objections and was not pursued. The recommended plans which follow include a more effective structure in NATO for both military and civil inputs regarding weaponry.

This has been singled out as a good example of successful argumentation in the military area because of the admitted military necessity for the best communications, command, and control. Nowhere has there been a better example of such a plethora of communications and related equipment and systems that there has been in NATO. Yet today, all the discouraging arguments have been overcome, and NATO possesses one of the finest integrated networks, including standardized or interoperable equipment and procedures, the world has yet to see equalled. Even now, more improvements on land, in the air, and in space are being accomplished.

The Military/Industrial/Governmental Complex

Thus far, these three areas have been addressed as single entities. To do so is something of an artificiality. They are not separate centers of power, but have joined naturally in producing a super-center of power which is more than the sum of each. If this fact is recognized, a demand could be reasonably made that national preagreement through such power centers can be accomplished in each member country, and each country should speak with a more common purpose and voice for national contributions and demands where the *Alliance* is concerned. As it is, one can still find evidence of each power segment speaking for its own cause, through its own channels, and at the expense of NATO.

NATO Arguments

A common argument is that NATO lacks "real power" to control or coordinate and always will. This is true only to the extent member nations continue to *withhold* such control or coordinative powers. NATO can be what NATO nations *want* it to be. The members must ask themselves tough questions, among them the crucial one, "Is there to be a real defense of Europe and of North America or not?" Lack of initiatives, institutional intransigence, the existing framework, lack of supra-national power, no joint economic authority or technological community — all these and more can be resolved.

Institutional/Organizational/Managerial Arguments

For NATO's problems, these arguments are well-presented in Tom Callaghan's "management orphans of NATO" and so will be addressed in the proposals which follow later. At this point, it is appropriate to address them in light of their more purely professional and principles aspects.

Institutional/Governmental/Industrial Shortcomings

Forgetfulness
Some institutions, like the Roman Catholic Church and the U.S. Marine Corps have been blessed with good institutional memories — and they have lasted. Some institutions, particularly governments and industrial organizations, seem to suffer from "institutional forgetfulness" when it comes to coalition and weapons codevelopment, coproduction matters. They seem doomed to repeat the mistakes and hard lessons learned in past efforts. At least, they have until recently. Industries doing business in commercial, world-wide, non-weapons enterprises seem to do remarkably well and to come up with workable, profitable patterns of organization and management. But it appears somehow that where governments and industry get into the business of coalition weaponry, each attempt is almost as if it were the first. Yet excellent records exist. The latest one to come to the writer's attention is an excellent report for posterity on lessons learned in several programmes participated in by the U.S. and published by the U.S. Army Procurement Research Office, U.S. Army Logistics Management Center, Fort Lee, Virginia, 1978, called *NATO Standardization and Interoperability: Handbook of Lessons Learned.* Although the weapons systems studied by the authors as a cross-section of some approaches are not identical to those used in this study, the similarity of most "lessons learned" is informative enough to include them in Appendix F. It should be noted that the thirteen categories into which they are placed and the lessons themselves could best be reviewed in context with the body of the report, which is too voluminous for inclusion in the Appendix. For those concerned with any or all of the RSI programmes, the full report is recommended.

Lack of Enfranchisement

A hindrance to progress has been the lack of proper enfranchisement of agencies and collaborative structures at the *highest* levels. The U.S. is taking direct action to remedy this in the Office of the President in the Congress by a new, specific committee on NATO affairs, and particularly by the new offices in the Department of Defense at Assistant Secretary level. It is a beginning. Other nations and NATO itself must continue to pursue this path toward effective structures and authority at the highest levels.

Management/Business Functions in Collaborative Efforts

Objectives and Planning

Starting at the beginning, determining objectives and carrying out planning in business is the function which should require almost 90 percent of top managements' time. In NATO, until now, it has been largely an ad hoc, reflexive function, often too late to really assist in weapons procurement. With the inauguration of the LTDP, GMOUs, Families-of-Weapons, and a refreshing, renewed interest, the functions should attain their proper importance and usefulness.

Research and Development

After objectives are agreed upon and plans made on how to reach them, including weaponry, controlled and deliberate duplication of research and development can follow. Within a given private business, R&D competition is either not tolerated or is directed toward definite company objectives. Competition does take place vis-à-vis other businesses. The situation is not quite the same in NATO. R&D are so important and so costly they must be planned, controlled, directed, and competition held to agreed projects and especially entered into with predetermination and deliberation.

Technology

NATO, with fifteen nations' weapons technology on tap, dwarfs the resources in that area of *any* business or political group in the world. It has, without question, the technological resources to surpass the Soviet bloc. But this resource has been wasted to the extent of 10, now 14, billion dollars a year as measured in dollar costs, to say nothing of more important *time* and *posture* losses. Technology is one of the Alliance's trump cards, which could easily blunt the effect of Soviet progress if it is put to directed use properly and right now.

Miscellaneous Managerial Arguments

1. *Technical data handling and data transfers*, held by many to be impossible tasks, have belied the pessimists and are now a matter of successful record for even the most complex weapons systems yet devised.

2. *Production methods* have been solved by impressive pro-grammes of exchange of expertise and are no longer looked upon as peculiarities of national production habits that cannot be modified, changed or accepted.

3. *Competition*, which to date has been pretty much unbridled in armaments, with the spoils going generally to the largest industry, would no longer be an impediment and waste, but if controlled and equitably directed, need *not* be eliminated as a source of superior quality armaments.

4. *Employee practices, wages, audit and accounting, ownership, taxes, tariffs*, and numerous other management hurdles, each of which has heretofore been used as an argument position of retreat or frustration in the past, now have been resolved sufficiently to convince all concerned they can be overcome. The General MOUs are evidence of the ability to overcome the toughest arguments, and now mark progress and readiness for members to agree on difficult management areas *beforehand*.

5. *Modes of Organization* for collaboration have proven them-selves adaptable to all efforts. Appendix G is a brief description of those tried to date and which appear feasible in the future.

Summary

Reflecting on the above argumentation, it would appear that most, if not all, reasons for not collaborating have been or can be over-come. Admittedly, coalitions of unequals, of free countries, in joint economic and industrial manner is a difficult undertaking. It would be so much easier if we were a totalitarian coalition! But, thank God, we are not.

However, if the fate of the future Atlantic Community is constantly kept uppermost in mind, we must prove that efficiency, excellence and superiority *can* come from democratic coalitions. Other "uppermosts" to be kept in mind are the future plans and recent moves of the Soviet Union as the realities of scarce resources and internal problems catch up with an adversary dedicated to superior defensive, *plus* offensive, capabilities. Nothing approaches these two facts in importance. The need to spread the "word" has never been so pressing. It would be criminal not to recognize for ourselves and to enlighten our people as to the alternatives: mentioned earlier national anarchy, blackmail, defeat, or an inglorious "preemptive surrender."

NATO's Management Orphans

As mentioned earlier, a listing of NATO's "management orphans" is included. Tom Callaghan's perceptions of 1977 are as clear and appropriate as any to close this chapter.[14] The previous treatment of argumentations has addressed these and answered them to some extent. That which follows in the next two chapters will attempt to offer remedies for them as well as problems which transcend management and organizational ones. His perceptive list, which could well have been the result of a true management scholar, begins and continues with the question of "who is worrying about each of these?"

1. Duplication and waste.

2. Research and development planning, assignment and coordination.

3. Production planning, assignment and coordination.

4. Loss of economies of scale.

5. Cost/effectiveness or both.

6. Principles of good management.

7. Loss of equipment, weapons and power.

8. Industrial abortions and stagnation.

9. Unfilled jobs, economic losses.

10. Underutilization of resources.

14. Callaghan, Thomas J. Jr., *U.S./European Economic Cooperation in Military and Civil Technology*. The Center for Strategic and International Studies, Georgetown University, September, 1975, passim.

11. Quantitative and qualitative weapons losses.
12. Destructive competition.
13. Time lost in lead time/production skills.
14. Logistics problems.

Chapter 6

The Challenge to NATO: A Time for Decisions and Action

The Story Thus Far

Thus far, we have learned of an impressionable record of accomplishments toward the goal of international military standardization and weapons supremacy. We have also been made aware of billions of dollars of waste, loss of effectiveness, and the fact that the Soviet bloc now surpasses us in armed strength. We have identified the keystones of problems and of future success. We have learned that management problems are surmountable, as are organizational ones for each programme and project. We realize that more authority, better lasting structures, and other agreements are mandatory in order to move forward. We know we are superior to the potential enemy in every way but numbers of arms in Europe. We have not answered the question of *why* we tolerate this?

Perhaps one cannot answer the question of why we do as we do except to blame ignorance, selfishness, and lack of willpower. If we were a dictatorship such as the Soviet Union, it would be done *for* us, through us, and at the expense of our living and dignity. Our faults are the faults of free men and free nations and will probably continue; but despite them, the problem here and now is to achieve military superiority over an inferior aggressor (in all ways but one). This problem *is* solvable through some tough, new agreements; some hard, organizational work; some sound, management techniques; some unselfishness; and the rededication of free nations and "men of goodwill" to act *now*. Let us begin by dispelling some of the obstacles and impediments to clear thinking, a truthful assessment of the situation, and a positive approach to problems, real and imagined.

Half-Truths, Myths and Certain "Deliberate" Thinking Which Have Prevailed

Here is a simple listing and a brief description of some popular excuses, myths, and "deliberate" thinking that have impeded the common goal:

—The myth that "not much can be done" under the existing charter. This is not so. Its wording is as open as most of the world's great constitutions are for interpretation. The mechanics of collaboration are all permissible with the possible exception of the proposal to make NATO supra-national only insofar as defense of Europe, weaponry, and equipment are concerned. However, a new charter or amendment can include that, if that must be a prerequisite for such authority.

—The myth that "our" requirements are "different" from those of NATO. This agreement cannot stand up to the fact that it is *NATO's* requirements that are at the heart of the matter. It does not prevent nations from procuring other weapons to defend other places.

—The myth that NATO strategic, theater nuclear, and tactical doctrine cannot be sufficiently standardized to permit coordinated decision making. Again, the objective is NATO's real estate defense, not world-wide.

—The fallacious thinking that a proliferation of duplicate weapons makes it harder for the enemy to destroy them or defend against them! This is a favorite myth of the "interoperability alone" proponents who oppose standardization.

—The myth and half-truth that business and manufacturing methods are "different"; that specifications differ, drawings differ, measurement systems differ, processes differ, scheduling differs, sales policies differ, etc. Every successful project to date rejects these beliefs.

—The myth that different replacement cycles of national armaments cannot be overcome. All it takes is a Long-Term Defense Programme and its supporting actions.

—The usual persistence of polarization of ideas, such as those who believe only in "purist" standardization to those who are "100 percent efficiency" exponents. The truth lies in the pursuit and ongoing *process* of standardization, while modifying it in the light of variables more important than cost or efficiency.

—The myth that it is impossible to set common criteria for weapons selection.

—The myth that it is impossible to arrive at comment test and evaluation criteria and methods.

—The fear of interdependence and that it would lead to a loss of "national" security.

—The myth that military/industrial/governmental complexes differ so much from one member nation to another that they cannot be relied upon to support the common cause.

—The sad truth that these military/industrial/governmental complexes have not yet changed their habit of favoring their own weapons. The open and undercover insistence on holding technological advantage and weapons stockpiles — the "fortress" syndrome.

—The fear and wishful thinking that NATO may neither be necessary nor "in business" in the future. This is one of the most dangerous of all when coupled with a pervasive inertia, feelings of futility, the false hope that the enemy will change his objective and be benevolent, and the attitude of depending upon the "other fellow" to do the job.

—The simple excuse that our cultures are "different".

—The half-truth that joint development and production has not *always* been successful — hence, should not be pursued. A corollary argument would permit interoperability of food, fuel, and ammunition — but maintains that all the remainder is a waste of time!

—The myth that joint production is a problem because of franchise disagreements, delays in transfers of technical material, changes in design, and that it produces military "camels" instead of "workhorses," etc. The record of these having been completely overcome by able men of goodwill, and the military workhorses that have been produced negate this whole area of beliefs. And besides, since when have free, bright people given up on *any* managerial/technological challenge?

—The myth that specialization is not practical or "safe".

—The myth that "comparative advantage" is sacrosanct and will prevail.

—The half-truth that the "economic threat" will always outweigh the military threat. This argument is blatantly wrong, as shown by the record of world history and by plain common sense.

97

—The truth that nations and industries deliberately hold on to technological advantage and employment.

—The half-truths and self-serving reasoning which Callaghan labelled as "intractable obstacles," but which by their very statement contain their own remedies:

1. The fundamental disagreement on strategy between the U.S. and Europe — i.e., defense versus deterrence — an argument which may soon become academic. The truth is that both have become necessary.

2. The American idea that we can "go it alone". Curiously, the U.S. war-making ability is *admittedly* underfunded and over-extended at the time of writing, but 1980 is seeing some changes for the better.

3. The European defense-industrial base is fragmented, budgets for defense inadequate, and defense markets too small to compete on a transatlantic scale. This is in process of change.

4. European/North American burden sharing/benefit sharing impasse continues unresolved. This, too, is changing.

5. There is no structure for Allied armaments cooperation; no structure for determining requirements; no structure for R&D; no structure for allocation of projects; no rules as to management of cooperative projects; no cooperative framework (structure). All these are included in the plan which follows.

6. Out-of-phase projects and sunk costs are viewed as untouchables and are never cancelled or swallowed on an equitable basis for the good of *all*. The plan would prevent these from occurring.

7. There is a reluctance to face up to the magnitude of the political, economic, and military effort required to remedy the situation. The plan calls for redressing the entire problem.

It is submitted, on the basis of past successes covered in this study, the evidence of fallibility of the half-truths, myths, and "deliberate" argumentation, and the will and momentum underway to move forward, that all of the above obstacles, are capable of change and open to remedial measures.

Chapter 7

Towards the Goal of Commonality: An Achievable Framework

National and NATO Self-Analyses and Agreements Required

At each national level and at NATO level, each member must take immediate, honest self-analysis of their policies, procedures, and attitudes and proclaim their complete willingness to participate in these actions:

—Agree to establish a common NATO identity — an Atlantic Community for defense — a real North American/European Defense Institution.

—Agree to establish institutional/organizational/enfranchised agencies and modes for collaboration. Set the structures and authority first; requirements will follow.

—Agree to establish the characteristics of a common military doctrine necessary to an Atlantic Community for Defense.

—Agree to establish the characteristics of weapons, equipment, and support to carry out that common NATO military doctrine.

—Agree to make every effort to bring Spain into NATO.

—Agree to consider inviting Japan (and eventually China) into a broadened North Atlantic/Pacific Treaty Organization.

—Agree to the goal of total alliance in four to five years.

—Agree to help cut national costs through the elimination of most duplication and *uncontrolled* competition.

—Agree to retain and go forward with managed, rational competition, and managed collaboration in research, development, and production.

—Agree to determine how to control and even modify the icons of cost-effectiveness and comparable advantage where necessary.

—Agree to faithfully follow a two-way street and multi-way

streets in trade and arms procurement, including variably-timed offsets and other practical adjustments.

—Agree that the objective of fairness and rationalization will be followed in order to balance contributions. There may not be equality, but there will be equity. If benefits are shared, so too must be costs and other burdens.

—Agree that the economic welfare or political welfare or any other "welfare" neither have priority over nor rank above the *common safety welfare* and the military force necessity to insure that common safety and survival.

—Agree that, while reality tells us that 100 percent commonality of weapons and standardization across the military spectrum may *not* be achievable, it is the *objective* and overrides all other factors, on balance.

—Agree that institutional strengthening and other procedural changes will be necessary, such as the removal of procurement restrictions where armaments or offsets are concerned.

—Agree that each member nation will strive for much more parliamentary/congressional participation; hence, more popular participation, and more top executive/ministerial participation as well.

—Agree to a joint, aggressive, rational and immediate exploration of research and development of weapons and equipments. Agree to control and direct the whole range of options in this crucial field from pure competition to assigned specialization.

—Agree to an aggressive programme, and actions to bring about "NATO thinking", *not* national, in all places of high authority and to all peoples. Agree to deliberately raise individuals and organizations involved in NATO to the highest possible levels of authority and expect action.

—Agree to build upon and reorganize certain present organizations; both NATO, national and industrial; create new ones where indicated; and dismantle or merge the efforts of older ones. The goal: to structure a top-to-bottom organization of national and espcially joint bodies, fully empowered to do their job, adequately staffed, and designed to be cooperative parts of a single purpose organization — a free-world armaments structure which can bring about collaboration, standardization, rationalization, interoperability — and all the other necessary parts of the total effort.

—Agree to emphasize the dire need for establishing structure *now* so it will be in place to manage future requirements. Agree that present projects be completed as soon as possible.

—Agree that the goal of International (NATO) Military Standardization (IMS) in its broadest context, which includes rationalization, standardization, interoperability, interchangeability, and all their nuances — commonality in all forms — is an absolute necessity.

—Agree to plan, not only short-range, mid-range, and long-range, but also ongoing, constantly updated, "rolling" operational and weapons plans.

—Agree to consolidate national and NATO political wills and commitments.

Without reciting again the record of obstacles overcome and collaborate projects given as evidence throughout this analysis, even the most complex ones, it is clear they *are* solvable. Substantive problems *have* proven consultable, negotiable, and manageable. Admittedly, the two most difficult areas to resolve at this point are the above necessary rededication suggestions and some instititional changes and restructuring recommendations which follow.

It is time to turn to a consideration of many excellent plans already proposed, their similarities and differences, and to take the best of each and propose a master plan as a point of departure for sincere, immediate agreement on such a plan, or on any modifications which would serve the same purposes.

Approaches/Options for Attaining International Military Standardization

The now familiar and popular concept of a "two-way street" for research, development, production, sales, and technology (ideas) can be realized, but not without determination, intelligence, and hard work.

Some broad avenues of approach which have been consolidated from the literature and research are these:

—Create a common defense market roughly divided into major and minor components based on capabilities first and on competition second.

—Create a NATO Weapons Procurement Agency (NWPA) responsible for all weapons and equipment procurements.

—Initiate a voluntary, cooperative exchange of civil and military technology of armaments and related areas.

—The United States, Canada, and all European members must divide equitably the total procurement costs and benefits of armaments. Initiate an open government procurement policy.

—The United States, Canada, and all European members initiate a substantial and equitable programme of research and development and then depend upon the designated member(s) to carry it out for all. Initiate an open government research and development exchange policy.

—The United States, Canada, and all European members initiate the same kind of designation and dependency for production within an agreed framework for competition (controlled as to numbers, capability, and equity). Initiate an open government procurement policy for production of armaments and related items.

—The above recommendations would be backed by a continuing programme of balancing sales on a dollar-for-dollar basis. The first offsets to be used would stem from armaments equipment and services, but *could* be followed by offsets and purchases of technically-advanced commercial products.

—All members commence immediately a multi-way street in the exchange of ideas, drawings, technical data not only for current projects but those slated for short- and mid-term procurement, until optimum traffic is achieved. This could well apply to major, high-pay-off items which may result in two equal, but different, weapons for the Alliance.

—Structure NATO organizations and member nations' organizations in order to be capable of taking action on ideas, negotiations, munitions/armament cycles and other initiatives well in advance of one nation or more becoming so deeply engaged that their investment, pride, reluctance to share, sunk costs, etc., defeat the IMS goal. Initiate sensible, common replacement cycles and reduce fluctuating demand.

—Accelerate and complete within rigorous time-frames all current ad hoc programmes and projects in order to clear the collaborative structure to take on the initiatives outlined above. Those that can and must be done now, under present procedures, must not be retarded.

—Apply the initiatives as soon as possible to the big pay-off items. The others will follow suit, but the need is to prove early in the total thrust that quality, major weapons "workhorses" *can* be realized with technological, military, economic, employment, and least cost per member benefits. The structuring of interim agencies is considered acceptable for big pay-off items if the most desirable ones may require some time. Competitive procurement should be used especially in R&D (without needless duplication due to lack of sharing technology), and to the maximum for production, especially for the big pay-off items. This means a big pay-off to the goal of *standardization* and not entirely to the producer. The principles and operations pertaining to fairness and *juste retour* can be handled by a suitable agency. Big pay-off item designations should be offset by (1) smaller items assigned to capable smaller members, and (2) the purchase of technically-advanced commercial products.

—Continue (and even modify or enlarge) successful standardization groups and agencies such as CNAD, NAMSO, NIAG, AGARD, NADGE, and many others. Modifications, changes or elimination of any of them will depend upon the accepted plans and actions of the future. The next chapter deals with existing and proposed organizational structures.

Existing and Proposed Structures and Responsibilities

There is a great amount of excellent structure that can be salvaged and also built upon in the current complex, and there is a need for some new structure to attain the goal of International Military Standardization. That which follows will be a mix of the two.

The point to be made is that while an objective may be agreed upon (and has been frequently), it is the *mechanisms* that make it possible. Indeed, this writer is of the opinion that in this, the most complex organizational and managerial area one can imagine, it is the mechanisms, the formal structural and *ongoing* mechanisms, that are more important to begin with than the particular armaments objectives. Let the structure be born and the requirements determinations will follow, not vice-versa, as has been the case. If the real culprits are institutional intransigence and lack of adequate structure to do the job, then let that be the first task to be met head-on and resolved.

We now have a record of highly complex consortia successes to build upon; we now have political awareness; we now have commitment to more funds; we now have successful, cooperative, industrial experience; we now have technological excellence. What we need is public awareness (the political will), and through that will, the necessary agreement to go forward.

Permanent, Enfranchised Organizations: Non-NATO and NATO

1. Starting at the top, institutionalize even more arrangements with the Eurogroup, the Four Power Group, and FINABEL to obtain full, necessary, and top-level governmental inputs to NATO. Such help will fill the need for multinational political, economic, and industrial advice as well for armaments matters, as at present. More frequent scheduled meetings with structured agendas should be sought. The International Staff, augmented by CNAD (civil side) and the Military Committee (MC) (military side), and a new joint policy-making group later discussed, should be the focal point and be responsible for the meetings and resulting decisions.

2. Strengthen the Independent European Programme Group (IEPG) in its relationship to NATO. As mentioned earlier, persuade France to return fully to the Alliance and thus drop the Independent part of the IEPG. Give NATO full recognition of and expectancy for the Group to make inputs for *all* European members. Agree on the need for full cooperation, advice and action by the Group for industrial/procurement matters. Give equal recognition to the U.S./Canadian Group and expect the same advice and support. Schedule frequent, structured meetings with the same NATO policy organization mentioned above for Eurogroup, especially the NWPA. The agenda would be mainly of an industrial/production nature. But both Eurogroup and the IEPG should be vital links with the European Economic Community.

3. All member nations take steps to establish stronger, enfranchised offices at ministerial or secretarial levels, to become high-level "Offices of NATO Affairs", so that CNAD representatives will be the most able individuals entirely concerned with NATO matters. Grant the super-CNAD power to make group decisions

for inputs into the new policy group and into NATO International Staff meetings. Emphasize the responsibility of direct advice to the Council if necessary, and vice-versa. Their inputs for the Long-Range Defense Programme and others should range from armaments planning policies, armaments community agreements, to technological and production matters which are their main concern within their own nations but which need exposure and agreement advantage taken of at the NATO level.

4. Strengthen NATO as the primary force and direction for all IMS by reorganizing the present organization by placing the International Staff (IS) in a coordinating chair position, above both the civil and military components, for all IMS matters. This is the nucleus for a top policy-making body for heading the entire new standardization thrust. This will not diminish in any way the current responsibilities of the CNAD, for example, or other interested civil committees, or of the Military Committee, and especially the MAS beneath it. The role of the expanded International Staff (IS) would be that of coordinator, controller, clearing house, initiator (if appropriate), and adjudicator for IMS matters which could either be agreed upon at that level, or if not, passed on to the DPC. There is nothing in the present NATO agreement and its several modifying understandings which would rule out the decision for this. It could be made in house, in NATO, just as present structures have been built. Indeed, it would be more in keeping with the wording of the NATO Treaty to do such better structuring towards the agreed goal of IMS.

5. Enlarge and invest authority in the most obvious divisions of the IS — namely, the Assistant Secretary General for Defense Support and the Assistant Secretary General for Defense Planning and Policy — to become the chief organizational units responsible within the IS and to the Secretary General and Council, to carry out the day-to-day responsibilities inherent in the recommendations in no. 4 above. The IS, through these two divisions, would be performing a necessary and, in the author's opinion, appropriate role as the best qualified organs through which both civil and military inputs could be handled in the IMS area for a total NATO approach.

Among the major duties these International Staff Divisions should be considered for are chairing and coordinating:

—Decisions on and coordination of the Short-, Medium-, and Long-Range Defense Programmes.

—Decisions on and coordination of matters of commonality ranging from standardization to interoperability to others.

—Decisions on and coordination of major standardization programmes.

Or, what is considered a broader and better approach, consider the next proposal:

6. Create a NATO Weapons Development/Production Management/Policy Council or Group. Consider how worthwhile a NATO Weapons Development/Production Management/Policy Council or Group or NATO International Military Standardization Group or Council, made up of *representatives* of the IS (International Staff) (Defense Suppport and Defense Planning), CNAD (Conference of National Armaments Directors), NMAS (NATO Military Committee, and International Military Staff), NWPA (NATO Weapons Procurement Agency), NIAG (NATO Industrial Advisory Group), and WFMs (Weapons Family Managers) could be. This should be chaired by the IS and would require no additional people but would rather provide a top advisory group at the operational/ policy level which could resolve problems and decisions *prior* to their entering the formal pattern or Council decision-making. Such a group could consider these policies and responsibilities to start the new thrust:

—Encourage and control ideas, negotiations, and policies on weapons collaboration.

—Prepare objectives and plans for short-term, medium-term, and long-term defense programmes.

—Decide on matters of rationalization, standardization, interchangeability, compatibility, and harmonization for review and approval by the Council.

—Develop the necessary accounting and audit groups to recommend decisions on ultimate offsets in either weapons, commercial, or dollar offsets. Final decisions would again be agreed upon by the Council. Coordinate recommendations with other such standardization and support agencies as NAMSO which also have an interest and capability for inputs.

—Become the main line of coordination and flow of information between the CNAD, MS (MAS), and the Secretary/Council.

106

—Decide on agencies, consortia or other organizations which may be required to carry out development and production which may lie outside the Family-of-Weapons framework.

—Act as the office to encourage and carry out cross-pollination of European/U.S./Canadian ideas.

—Become the contact point for other major multination organizations and weapons organizations which lie outside the NATO framework, such as a European Common Arms/Equipment Market, a Production Policy Group of Nations, Euromissile, Panavia, etc.

—Prepare production policies and the national/industrial inputs.

—Assist in designing multinational organizations for an item of a family or a complete family of weapons.

—Recommend policy on engineering management controls, drawings, conversions, mathematical systems, accounting and audit, wages, hours, production rates, scheduling, capital, economics of scale, sharing, etc., etc. — all the hard areas of managerial expertise and cooperation.

—Make decisions on and coordination of rationalization.

—Make decisions on and coordination of interoperability.

—Make decisions on Families of Weapons and Managers.

—Allocate Families of Weapons, or items within families based on capability, specialization, fairness, etc.

—Make recommendations to the DPC on and coordinate all defense policies related to IMS.

7. Among the duties a Weapons Family Manager (WFM) might be considered for are to:

—Coordinate and serve as an interface in dealing with the member nations military forces, with NATO intelligence, with NATO and civil service agencies, and most importantly, with a new NATO Procurement Agency.

—Determine the functional requirements for weapons systems within their family.

—Determine future plans for NATO weapons, equipment, and support material.

—Assess new weapons candidates in the conceptual and developmental stages.

—Develop, recommend, and assign priorities — for recommendation to the IS (and CNAD and MC jointly) through the Defense Support

107

Division — to a coordinated plan for their own Family of Weapons based on cost and effectiveness. Decisions on acceptance of family items vis-à-vis other family items would be the ultimate charge of the IS and Council.

—Establish mixes of weapons in each family when appropriate and decide upon extensions of current weapons systems.

—Serve as the NATO point of contact for all information concerning a family.

—Senior positions in each family to have civil *and* military representation, at high rank, from the dominant (larger-share, larger-use nations). Rotation of command or management is both feasible and desirable.

—Suggested Families of Weapons from two different sources were listed earlier, however, a broad-gauge suggestion for a "family organization" follows, taken from Lidy:

Weapons Family Manager[1]
(Senior Member Nation)

Deputy for Concept & Validation	Deputy for Full Scale Development & Testing	Deputy for Production/Deployment
Engineering	Integrated Logistics	Configuration Management
Planning	Procurement	Production

Lidy foresees not more than twenty-five to forty military and civilian personnel with proper experience as being necessary to carry out a Family of Weapons Office, a minimal cost for what might be expected of such a step forward. Likewise, the number required to expand the Defense Support Division and Planning and Policies Division should be reasonable but adequate to perform the interface/cooperative/decision-making tasks at their levels.

—FoW is progressing nicely, although with some differences from initial plans.

8. Create a NATO Weapons Procurement Agency (NWPA). This would be a permanent, independent organization reporting to the Council, serving as the focal point for all weapons procure-

1. Lidy, A. Martin, Lt. Col., U.S.A., "NATO Standardization — An Alternative Approach." *Defense Systems Management Review*, Summer, 1977, p. 54.

ment by NATO. It should, among other functions:

—Become the centralized management office for all common procurements of international (NATO) armaments and equipment on a competitive basis.

—Become the agency responsible for the task of balancing the accounts of the member nations for use in the offset process mentioned earlier.

—Eliminate the need for procurement agencies except for special cases outside the overall framework.

—Be responsible to structure for communication with all interested national defense industries (a) through NIAG-CNAD for Europe; (b) through the U.S. and Canadian counterparts; and (c) through independent industries.

—Vigorously develop competition, coordination and a new thrust toward R&D and Production by rationalized sources and be the repository of information on procurement capabilities.

—Insure fairness in R&D, production, costs, schedules, technological capability, and member awareness, while taking into account the diversification of the bases for all of these.

—Recommend balance of procurement dollars or offsets, not on a "forced" schedule but on a flexible timetable that will insure equitable completion at an agreed time.

—Be responsible to the Council, perhaps through the new weapons policy council, rather than through purely civil or military channels.

—Receive advice, support, and in turn support the inputs from CNAD and NAMSO.

9. Continue NAMSO and enlarge as necessary its capability to facilitate the optimum supply of spare parts, maintenance, and repair facilities. No change in place or status is recommended except that the United States should be a primary user. The aims are to:

—Continue under the Defense Support Division.

—Interpret national logistics responsibility to mean what it should — responsibility for providing for logistics support — and get rid of the traditional allegiance to the idea that each nation must perform its own logistics. The principle has already been tried successfully of having common items, even technical ones, supplied by a common agency.

—Insist on logistics being a collective agency.

10. Continue the MAS and the newly-formed ASI (an advanced

systems integrating group) to inject military requirements for planned, future weapons. Continue AGARD because of the importance of air and space technology in warfare. Continue to rely on its consultations, panels and exchange programmes. The Military Committee would continue as its point of contact, and the committee would be empowered to request studies and assistance from AGARD within their role of providing advice on major weapons and space vehicles.

A Beginning – U.S. Examples

With some important exceptions, the United States has already proclaimed a strategy, treated earlier, which is in keeping with the above agreements, goals and organizational structure. Within the past three years, it also has:

1. Agreed to mutual planning of national Research and Devlopment within the Alliance.

2. Agreed to standardization of weapons if at all possible, and if not, to achieve interoperability.

3. Decided to concentrate on a smaller number of really important high-pay-off items for standardization and interoperability.

4. Agreed to the Family-of-Weapons concept even to recommending these members: airbase warning, fighter aircraft, air-to-air missiles, ammunition (all sizes), communications, electronic warfare, aircraft cross-servicing, logistics and standard parts material, and antiship missiles.

5. Proclaimed a willingness to give considerable weighting in the competitive process to equipment that Europeans collectively agree upon as their standard.

6. Agreed to pursue simpler procedures to expedite government approval for competitive and cooperative development and production programmes.

7. Increased its armament budget to fairly close to the 3 percent agreed upon by the Alliance. At this writing, the President has asked for $3 billion more in the present budget to make it a true increase in expenditures and not merely a matter of keeping up with inflation. He won his point and more.

8. Agreed to policies to better tap Allied capabilities and techniques.

9. Agreed to disapprove programmes if NATO standardization/interoperability goals are not met when the system or weapon is a NATO one.

10. Passed legislation by the Congress requiring an annual NATO Readiness Report from the Secretary of Defense.

11. Agreed to base U.S. decisions on complete and validated data on foreign-made items.

12. Commence a Department of Defense Triad of Initiatives.

The policies may not all emanate from the same source, but all can be traced to a growing, legal administrative and legislative backing. This brief recital of some U.S.-proclaimed policies is not intended to indicate it is the "ideal" partner to be followed at any cost, but to indicate the need for *all* members to seriously analyze, publically proclaim, and then follow through on the essential agreements to do the job we all know must be done. Common political effort is still at the heart of things. Even strategy has its roots in political support. If the political will is forthcoming; economic, strategic, and technical cooperation will follow.

A Recommended Timetable

Several authorities have recently made the observation that, by 1983 at the latest, the Soviets will overtake the Alliance in technology. Some say they have already. If this is true, and when coupled with the undeniable truth that no one can *afford* to go it alone any longer, a rigorous timetable for agreement and organizational functioning must be followed. Again, after reviewing the opinion of many authorities, they seem to agree on:

1. One to two years for completing short-range projects, and a rigorous one- to two-year time schedule for commencing production on those now approved by two or more nations.

2. For mid-range projects which could hopefully be commenced under the new, more effective cooperative structure, three to four years at most.

3. For long-range projects, all of which should come under the new structure, five to ten years at most. Fifteen years is perhaps closer to reality for major weapons.

All this requires that the structure and functions be immediately agreed upon nationally, and as an Alliance in the coming year. It will then require a year to place them in commission. Meanwhile, those recommendations having to do with weapons planning and weapons planning structures must receive first priority to commence as soon as possible.

Chapter 8

A New Spirit or a New Treaty?

Possibilities Under the Present Treaty

All the proposals for agreement set forth in this analysis thus far are deemed possible, if not probable, under the wording of the present Charter. Article 2 states, "eliminate conflict in their international policies and will encourage *economic collaboration* between any or all of them" (italics mine). Article 3, one of the most appropriate, states, "the Parties, separately and jointly, by means of continuous and effective self-help and mutual aid, will maintain and develop their individual and *collective capacity* to resist armed attack." Article 9, which establishes the Council, states, "The Council shall set up *subsidiary bodies as may be necessary*" to implement the provisions of the Treaty. Article 10 opens the door to other European members. Article 12 has this little quoted power, ". . . including the *development of universal as well as regional arrangements* under the Charter of the United Nations for the maintenance of international peace and security." It is largely Article 3 which permits the *development of joint capacity*, from which stems, among other things, the *coordination of military instruction and training, joint programmes for equipment, and the infrastructure programme*. It is mainly by reference to Article 9, buttressed by the others, that the organization has gradually been built up and could continue to be built to incorporate the recommendations of the previous chapter and this one, if it were determined to construe the wording to that end, just as it is with any fine constitution.

Possibilities Under a Revised or New Treaty

However, if it is felt by the members, as it is by many leading proponents of a strong NATO, that the first treaty is flawed because it called for a military effort only, then either revisions to the treaty, as provided for by Articles 12 and 13 could be the route, or indeed, a new treaty could be begun in NATO's 4th decade. If a revised or new treaty were acceptable to the members, the provisions to make it truly a military/industrial/economic (as related to defense) agreement have already been concisely set forth by Thomas Callaghan, Jr., among others, and should provide for the following:

1. General Agreements:
—To join the technological and industrial resources in a North Atlantic Defense Market.
—To establish a continental European defense industrial base.
—To provide for the equitable sharing of Allied defense burdens and benefits as a pro rata share of combined NATO GNP.
—Employ the formula (56 percent North America, 44 percent Europe) to provide support to the less-developed Southern Flank nations.
—Encourage the less-developed members to participate soonest.
—Permit Japan, Australia, and New Zealand to accede to the treaty.

2. Establishment of a North Atlantic Defense Market. Building upon the first agreement, the United States should:
—Offer to join Europe and Canada in determining all new weapons and requirements for the collective defense.
—Offer to agree with Europe and Canada on an efficient and equitable assignment of new weapons development and production projects.
—Offer to open all American subcontracts for competition on a reciprocal basis for competitive award on both sides of the Atlantic.
—Offer to share equitable the costs of assistance to less-developed members until they can provide their own share.
—Offer to increase the total American defense budget by at least 4 percent in real terms for five years.

3. Europe should agree to:
—Organize its defense procurement on a united and collective

basis, including a collective Independent European Programme Group to finance and manage multinational research, development, and production/support programmes with the U.S. and Canada.

—Increase its collective defense expenditures by 5 percent a year until its total defense expenditures equal its pro rata share of total GNP.

—Make the same offers and join with the U.S. and Canada in those agreements listed above for the U.S.

—Take specific steps to compensate fully for the United States' annual balance of payments deficit on military account.

—Agree to permit Japan, Australia, and New Zealand to accede to the treaty.

4. Other critical problems to be addressed in a revised or new treaty:

—Establish fixed minimum percentages of defense budgets to investment and support of NATO.

—Establish minimum percentages of Allied defense procurement funds for research and technical building blocks.

—Require reliable statistics be kept.

—Establish security policies.

—Provide that military trade need not be balanced at a project or on an annual basis.

—Establish a senior and junior NATO Industrial College.

—Establish short-term goals and funds pledged for the next five years, over and above current budgets. The goals should call for implementing STANAG's and provide fixed goals of procurement orders from each other.

—Establish mid-term and long-term goals; three years for harmonized basic research; three years for development of complementary projects; four years of common logistic support for present weapons; and military-industrial interdependence by the twelfth year.[1]

Most of the above is identical to the recommended agreements listed earlier as being possible *within* the present treaty. Thus, it appears that, in general, those who have dealt with and studied

1. Taken from Callaghan, Thomas A., Jr., *A New Atlantic Treaty of Technological Cooperation and Trade.* Allied Interdependence Newsletter No. 17, 20 Nov. 1979. The Center for Strategic and International Studies, Georgetown University.

the requirements are fairly well in accord with what needs to be done. It is now a matter of getting on with initiatives and concensus. For a sensational kick-off date, as Tom Callaghan recently said in the author's presence, "I can think of no better initiative to begin with than the President of the United States' *State of the Union* message to the Congress." The author agrees that it is the United States which *must* take the initiative.

The Way Ahead — or The Way to Retreat

Let us commence now with an admission that IMS and collaborative programmes and projects *can* be done and *have been* done successfully — but do we really *want* to do it? Let us commence with a clear picture of the alternatives always in mind. Let us commence with a sincere desire to persevere, to grow and to maintain a world wherein the free person, the individual, may still exist. There is nothing *in* the Charter to *prevent* organizational change; nothing *outside* the Charter but national pride, the political will, and public unawareness which could prevent a change in attitude and spirit; nothing but half-truths and myths to prevent the world's greatest governmental/industrial/military Alliance from full cooperation. As Mr. Carl Damm of the Federal Republic of Germany wrote in May, 1979, "NATO is no supranational enterprise. The fifteen partners are, and remain, sovereign nations. However, as long as NATO exists, the participating governments and parliaments *must act more and more in a spirit as if we had already transferred rights to NATO*"[2] (italics mine). But if a new charter really is deemed necessary, let us get on with it. There is nothing to prevent an Atlantic Community but past limited vision, thinking, and actions. NATO's future is *not* uncertain. What is needed is a determination now by all members to go forward with the excellent plans now underway and proposed and to readdress their enormous collective potential and ability to provide for superiority in any kind of conflict. The stakes are higher than sovereignty, or one-upmanship, or economic welfare, or even a balance of power. The ultimate goal at stake is to provide the

2. Carl Damm, Chairman of the NATO Military Committee's Sub-Committee on Defense Cooperation. Supplement Report to the Report of the Sub-Committee on Defense Cooperation, May, 1979.

security to maintain Western civilization's most important product, as Robert S. Ritchie so aptly concluded as early as 1956 after analyzing the economics of an alliance: "its emphasis on the significance and value of the individual."[3]

An authority once said that the real written record of man is about 5,500 years, and in that time, 15,000 acknowledged *wars* have been fought — an average of three per year. It is mindbending to think of where we might have progressed without having to resort to violent power. However, statistically, rationally, and practically, one cannot believe that such a record of man and nations having to resort to violent power will cease in our lifetime. But as intelligent, supreme beings are we afraid to be laughed at if we look to "one world" for our descendants? Power, *balances of power,* and even wars may be necessary to reach that objective — but let the world know it *is* our objective! Meanwhile, we must acknowledge that power is *real*, it has and will be used, and we — not they — must achieve adequate power to prevail because we believe in peaceful coexistence.

3. Ritchie, Robert S., *NATO, The Economics of An Alliance*, The Ryerson Press, Toronto, 1956, p. 144.

Appendices

Appendix A
Organization and Component Charts*

NATO ORGANIZATIONS
CONCERNED WITH COLLABORATIVE WEAPONS EFFORTS

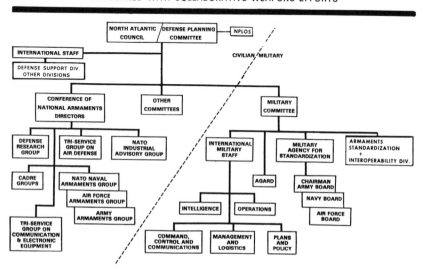

Chart 1

*These charts are from the *Multinational Program Management Course*, at the U.S. Department of Defense Systems Management College, Fort Belvoir, Virginia, Fall, 1979.

120

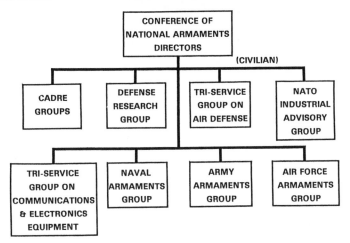

Chart 2

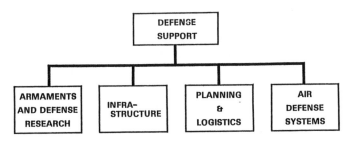

Chart 3

NAMSA - SUPPORTED SYSTEMS

NIKE	FORWARD SCATTER
HONEST JOHN	AND SATELLITE
	COMMUNICATIONS
SIDEWINDER	STATIONS
BULLPUP	NADGE
HAWK	NAMFI (NATO
LANCE	MISSILE FIRING
	INSTALLATION)
TOW	
	MARK 37/44
F-104	TORPEDOES

Chart 4

NATO PRODUCTION, LOGISTIC AND MANAGEMENT ORGANIZATIONS

STANDARDIZATION

NATO HAWK PRODUCTION & LOGISTICS

NATO MULTI-ROLE COMBAT AIRCRAFT DEVELOPMENT AND
PRODUCTION MANAGEMENT (NAMMO)

CENTRAL EUROPE PIPELINE SYSTEM

NATO MAINTENANCE AND SUPPLY (NAMSO)

NATO AIRBORNE EARLY WARNING PROGRAM OFFICE

NATO INTEGRATED COMMUNICATION SYSTEM MANAGEMENT

Chart 5

122

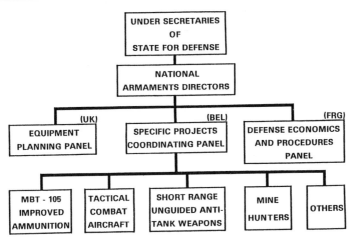

Chart 6

EUROGROUP ORGANIZATION

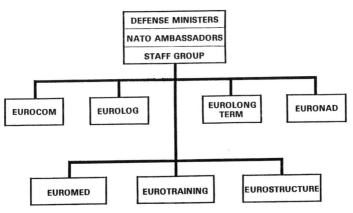

Chart 7

123

NATO (1949)	EUROGROUP (1968)	WEU (1948)	FINABEL	IEPG (1976)
BELGIUM	BELGIUM	BELGIUM	BELGIUM	BELGIUM
CANADA	--	--	--	--
DENMARK	DENMARK	--	--	DENMARK
FRANCE	--	FRANCE	FRANCE	FRANCE
GERMANY	GERMANY	GERMANY	GERMANY	GERMANY
GREECE	GREECE	--	--	GREECE
ICELAND	--	--	--	--
ITALY	ITALY	ITALY	ITALY	ITALY
LUXEMBOURG	LUXEMBOURG	LUXEMBOURG	LUXEMBOURG	LUXEMBOURG
NETHERLANDS	NETHERLANDS	NETHERLANDS	NETHERLANDS	NETHERLANDS
NORWAY	NORWAY	--	--	NORWAY
PORTUGAL	--	--	--	--
TURKEY	TURKEY	--	--	TURKEY
UNITED KINGDOM	UNITED KINGDOM	UNITED KINGDOM	UNITED KINGDOM	UNITED KINGDOM
UNITED STATES	--	--	--	--

Chart 8

Chart 9

Appendix B

NATO Military Agency for Standardization: Working Panels

Naval Panels

1. Maritime Technological Data
2. Helicopter Operations from ships other than A/C Carriers
3. Replenishment at Sea
4. Amphibious Warfare
5. Naval Fuels and Lubricants
6. Mine Warfare, Technical Publications, Tactical Publications, Exercise Evaluation
7. Naval Medical
8. RADHAZ

Army Panels

1. Army Fuels and Lubricants
2. Combat Clothing and Equipment
3. Materials Handling
4. NBC Material
5. Movements and Transport
6. Land Force Air Mobility
7. Camouflage and Concealment
8. Explosive Ordnance Disposal Interservice
9. Combat Engineering
10. Ammunition Interchangeability
11. Artillery Procedures
12. Land Force Operational Procedures
13. Intelligence Procedures
14. Land Force Tactical Doctrine
15. Land Force Logistics

Air Panels

1. Air Traffic Control
2. A/C Instruments and Aircrew Standardization
3. Interservice Laser Interoperability
4. Air Electrical
5. Search and Rescue
6. Flight Safety
7. Electromagnetic Capability
8. Maps and Charts
9. Lasar Panel on Safe Exposure Levels
10. Photo Equipment and Materials
11. Photo Recce Interpretation
12. Aeromedical
13. Air Transport
14. Air Armament
15. NATO Tactical Air Doctrine
16. A/C Gasious Systems
17. Airfield Marking and Lighting
18. Aircraft Standard Parts
19. Aviation Fuels and Lubricants
20. POL Handling Equipment
21. Aircraft Cross Servicing
22. Interservice Tactical Air Operational Procedures

Progress Report:
CNAD Ad Hoc Study Group for a Possible Periodic Armaments Planning System (PAPS)

1 November 1979

In the fall of 1976 the Conference of National Armaments Directors (CNAD) established an Ad Hoc Study Group to examine a possible Periodic Armaments Planning System (PAPS) for use by NATO. This action stemmed from a general concern on the part of the National Armaments Directors (NADs) that national equipment programmes were not sufficiently responsive to the needs of NATO forces, especially in the areas of standardization and interoperability of weapons.

NATO Armaments Planning Review (NAPR)

The first year of study resulted in a procedure called the NATO Armaments Planning Review (NAPR). This procedure (Figure 1) consists of an annual input from nations of their plans to replace currently deployed equipment. A second input is an assessment by the NATO Military Authorities (NMAs) of the priorities for standardization and/or interoperability in key categories of equipment (mission areas). The European input is provided through the Independent European Program Group (IEPG) and the U.S. and Canadian inputs are provided separately. The replacement schedules and NMA inputs are provided to the NATO International Staff and the Main Groups[1] to be reviewed for opportunities for cooperation not previously exploited. The review can also identify areas where nations are diverging from standardization or interoperability as a result of independent national

1. NATO Army Armaments Group (NAAG): NATO Naval Armaments Group (NNAG); NATO Air Force Armaments Group (NAFAG); Tri-Service Group on Communications and Electronic Equipment (TSGCEE); Tri-Service Group on Air Defense (TSGAD).

decisions. The conclusions and recommendations drawn from this review are then provided to the CNAD for action.

At the fall 1977 meeting the CNAD directed that a trial be conducted using a few equipment categories to determine the utility of these procedures. The results have now been analyzed by the National Armaments Directors' representatives (NADREPS) and final procedures were approved by the CNAD this fall. With these procedures adopted by the CNAD, NATO planners will gain better insight into national equipment replacement plans (a process which has been random at best in the past) and national perspectives should be better reflected in NATO decisions.

Two other benefits should accrue: first the NMA's judgment on priorities will be considered at an early point in the CNAD's decision process, thus having more impact on equipment decisions. In many cases collaborative projects have suffered because the NMA's military judgment has been available too late in the decision process. A second benefit is that NAPR elevates progress or lack of progress towards standardization and interoperability to high-level national authorities (NADs) who can take appropriate action at home or within NATO if things aren't getting done.

Structure for NATO Planning

A drawback of NAPR is that the data reflect a rather mature stage of national planning. When national equipment replacement schedules are firm it is difficult to accommodate programme changes brought about via attempts to collaborate. A major problem has been a lack of early visibility into national military requirements and a NATO review before national commitments were made. A second but related problem was incomplete information on national plans and a lack of discipline in the reporting process for collaborative programmes. Since NAPR partially addressed the second problem area and was under trial, the Study Group focused on developing a solution to the first problem; that of encouraging early discussions of military requirements.

The first task was to reach agreement on what was meant by early. This was achieved by defining the phases of a weapon system's life cycle and the activities embodied within those phases. Six phases were agreed as representative of a typical weapon

system life cycle: (1) Prefeasibility; (2) Feasibility; (3) Development; (4) Production; (5) In-Service; and (6) Disengagement.
These are shown graphically in Figure 2 with reference to the equivalent phases of the DoD Acquisition Process (DSARC).

There is a great deal of similarity between PAPS and the DSARC process, but two differences are worth noting. First, PAPS defines the start of the weapon system life cycle as the point when military authorities forward the mission need. This is somewhat earlier than the DoD, since we define the start as the point when approval of the need is obtained from the Secretary of Defense. PAPS also recommends attention be given to the in-service and disengagement phases at the mature stages of the weapons system life cycle, whereas DSARC visibility terminates at the production decisions.

The CNAD agreed that procedures for the joint conduct of the first two phases of PAPS should be developed, underlining a concern that national programmes were often begun without considering the needs of NATO. There was, however, disagreement on whether a structure for the subsequent phases would be of value. Some NADS believed that an effective NAPR would provide sufficient information to augment existing reporting procedures and provide adequate oversight of mature programmes. At the fall 1978 meeting the CNAD directed further development of the procedures for Phases 1 and 2 and preparation of a trial plan to evaluate their utility. Further work on Phases 3 through 6 was to take second priority.

Trial Objectives

Within Phases 1 and 2 of PAPS, there are four decision points or Milestones (Figure 3): the first is the point where a Mission Need Document (MND) is forwarded by a military authority through NATO to NADs for review and possible action. The second milestone occurs when two or more nations have agreed to an Outline NATO Staff Target (ONST). This document restates the mission need and identifies technical, financial, and schedule factors which form the basis of joint prefeasibility studies. The ONST is roughly the equivalent of the DoD Mission Element Need Statement (MENS). The third milestone occurs at the conclusion of prefeasibility studies, which, in the DSARC would be equivalent to reaching Milestone I. At this time a NATO Staff Target (NST) is completed which forms the basis for feasibility studies. A Memorandum of Understanding (MOU) is also signed by those nations which agree to conduct feasibility studies. The fourth milestone occurs at the completion of the feasibility studies and the drafting of a NATO Staff Requirement (NSR) which details the performance goals of the system to be designed. In the U.S. DSARC process this is equivalent to the completion of the validation phase and Secretary of Defense approval to enter full-scale development (Milestone II).

The trial has two basic objectives. First, to assess the impact of mission needs which are directly transmitted from national or NATO military authorities to the NADs. The second objective is to examine the utility of direct NAD involvement in the decisions that occur at subsequent milestones. This second objective addresses a perceived decoupling between decisions made by subgroups of the Main Groups on weapons programmes and decisions made by the NADs. Decisions now made at the subgroup level may not reach the NAD, who may inadvertently make recommendations or take actions which are contrary to the subgroup agreements. Further, agreements on major programmes by MAG Subgroups affect national programmes and must have high-level national support to be successful. This report can be provided by the NADs and their staffs thus adding momentum to important cooperative programmes. The communication channels established by PAPS on major programmes should help keep the NADs and Main Groups closer together.

Trial Plan

Given a trial period of reasonable length it is not possible to follow a programme from its introduction as a mission need through the decision to enter full-scale development. The trial examines the decision process in time segments surrounding each milestone (Figure 3) and the flow of information between NATO working groups and the decision levels within nations. The methods of work employed by the Main Group subgroups between these time segments will not be evaluated. These are a function of the problem at hand, the technology involved and the acquisition strategy followed by the nations and are not an issue for the trial.

Because mission need preparation and processing have characteristics unique from the decision processes at other milestones, this activity is being treated separately in the trial. Also, because the decision processes at subsequent milestones have similar characteristics, the three were combined. For the mission needs, all NATO organizations and nations were requested to provide examples for the trial. It was important that these be actual mission needs and not simulated ones because high-level officials will be asked to make decisions on national involvement in cooperative efforts and Main Group subgroups will be tasked accordingly. In this sense the utility of mission needs is being evaluated but with "live ammunition". A total of nine Mission Need Documents (MNDs) were received for use during the trial and two or three more are anticipated.

To obtain candidate programmes for evaluating NAD involvement at subsequent milestones, the Chairmen of the Main Groups were requested to identify programmes which were expected to reach one of the three milestones during the trial period. Again, the intent was to use only actual programmes which were planned targets for cooperation. Ten programmes were selected to monitor. When decision points are approached, a parallel decision channel will be activated through the NATO structure to the National Armament Directors and back to the action group. Through this channel the NADs will provide decisions on the degree that their nations will participate in the next stage of these cooperative programmes.

The trial is scheduled for completion by summer 1980. The processing of the Mission Need Documents and subsequent evaluation should be completed by that time so firm recommendations can be made at the fall 1980 CNAD meeting. If the Main Group subgroups encounter delays in reaching milestones, final recommendations for these milestones may not be available until the spring 1981 CNAD meeting. However, since the mission need processing is largely independent of the events that follow, a two-stage implementation should cause no special problems. In fact, it may be beneficial to gain acceptance of the first process (mission needs) before adding the second (NAD involvement).

Integration of PAPS and NAPR

With the conclusion of the trial and possible implementation of procedures for PAPS Phases 1 and 2 by the spring of 1981, one additional item needs attention – the integration of NAPR into the PAPS structure. By fall 1980, sufficient information should be available on the success of NAPR and the potential acceptance of PAPS procedures that the CNAD may direct an examination of ways to integrate the two. NAPR should provide the so-called "feedback" on replacement plans and augment other existing reporting procedures within NATO, thus providing the CNAD with sufficient information on the major programmes, regardless of their state of maturity.

This examination should naturally resolve the disagreement now surrounding the need for further structuring of PAPS Phases 3 through 6. If the process of involving the NADs and obtaining their decisions at early milestones is adopted, it may be applied to the decisions at the final milestone prior to production. This would provide a method whereby nations who have not participated in the research and development phase of a major programme will be able to obtain information to make decisions on entering into co-production or dual-production agreements or to simply procure the weapon. This process occurs today, but on an Ad Hoc basis and opportunities for co-production or common procurement are missed because information is not available or is too late to be of value.

If integration is completed along these lines the PAPS process will include three elements:

1. The receipt and processing of Mission Need Documents from NATO or National Military Authorities with NAD involvement in the initial decision by nations to participate;

2. A method whereby National Armaments Directors provide the CNAD with national positions on the degree of participation in cooperative activities such as prefeasibility (concept formulation), feasibility (validation) and full-scale development; and

3. A periodic review of national equipment acquisition plans and assessment of progress made towards enhanced cooperation. This includes the identification of areas where divergence is beginning to occur so that proper action can be taken.

131

The goal is to provide this complete package for CNAD approval by spring 1981.

The DSARC/PAPS Interface

Because of similar definitions and procedures, PAPS and the DoD Acquisition Processes should complement one another. Under DoDD 5000.1 a Service identifies needs and develops a draft MENS for each of those which may become major programmes. The MENS is first coordinated within the Service staffs resulting in a document which represents the Services position with regard to the mission need. The MENS is then forwarded to OSD for comment and finally to the Secretary of Defense for approval.

If a particular need has potential NATO application and may represent a target for cooperation within the Alliance, the Under Secretary of Defense for Research and Engineering, acting in his capacity as the U.S. NAD, could forward the draft MENS to NATO as a Mission Need Document (MND) under PAPS. Specifically, the draft MENS (now an MND) would be sent to the Assistant Secretary General for Defense Support. The MND would be transmitted to other nations for review and a decision on their degree of initial participation. The DoD review of the MENS would proceed as usual and in parallel a meeting would be called for a Main Group subgroup to take action on the MND.

The results of a U.S. and a NATO review can then be reflected in the final approved MENS providing a sound basis for collaborative R&D from the start. (The MENS would have a NATO equivalent in an Outline NATO Staff Target.) If this process is conducted in parallel, time will not be lost; in fact, it may preclude delays in new starts due to concerns raised regarding NATO standardization goals in the MENS and specific plans for Concept Formulation (Phase 0).

The process of approval of the DCP for Milestone I, II and III parallels NAD reviews under PAPS. Activation of the PAPS process could form a part of the normal DCP coordination process prior to a DSARC. Although the PAPS trial only considers activities up through completion of feasibility studies (DSARC Milestone II) the concept should be valid through full-scale development (DSARC

132

Milestone III), providing DSARC/PAPS compatibility from the draft MENS to the completion of full-scale development.

PAPS/European Interface

The PAPS structure being developed is compatible with a number of European systems and a concept recently developed within the IEPG. Therefore, the similarities noted between PAPS and DSARC will likely hold for most other nations and the procedures could be widely adopted without major structural changes to national systems.

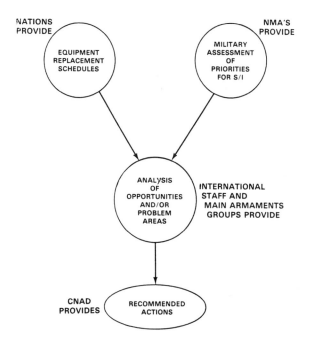

Figure 1. NATO Armaments Planning Review.

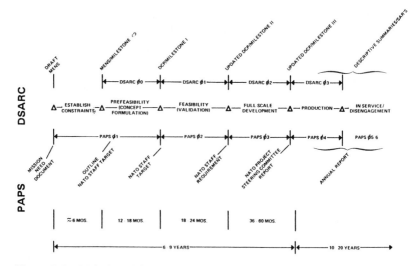

Figure 2. PAPS/DSARC Structure.

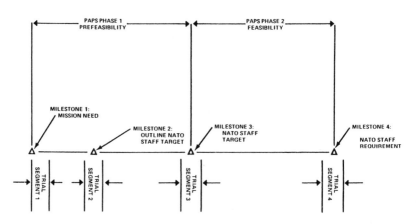

Figure 3. Milestones and Trial Segments for PAPS Phases 1 and 2.

134

North Atlantic Assembly

REPORT of THE SUBCOMMITTEE ON DEFENSE
COOPERATION Presented by
Mr. A. Hamilton McDONALD (Canada) Rapporteur

II. Long-Term Defense Programme

Background

6. At the meeting of Heads of State and Government held in Washington on 30-31 May, 1978, the leaders of the states participating in the integrated defense structure of NATO approved the Long-Term Defense Programme.[1] The LTDP was developed by the Defense Ministers of the participating states in response to directives issued at the NATO summit meeting in May 1977. The LTDP, which incorporates 123 measures divided into nine functional areas related to conventional defense, as well as a functional area related to theater nuclear defense, provides an agreed blue print for strengthening NATO force planning and national programmes in the face of the threat posed by the build-up of Warsaw Pact military forces. NATO has stressed that with its emphasis on long-range planning and cooperation, the LTDP marks a significant milestone for the Alliance.

---

*In Appendix D, Part I of the Report, which deals with other cooperative matters, has been omitted, and the displayed Appendix is an excerpt beginning with Part II, paragraph 6, which part is concerned with the subject, The Long-Term Defense Programme.

1. All Alliance members except France and Greece participate in the integrated defense structure. In endorsing the LTDP, Turkey appended a statement pointing out the importance to her participation of sufficient support from her Allies, as well as of the complete removal of existing restrictions.

7. The 123 LTDP measures vary greatly in their degree of specificity. Measures in the readiness and electronic warfare areas tend to be very precise, while others are much more general. A number of measures must be further refined, and some must be studied further before they can be approved. An action body for each measure has been appointed and tasked with providing the necessary fine print. It must be appreciated that the LTDP is *selective* and not all-inclusive. For example, the LTDP per se does not call for additional aircraft or ships. In brief, the LTDP is only part of the solution to NATO's current force deficiencies. The following paragraphs describe major LTDP measures, grouped according to the ten functional areas.[2]

Readiness

8. Readiness initiatives under the LTDP are aimed at increasing force responsiveness through a number of measures including increased cooperation, especially higher levels of standardization and interoperability, and more efficient use of available resources. The readiness portion of the LTDP is divided into twelve major initiatives with a separate group of minor measures (no-cost and low-cost items for the most part), involving multinational actions in co-ordination with various NATO civilian and military agencies.

9. *Increase in Anti-tank Guided Missile War Reserve Stocks and Development of Planning Factors for Densities and Consumption Rates.* Under this measure nations initially have agreed in principle to increase their anti-tank guided missile war reserve stocks to minimum levels based on existing national rates of consumption. At a later date, nations will undertake to maintain/build their stocks in accordance with new NATO-wide standards developed by SACEUR.

10. *Anti-armour Weapons Programme.* This initiative calls for expanding and modernising anti-armour capabilities in the mid-

2. Description of LTDP measures taken from the January 1979 U.S. Defense Department report to Congress on Rationalization/Standardization within NATO.

term (1979-1984) and continuing that effort into and through the long-term (1985-1990).

11. *Defense against Chemical Warfare.* This initiative includes two major measures — one dealing with provision of standardized protective equipment and a second concerned with special protective equipment for aircrews.

12. *Ammunition Loading Programme.* The goal of this programme is to improve and modernise ammunition storage and handling facilities and procedures. Individual measures involve procurement of modern handling equipment, modernisation of facilities, revised personnel manning for ammunition handling units, real estate procurement and construction of facilities, combat loading of selected units and tests of procedures.

13. *Air-to-Surface Munitions Purchasing Programme.* This initiative involves achieving agreed stockage levels of air-to-surface munitions based on an interoperable family of munitions.

14. *Recategorisation of Forces.* This initiative proposed an increase in force commitment to NATO by recategorising certain member nation forces to permit earlier transfer of authority.

15. *Pursuit of Current Cooperative Development of a Common Family of Anti-armour Weapons.* A cooperative review and development programme for a common family of anti-armour weapons was endorsed by NATO Defense Ministers in May 1978.

16. *Protection of NATO Headquarters Against Chemical Warfare.* The U.S. has notified NATO that it will provide its personnel in these headquarters with the minimum nuclear/biological/chemical (NBC) defense equipment required under NATO standards and also that NBC defense training for personnel will be upgraded. The U.S. has also recommended that all international headquarters develop NBC defense plans, conduct training for command post personnel and NBC defense teams, conduct NBC exercises in conjunction with major exercises, and organise and conduct NBC defense evaluations in headquarters.

17. *Improvement of Reaction Time, 1st Netherlands Corps.* This measure calls for accelerating the movement to Germany of additional Netherlands forces in time of war or crisis.

18. *Cooperative Development of a New Family of Air-Delivered Weapons.*

19. *Improved Responses to the NATO Alert System.* This

initiative includes some 15 different measures, all designed either to effect transfer of authority (to NATO from national command) earlier than is currently agreed or to provide the means by which earlier decisions may be rendered.

Reinforcement

20. Reinforcement proposals entail basically two programmes. The first is principally designed to accelerate the movement of significant fighting power to the forward areas in the critical early phase of a crisis or hostilities. The second involves primarily a broad study of the overall problem.

21. A major item in the first programme is the prepositioning of equipment for three additional United States heavy divisions in the Central Region of Europe.

22. Another major item in the first programme is the United States initiative to modify long-range, wide-body civil passenger aircraft to carry military cargo.

23. Additionally, Norway has earmarked modern multipurpose ships for the movement of the Canadian Air/Sea Transportable Combat Group, thus reducing deployment time. These ships will be replaced in two to three years by new modern roll-on/roll-off vessels, further reducing deployment time. Norway has also purchased and prepositioned significant stocks of military equipment for use by Norwegian forces. This action has materially reduced reinforcement reaction time and therefore improved Norway's defensive posture. The United Kingdom has identified a number of merchant ships suitable for employment with the UK/Netherlands Marine Force.

24. The second programme involves Allied planning to identify suitable merchant ships and civil aircraft and to resolve the technical and legal problems involved in making them available for reinforcement purposes.

Reserve Mobilisation

25. The reserve mobilisation programme recognises that national reservists and reserve units are indispensable components of NATO's forces providing a significant portion of the war-authorised strength

of ground forces. The programme further recognizes that, in view of the Warsaw Pact's capability to attack with little warning, the mobilization of reserves by NATO member nations must be quick and effective. Moreover, the reserve forces must be adequately postured and sized to meet the requirements of the NATO strategy on the modern battlefield.

26. With the importance of national reserve forces in mind, the Reserve Mobilization Task Force conducted an analysis of the responsiveness and capabilities of national reserve forces. The effort concluded that NATO's ability to mobilize its reserves rapidly and in a coordinated manner needs to be improved. In addition, the data supplied by nations have revealed a number of force-related deficiencies. Further, the study found that there are a number of uncommitted reservists who could be used to create additional reserve component formations.

27. These conclusions led to the identification and subsequent approval of a number of remedial measures which emphasize ground force units and individuals. They can be grouped into three broad categories of national action:

(1) To coordinate and synchronize, as far as possible, national policies with the NATO alert system to insure that NATO-allocated reservists and reserve units will be available when required.

(2) To bring national reserve forces up to NATO standards.

(3) To consider plans, in the case of certain European Allies, for the provision of extra units from uncommitted reserve manpower.

Maritime Posture

28. The measures approved in the LTDP for improving NATO's maritime posture are directed principally to enhancing survivability and combat effectiveness in five selected functional areas.

29. *Maritime Command, Control and Communications.* These measures concern the fitting of Link II terminals into certain ships, the development of NATO common message language for tactical data links, the installation of secure voice and ECM-resistant communications, the fitting of satellite communications (SATCOM) in appropriate ships and the development of broadcast

equipment for shore stations and suitable reception facilities in submarines.

30. *Air Defense.* One measure calls for a programme for point defense missiles systems (PDMS).

31. *Anti-Submarine Warfare (ASW).* The majority of nations are prepared to provide their ASW-capable ships with an effective medium-range sonar which will be effective against torpedo-firing submarines. For the mid- and long-term, the development of future lightweight torpedoes is being studied by the CNAD. A European collaborative effort in the long-term may also be expected. In the long-term there is the programme for an advanced acoustic sonar system which CNAD has under discussion.

32. *Mine Warfare.* This programme includes three measures for early implementation. Two or them, those concerning existing minelaying/mining capabilities and a production programme for mine countermeasure (MCM) systems, are well supported. The MCM production programme is designed to increase the quantity of MCM ships. A programme for retaining MCM vessels in reserve status is supported by three nations. Most NATO MCM ships are old, however, they do possess a limited capability and some could be fitted with modern gear. In the long term, CNAD is actively engaged in considering opportunities for cooperation in the development of new generation mines.

33. *Surface Warfare.* The LTDP calls for nations to give their ships an improved anti-surface ship missile capability. Another mid-term measure involves equipping additional aircraft with improved anti-surface ship missiles (ASSM).

34. *Maritime Concept of Operations.* The terms of reference for the Tri-MNC Concept of Maritime Operations have been prepared by the Military Committee.

Air Defense

35. NATO has begun activities to refine and implement the programme to improve its integrated air defense. The major measures are as follows:

—Adoption of an Improved Identification Capability for All Nations and Agreement to Cooperative Development of a Long-term Solution.

—Agreement on a Multifunctional Information Distribution System (MIDS).

—Phased Improvement of an Integrated Air Command and Control System in Allied Command Europe.

—Improvements to the Interface Between Land-based Elements of the Air Defense System and NATO Maritime Elements Operating in Close Proximity.

—Provision in the Mid- to Long-Term of Interceptor Aircraft Having Enhanced Capability and Operating under NATO Command.

—Strengthening of Forward SAM Defenses and Provision of Additional Surface-to-Air Capability in Other Areas.

—Air defense Requirements of Portugal. The Portuguese air defense system needs strengthening. For Portugal to strengthen her air defenses and meet NATO force goals, external assistance into the mid-80s is necessary. It is important to continue current military assistance programmes to enable further Portuguese force modernization, of which air defense is an integral part.

Communications, Command, and Control

36. Integrated or at least interoperable communications, command, and control (C^3) is central to effective Alliance conduct of coalition defense. Although a number of C^3 programmes have been under way within NATO for years, approval of the NATO Long-Term Defense Programme in May 1978 formed the diverse projects into a cohesive coordinated whole. This demonstration of political will gave NATO and national C^3 efforts an increased sense of purpose and urgency. Of the ten LTDP programme areas, C^3 is an essential element in four: maritime posture, air defense, electronic warfare and, of course, the programme specifically devoted to C^3. Major C^3 LTDP measures are development and approval of operational, procedural and technical interoperability standards for communications and ADP systems; NATO Integrated Communications System Stage II; Maritime Communications Programme; Tactical Trunk Network; Single Channel Radio Access; NATO/National Area Interconnection Programme; Strategic ADP system; War Headquarters Improvement Programme; Tactical ADP Programme; and Warning Improvement Programme.

37. LTDP initiatives and other related EW measures have been undertaken to provide for important improvements in NATO's EW capability and NATO's capability to counter the sophisticated EW threat posed by the Warsaw Pact. These measures cover land, air, and maritime forces together with improvements in NATO's EW organization and procedures, including close cooperation in research and development.

—Provision of EW Units in Support of Assigned/Earmarked Corps in Divisions.

—Provision of Basic EW Self-Protection Capability for Army Aircraft and Combat Vehicles and Troops.

—Provision of Self-Protection Suit for Tactical Aircraft.

—Provisions in the Mid-Term of Chaff and Decoys and a Dispensing System for All Ships.

—Provision in the Medium Term of Shipboard Threat Alert Receivers.

—Provision in the Long-Term of Jamming Equipment for Major Combatants.

—Provision of Expendable Jammers in Support of Corps and Divisions.

—Provision for EW Direct Support of Combat Operations.

—Provision of NATO-Assigned Expendable Drone Force.

—Provision of NATO EW Software Facility.

—Development of a Concept to Counter Soviet/Warsaw Pact Command, Control and Communications (C^3) Systems.

—Reorganization of NATO Intelligence Organizations in Order to Give Adequate Support to EW.

—Provision of EW Staff at NATO Headquarters.

Rationalization

38. As the principal forum for armaments cooperation within the Alliance, the Conference of National Armaments Directors (CNAD) is responsible for monitoring the weapons acquisition activities of the nations and for providing a structure for cooperation and information exchange through its subordinate bodies. The CNAD has continued to stress the need for greater

standardization/interoperability through improved cooperation, more efficient procurement of military equipment, and promotion of a strong Alliance-wide industrial and technological capability. At its fall 1978 meeting, the CNAD, having reviewed those aspects of the LTDP which offered areas for greater equipment cooperation, tasked its Main Groups to pursue vigorously 38 LTDP measures and will continue to review the LTDP for additional opportunities in this regard. In addition, the CNAD has been assigned action on most of the agreed measures in the rationalization programme area of the LTDP.

Logistics

39. NATO approved a series of logistics recommendations as a part of the LTDP:
(1) Harmonization of logistics arrangements in the Communications Zone.
(2) Establishment of a logistics coordinating capability in Headquarters Allied Forces Central Europe (AFCENT), and study a capability at Allied Forces Northern Europe (AFNORTH) and Allied Forces Southern Europe (AFSOUTH).
(3) Establishment of Ammunition War Reserve Stocks for an adequate number of combat days.
(4) Provision of additional well-located storage facilities for ammunition stocks, including acceleration of the forward storage site programme.
(5) Remedial measures to resolve problems arising from the discharge of ammunition cargoes.
(6) Clarification/simplification of procedures for the authority of Major NATO Commanders (MNCs) to reallocate war reserve ammunition stocks.
(7) Agreements between MNCs and nations to earmark ammunition for use in war by NATO commanders on a regional basis.
(8) Arrangements to guarantee fuel requirements for Allied forces prior to hostilities.
(9) Strengthening of logistics staff support at NATO Headquarters and within NATO military commands, including a new Assistant Secretary General for Infrastructure and Logistics.

(10) Study the establishment of NATO command-controlled stocks of selected ammunition items.

(11) Study the improvement to reserve stocks of selected heavy equipment.

(12) Build-up of war reserve stocks of jet, ground and naval fuel for Allied forces, including reinforcements for an adequate number of combat days in dispersed, protected or hardened facilities.

Theater Nuclear Forces (TNF)

40. The TNF task force is essentially the NATO Nuclear Planning Group (NPG) and is concerned with modernizing NATO's theater nuclear forces, that is, those nuclear weapons and supporting posture deployed in Europe or in support of deterrence of attack on Europe. This vital area was included in the NATO Long-Term Defense Programme to ensure that the NATO triad of capabilities — conventional, theater nuclear, and strategic nuclear — continues to provide balanced, mutually supporting deterrence.

Implementation

41. The LTDP can best be described as a complement to, rather than a substitute for, NATO's established force planning system. Thus in order to understand NATO's machinery for following through on the LTDP, one must first be familiar with the normal two-year cycle that results in specific NATO Force Goals, as well as with the system of annual reviews of each country's performance in meeting NATO Force Goals.[3]

42. The first step in the cycle is the issuance of Ministerial Guidance. In the spring of odd-numbered years, the Ministers of states participating in the integrated defense structure collectively agree on a set of general directives which provide NATO Military Authorities with a broad outline for defense planning. This Ministerial Guidance takes account of all military factors and considerations likely to affect force structures, deployments, and equip-

3. This section draws in part on the chapter on defense planning and policy in "NATO Facts and Figures," NATO Information Service, Brussels, January, 1976.

ment — both in NATO and in the Warsaw Pact — during the period under review, implications of technological and demographic developments, and economic and political factors affecting the development of NATO forces. Since Ministerial Guidance must be coordinated between and approved by all states participating in the integrated defense structure, it is generally not very specific. Examples of recent Ministerial Guidance include the commitment to a 3% annual increase in defense spending and the priority assigned to RSI.

43. Upon receiving the Ministerial Guidance, NATO Major Commanders draw up specific force improvement recommendations, called Force Proposals, for each country participating in the integrated defense structure. These Force Proposals vary in their degree of specificity and the total number can be quite extensive. For example, in 1977 SACEUR put forward well over 1,000 Force Proposals. To the extent possible, Major Commanders estimate the costs associated with each Force Proposal.

44. After being coordinated and reviewed by the Military Committee, the Force Proposals are forwarded to the Defense Planning Committee (DPC). Each Force Proposal is accompanied by a statement of justification and associated risk. Next the Defense Review Committee (DRC), acting on behalf of the DPC, assesses the financial, economic and political implications of the overall Force Proposal package. The DRC is composed of representatives from each country and from the NATO Military Authorities. The DRC then submits the proposals to the DPC and recommends any adjustments needed to ensure that they are fiscally realistic and in full compliance with Ministerial Guidance. Once the DPC approves the Force Proposals, they become formal NATO Force Goals, which countries are to use as the basis for their Force Plans for the next seven-year period.

45. In determining the degree to which they will comply with the specific NATO Force Goals, member states retain full independence of action. They must bear in mind, however, that the collective nature of NATO's defense requires that in making these decisions, governments must take into account the overall force structure recommended by NATO, as well as the long-term military plans of their Allies. In this respect, then, Force Goals are accepted as challenges to be met *if possible.*

46. The principal instrument for measuring national compliance with Force Goals is the Defense Planning Questionnaire (DPQ). Using the DPQ, NATO each year formally asks each country to indicate what it is doing to meet each Force Goal, the time schedule the country envisages for meeting the goals, and if compliance is not anticipated, the DPQ requires an explanation for the country's non-compliance. In addition, to Force Goals, the DPQ also requires information on force structure, unit readiness levels, research and development plans, equipment and ammunition stockage levels, and financial projections. Importantly, the DPQ replies are the formalized way in which a country commits its forces to NATO, categorizing them as "earmarked", "assigned", etc. The DPQ is extremely detailed. For the case of the United States, the reply will run well over five hundred pages. Taken together, the DPQ replies received from all countries provide a comprehensive NATO data base on force levels, war reserve stocks, training levels, plus financial and economic information on national defense planning. DPQ replies are due in to NATO by 31 July each year.

47. Upon receipt of the DPQ reply, the NATO International Staff prepares an assessment, or "report card", of each country's performance in meeting the Force Goals. Each country then takes its turn in the "hot seat" to reply to this assessment. The forum for this consultation is the DRC. After these multilateral examinations, the DRC prepares an overall report on NATO's success in meeting its Force Goals, including individual country chapters and specific recommendations in cases where better performance is believed possible. This report is reviewed by the DPC at the level of Permanent Representatives and forwarded to the Minsterial level for consideration at their annual December session, who then approve a NATO five-year force plan.

48. The DRC annual performance report provides an effective pressure mechanism that can lead to some finger-pointing at the Ministerial level. In brief, countries can be called on the carpet in instances where NATO believes that greater efforts could and should have been made. In attempting to obtain greater compliance with Force Goals, there are, however, limits to NATO's influence. It can beg, cajole or squeeze; it cannot direct or order. In many cases, though, countries have taken a tasking to heart and decided to increase funding for or continue with vital programmes.

49. How then, does the LTDP fit into this system? While the follow-through on the LTDP draws heavily upon established force planning procedures, in view of the high-level political commitment to the programme and its functional and longer-term aspects, extraordinary monitoring procedures have been developed. Programme Monitors have been appointed for each of the nine conventional LTDP areas. For example, SACEUR is monitor for readiness, C^3, and air defense, CINCHAN monitors EW, and the NATO Assistant Secretary General for Defense Planning and Policy monitors reinforcement. The tenth LTDP area, theater nuclear modernization, is being coordinated by the Nuclear Planning Group.

50. On the basis of data on national action reported in DPQ-79 and on information provided by various NATO committees, the Programme Monitors submitted reports on October 1, 1979 to the Secretary General assessing progress in implementing LTDP measures, identifying problem areas, and recommending remedial action. Drawing upon these reports, the International Staff will prepare a comprehensive LTDP progress report which the Executive Working Group of the DPC, chaired by the Deputy Secretary General, will address early in November and forward for Ministerial review in December.

51. The Fall multilateral reviews will address national actions on LTDP measures in detail, and the resulting country chapters and general report to Ministers will contain distinct sections on LTDP progress. Further, the Force Proposals/Goals process will provide a useful tool for the further definition and refinement of LTDP measures.

52. Major Commanders have been directed to incorporate formally the LTDP measures in the next round of Force Proposals. Thus the Force Proposals to be put forward by the Major Commanders in November 1979 (reflecting the Spring 1979 Ministerial Guidance) will include, but not be limited to, all applicable LTDP measures. Moreover, the Major Commanders have agreed that in assigning priorities to the various Force Proposals, they will ensure that most LTDP measures receive Priority One ratings. It should be noted, however, that whereas countries participating in the NATO integrated defense structure accept Force Goals as challenges to be met if possible, these countries have already

formally pledged to implement the LTDP. Thus LTDP-related Force Goals should carry a higher degree of political commitment than Force Goals not in the LTDP package, and thus should experience a higher rate of fulfillment. Many non-LTDP Force Goals are, of course, of the highest inportance and should be implemented in parallel with LTDP-related Force Goals.

General Comments

53. As an act of political symbolism, the May 1978 NATO endorsement of the LTDP clearly represents a significant achievement. By committing itself at the highest levels of government to carrying out this ambitious collective defense effort, the Alliance has signalled its firm intention to act decisively and cohesively in the face of escalating Warsaw Pact military capabilities. Nonetheless, it is well understood that if this initiative is to transcend the purely symbolic and actually produce enhanced in-place assets and more streamlined organizational processes, a determined and sustained follow-through effort will be required.

54. If the LTDP initiative is to remain credible a number of obstacles will have to be overcome. First, in many cases the general blueprint must be fleshed out and transformed into concrete requirements, in order to incorporate specific quantities, milestone dates and costs. Those measures which participating states have only agreed to in principle must in fact be refined further and finalized. And other measures designated as requiring further study must be expeditiously integrated into the blueprint. In short, the LTDP must be turned into hard and fast requirements. As Defense Secretary Brown has warned, "Without such a baseline, it will be difficult to ensure coordinated action and to monitor implementation."[4]

55. Producing such a baseline entails more than just a technical drafting exercise. It requires a deliberate political effort by the participating states to narrow progressively the range of conditions, caveats, and reservations with which they entered into the LTDP commitment. NATO's actual fighting capabilities can hardly be said to have been enhanced by even 100% "compliance" with the

4. 1979 Department of Defense RSI Report, *op. cit.* p. 9.

LTDP if a number of the measures are defined as "continue to study this problem".

56. Second, the LTDP must sooner or later come to grips with realistic costing. The simple truth is that there is not direct correlation between NATO's commitment to a 3% spending increase and its endorsement of the LTDP. No supporting studies were presented to Heads of State and Government in May 1978 establishing that the LTDP could be "bought" without requiring more than a 3% spending increase. No trade-off options were presented analysing what the 3% rise would buy in LTDP measures versus priority, but non-LTDP, force improvements.

57. Indeed it is clearly recognized at NATO that there are not sufficient funds in current national defense forecasts through 1985 to buy all those LTDP measures which call for completion by then. Thus there is every incentive for slippage. Again, NATO will gain little militarily in the next decade from even 100% "compliance" with a programme in which all the really hard fiscal burdens have been pushed back into the 1990s. Thus the action bodies charged with establishing time schedules for each LTDP measure must do all they can to hold the line against slippage, and Programme Monitors must be firm in scoring non-compliance where non-compliance does in fact occur.

58. Third, states participating in the LTDP must devise mechanisms for integrating the measures into their own national defense planning systems and for developing parliamentary support for funding the programmes. In this regard, the United States and Canada have made the LTDP measures mandatory programming guidance for their armed services. Nonetheless, NATO will gain little from the LTDP no matter how detailed and comprehensive, if parliaments, by either omission or commission, fail to approve the necessary funding. The North Atlantic Assembly is especially well-suited for promoting broader parliamentary familiarity with the LTDP.

59. Lastly, NATO must ensure that the political, military and bureaucratic strands of the organization do not come unraveled over the LTDP initiative. If only grudging support is forthcoming from any of these levels, there will not be a sufficiently powerful fusion to propel the LTDP past the formidable obstacles outlined above. Political authorities must be courageous in bringing pressure to bear on recalcitrant states and in avoiding the temp-

tation to leave some LTDP measures "under review" indefinitely. Major NATO Commanders must not undermine the LTDP by letting it be known that they would be just as pleased if non-LTDP-related Force Proposals were funded by national governments in lieu of LTDP-related Force Proposals. This is not to say that a large number of non-LTDP Force Proposals are not extremely important; but rather that these measures should be implemented in parallel with LTDP measures and not become competitors. Finally, the International Staff at NATO must regard the LTDP not as a repudiation of their established planning system and previous efforts, but rather as an extraordinary programme needed to mobilize the Alliance in these extraordinary times. While the LTDP is admittedly a "glamour item", it remains selective and does not depreciate the need for systematic NATO force planning across-the-board.

60. In summary, NATO is to be commended for launching the LTDP initiative. But if this exercise is to be translated into a cutting edge of enhanced fighting capability, hard decisions will have to be taken and associated fiscal burdens shouldered. In this effort, strong support will be required at all levels of the Alliance — national, international and parliamentary.

Appendix E

The Secretary of Defense

Washington, D.C. 20301
April 10, 1979

MEMORANDUM FOR SECRETARIES OF THE MILITARY
DEPARTMENTS
UNDER SECRETARY OF DEFENSE
FOR POLICY
UNDER SECRETARY OF DEFENSE
FOR RESEARCH AND ENGINEERING
ASSISTANT SECRETARIES OF
DEFENSE
DIRECTOR, DEFENSE COMMUNI-
CATIONS AGENCY
DIRECTOR, DEFENSE LOGISTICS
AGENCY
DIRECTOR, DEFENSE SECURITY
ASSISTANCE AGENCY

SUBJECT: U.S.-Netherlands MOU on Reciprocal Defense Procurement

On 24 August 1978 the U.S. and the Government of the Kingdom
of The Netherlands entered into a reciprocal defense procurement
Memorandum of Understanding (MOU) (enclosure 1) with the
objective of facilitating the mutual flow of defense procurements.
The primary purpose of this agreement is to promote greater
U.S.-Netherlands cooperation in research and development (R&D),
production and procurement in order to enhance NATO rationalization and standardization, and thereby to achieve the greatest
NATO capability at the lowest possible cost. Annexes I, II, and
III to this MOU (enclosure 2), contain procedures for carrying out
on the implementation of the MOU. The Netherlands will in turn
take necessary steps within its own acquisition framework to

151

ensure that U.S. contractors have access to the Netherlands defense market, in keeping with the purposes of the MOU.

Applicability

This guidance shall apply to all acquisitions of defense items and related services (to include components, subsystems, and major systems at all technology levels, and at any phase of the acquisition cycle from concept definition through production), except where restricted by (1) provisions of U.S. National Disclosure Policy (NDP); (2) U.S. laws or regulations; or (3) U.S. defense mobilization base requirements and subject to U.S. Industrial security requirements all as further discussed herein.

Responsibility for Implementation

The MOU states that it is principally the responsibility of the industry of each country to seek a market for its products. Department of Defense (DoD) personnel shall nonetheless, whenever possible, take positive action to facilitate this effort. Netherlands sources are to be provided every opportunity to compete on a fair and equal basis with U.S. sources for both R&D and production contracts, consistent with National Disclosure Policy and legal or regulatory restrictions.

Security

The U.S. and the Netherlands entered into a general Security of Information Agreement on 8 Sept 1960 and an Industrial Security agreement on 3 April 1969. The agreements cover aspects and details concerning protection of U.S. and Netherlands classified information exchanged between both countries. The primary document which implements procedures for safeguarding classified information within industry under bilateral agreements is Section VIII of the Industrial Security Regulation (DoD 5220.22-R). This section, entitled, "International Security Programme," also includes detailed requirements concerning security of foreign classified contracts or subcontracts in the U.S. (para. 8-103), and security of U.S. classified contracts or subcontracts awarded to a foreign contractor (para. 8-104).

All recipients are reminded that the Directorate of Industrial Security, Headquarters, Defense Logistics Agency, must be informed whenever a U.S. contractor is authorized to place a U.S. classified contract in a foreign country involving disclosure of U.S. classified information to the foreign country (para. 8-104c).

Foreign Licenses and Technical Assistance Agreements

Technical assistance in the form of data, foreign patent rights, manufacturing aids, etc., necessary to enable Netherlands sources to produce supplies or perform services may be exported by means of Foreign Licenses and Technical Assistance Agreements using either Foreign Military Sales (FMS) or International Traffic in Arms Regulations (ITAR) procedures. The cognizant DoD Component will insure that proper coordination and approvals are obtained. Such coordination should be done expeditiously to enable timely teaming relationships between U.S. and Netherlands firms. (Reference DoD 5030.28).

For major programmes where exports of large amounts of data would be involved, creation of a "U.S. Government Approved Project" (reference 22 CFR 125.11 (a) 10) should be considered for proposal to the Department of State as a potential mechanism for simplifying the Governmental approval process for information released. In cases where this mechanism is determined to be appropriate, as well as in cases involving sensitive design and manufacturing technologies, technology release guidelines will be prepared to provide necessary guidance to the U.S. project office or other implementing activity. Such guidelines must be coordinated with OUSDRE, OASD(MRA&L), and OASD(ISA) which in turn will coordinate with the Department of State. It should be noted that the provisions of the National Disclosure Policy apply to the export of U.S. classified military information through direct commercial channels (ITAR) as well as under FMS procedures. Specific guidance is provided in the Industrial Security Regulation DoD 5220.22R; DAR Section IX, Part 3; DoD Directive 5230.11; and 22 CFR 121-128 (ITAR) as implemented by DoD Directive 5030.28.

Issuance and Evaluation of Solicitations

When Netherlands sources are provided copies of Requests for Proposals (RFP) or Invitations for Bid (IFB), Procurement Offices will ensure that a reasonable period is permitted for all sources to respond to solicitations.

Where the possibility of competition from Netherlands sources exists, notification shall be given to all potential competitors by the inclusion of an appropriate clause in the solicitation document. A sample clause entitled "Notice of Potential Foreign Source Competition" is attached as a guide (enclosure 3), until such time as an approved clause is published in the DAR.

Netherlands sources competing for DoD requirements must be responsive to all normal terms and conditions of DoD solicitations (e.g., quality, performance, delivery, logistic support, etc.). If unusual technical or security requirements would preclude the acquisition of otherwise cost effective Netherlands defense items, the need for such requirements should be specifically reviewed. Under no circumstances will unusual technical or security requirements be imposed for the purpose of precluding the acquisition of Netherlands defense items.

In addition, Netherlands sources will not be automatically excluded from submitting bids or proposals because their defense items have not been tested and evaluated by a U.S. DoD Component. Components which find it necessary to limit solicitations to sources whose items have been service tested and evaluated by the Component, should make provisions for considering Netherlands items which have been tested and accepted by Netherlands for service use, subject to U.S. confirmatory tests if necessary. Where it appears that these provisions might adversely delay Service programmes, the concurrence of the DoD Acquisition Executive will be obtained prior to the exclusion of Netherlands items from consideration. Sufficiency of Netherlands service testing should be considered on a case-by-case basis. When U.S. confirmatory tests are deemed necessary by the Component, U.S. test and evaluation standards, policies, and procedures will apply.

In furtherance of the objectives set forth in the attached MOU and Annexes I, II, and III thereto, it has been determined (see enclosure 4) pursuant to section 2 of title III of the Act of March 3, 1933 (47 Stat. 1520; 41 U.S.C. S10a, Buy American Act) that it would be inconsistent with the public interest to apply the restrictions of that Act with respect to any defense items of Netherlands origin or manufacture procured to meet U.S. DoD requirements, unless specifically restricted. Accordingly, bids or proposals submitted by Netherlands sources shall be evaluated without the application of the price differentials normally applied pursuant to the Buy American Act requirements contained in Section VI of the DAR. In addition, these bids and proposals shall be evaluated without the application of the price differential normally applied pursuant to the Balance of Payments requirements contained in Section VI, parts 1 and 8 of the DAR. In those instances susceptible to issuance of a duty-free entry certificate, as provided in Section VI, part 6 of the DAR, bids and proposals submitted by Netherlands sources shall be evaluated without application of duty. If, when evaluated in accordance with the above, a Netherlands source is determined to be the lowest, responsive, responsible bidder or offeror, or submits the best technical proposal in accordance with the factors outlined in the solicitation, the cognizant Procurement Office shall normally proceed to make award to that source.

Nothing contained herein and in the Determination and Findings (D&F) (enclosure 4) pursuant to the Buy American Act, 41 U.S.C. §10a (1970), shall affect the authority or responsibility of the cognizant Military Department Secretary or head of a Defense Agency to reject an otherwise acceptable Netherlands bid or proposal in those instances where such rejection is considered necessary for reasons of the national interest. In instances where such a rejection of a Netherlands bid or proposal is contemplated, a copy of the proposed decision shall be forwarded to the DUSD(AP), ten working days in advance of issuance. In those instances where award is to be made to the Netherlands source and where a duty-free entry certificate is susceptible to issuance, the contract shall provide for duty-free entry by inclusion of the appropriate clause(s) referenced in DAR 6-603.3

Utilization of Netherlands Sources

In furtherance of the MOU, each DoD Component is requested to (1) publicize the existence of the MOU among its prime contractors and request that they consider Netherlands sources for subcontracting opportunities; (2) permit attendance by Netherlands industry (subject to the provisions of the paragraph above entitled, "Applicability") at symposia, programme briefings, presolicitation and pre-award conferences which address U.S. defense equipment needs and requirements; and (3) in connection with the review of prime contractor subcontracting procedures, assure that Netherlands sources are not precluded from obtaining subcontracts for reasons that would contravene the MOU. (See enclosure 2, appendix 1 and 2 to annex 1 for a sample of items produced by the Netherlands Industry.)

Restrictions on Netherlands Participation

Except where the quantity being procured is greater than that required to maintain the U.S. defense mobilization base, the Netherlands sources shall be excluded from consideration for (1) participation in the production of items for which contracts are negotiated pursuant to the authority of DAR 3-216, and (2) the restricted items set forth in DAR 1-2207. In accordance with paragraph III of Annex I to the MOU, a list of such items has been developed (see enclosure 2, appendix 3, annex 1). The list will be periodically reviewed with representatives of Netherlands Ministry of Defense (MOD) in order to apprise them of those procurements for which Netherlands sources will normally be excluded. From time to time new items may be identified for inclusion in this list and items already included may be deleted. All proposals for additions and deletions shall be coordinated through DUSD(AP). Acquisition of the items noted above are the *only* ones for which Netherlands sources shall be prohibited from participation on the basis of protecting the defense mobilization base.

Netherlands sources may also be excluded from participating in the acquisition of other items because of legally imposed restrictions on their purchase from non-national sources. This

156

category of items includes, but is not necessarily limited to, the items contained in DAR Section VI, Part 3, and the DoD Appropriation Act prohibitions concerning the construction of Naval vessels or major components of the hull or super-structure thereof.

Applicable exclusions will be determined in accordance with the technology release guidelines developed pursuant to the paragraph above entitled, "Foreign Licenses and Technical Assistance Agreements."

Netherlands sources shall not be excluded from participating in the acquisition of any items where such participation would be permitted by existing exceptions.

Implementation by DoD Components

The guidance contained in this memorandum will be incorporated in the Defense Acquisition Regulation (DAR) as soon as possible. In the interim, it is requested that each addressee give broad distribution to this memorandum within his component, as well as to major prime contractors; and take any additional action considered necessary to ensure that the spirit and intent of this agreement is fulfilled. It is further requested that information copies of departmental instructions promulgating this guidance within your respective components be forwarded to DUSD(AP) within 45 days from the date of this memorandum.

U.S.-Netherlands Memorandum of Understanding

Preamble

The Government of the United States of America and the Government of the Kingdom of the Netherlands, duly represented by their Ministers of Defense:

Intending to increase their respective defense capabilities through more efficient cooperation in the fields of research and development, production and procurement in order to:

—Make the most cost-effective and rational use of the resources available for defense,

—Ensure the widest possible use of standard or interoperable equipment,

—Develop and maintain an advanced industrial and technological capability for the North Atlantic Alliance, and particularly with respect to the parties to this Memorandum of Understanding (MOU), and

Seeking to improve the present situation and to strengthen their military capability and economic position through the further acquisition of standard or interoperable equipment, and

Recalling that they had agreed, as members of the Alliance, to maximum cooperation in procurement as set forth in Annex A to NATO Document C-M(73)51 (revised), dated 20 August 1975.

Have entered into this Memorandum of Understanding in order to achieve the above aims.

This Memorandum of Understanding sets out the guiding principles governing mutual cooperation in research and development, production and procurement of conventional defense equipment.

The two Governments conclude this MOU to strengthen the

North Atlantic Alliance. In so doing, the Governments are fully aware that the Independent European Programme Group (IEPG) wants to enhance equipment collaboration by more comprehensive and systematic arrangements. They therefore agree that in the event of a possible conflict between agreements entered into between the IEPG and the Government of the United States, and this MOU, the parties hereto will consult with a view to amending this MOU.

The two Governments further agree that this MOU should be viewed in the larger context of the cooperation between Europe and North America within the Alliance and that this cooperation will be carried out pursuant to the Mutual Defense Assistance Agreement between the Government of the United States of America and the Government of the Kingdom of the Netherlands, signed 27 January 1950.

Article I

Principles Governing Reciprocal Defense Cooperation

1. Both Governments intend to facilitate the mutual flow of defense procurement, taking into consideration relative technological levels of such procurement, and consistent with their national policies. This facilitation shall be sought through the provision of opportunities to compete for procurements of defense equipment and services as well as through the coproduction of defense equipment and defense R&D cooperation.

2. This MOU is intended to cover areas in which possible bilateral cooperation could be achieved in research and development, production and procurement of conventional defense equipment, complementing the work of the Conference of National Armament Directors (CNAD) and the Independent European Programme Group (IEPG).

3. The two Governments will, consistent with their relevant laws and regulations, give the fullest consideration to all requests for cooperative R&D, and to all requests for production and procurement which are intended to enhance standardization and/or interoperability within the Alliance.

4. In the interests of standardization and the effective utilization

159

of scarce resources, the two Governments shall, to the extent possible, adopt qualified defense items that have been developed or produced in the other country to meet their requirements. Defense items or services are those items or services which may be procured utilizing appropriated funds of the U.S. Department of Defense or budgeted funds of the Netherlands Ministry of Defense.

5. The two Governments shall mutually determine the counting procedures to be laid down in an Annex to this MOU that will apply to all defense items and defense services purchased by them directly or through their relevant industries under this MOU.

6. Each Government shall from time to time notify the other Government of defense items that may not be acquired by the notifying Government from other than domestic sources, as well as those defense items that may be particularly suitable for acquisition by the other Government.

7. Both Governments will provide appropriate policy guidance and administrative procedures within their respective defense acquisition organizations to facilitate achievement of the aims of this MOU.

8. Competitive contracting procedures shall normally be used in acquiring items of defense equipment developed or produced in each other's country for use by either country's defense establishment.

9. The detailed implementing procedures, to be agreed, will, consistent with and to the extent permitted by national laws and regulations, incorporate the following:

a. Offers or proposals will be evaluated without applying price differentials under buy national laws and regulations and without applying the costs of import duties;

b. Full consideration will be given to all qualified industrial and/or governmental resources in each other's country;

c. Offers or proposals will be required to satisfy requirements of the purchasing Government for performance, quality, delivery, and costs.

10. Both Governments will review items submitted as candidates for respective requirements. They will indicate requirements and proposed purchases in a timely fashion to ensure adequate time for their respective industries to qualify for eligibility and submit a bid or proposal.

11. Each Government will ensure that the technical data packages (TDP's) made available under this MOU are not used for any purpose other than for the purpose of bidding on, and performing, a prospective defense contract without the prior agreement of those owning or controlling proprietary rights and that full protection shall be given to such proprietary rights, or to any privileged, protected, or classified data and information they contain. In no event shall the TDP's be transferred to any third country or any other transferee without the prior written consent of the originating Government.

12. Both Governments will use their best efforts to assist in negotiating licenses, royalties and technical information exchanges with their respective industries or other owners of such rights.

13. Arrangements and procedures will, at the request of the purchasing government, be established concerning follow-on logistic support for items of defense equipment, purchased pursuant to this MOU. Both Governments will make their defense logistic systems and resources available for this purpose as required and mutually agreed.

Article II

Implementing Procedures

1. Representatives of the two Governments will be appointed to determine in detail the procedures for implementing this MOU and the terms of reference for a Netherlands-U.S. Committee for Procurement Cooperation.

2. The Under Secretary of Defense for Research and Engineering, in cooperation with the Assistant Secretary of Defense for International Security Affairs, the Assistant Secretary of Defense for Manpower, Reserve Affairs and Logistics, the Director, Defense Security Assistance Agency, and other appropriate Department of Defense officials, will be the responsible authority in the United States Government for the development of implementing procedures under this MOU.

3. The Director General for Material in the Ministry of Defense, in cooperation with other appropriate government authorities, will be the responsible authority of the Government of the Nether-

lands for the development of the implementing procedures under this MOU.

Article III

Industry Participation

1. Each Government will be responsible for calling to the attention of the relevant industries within its territory the basic understanding of this MOU, together with appropriate implementing guidance. Both Governments will take all necessary steps so that the industries comply with the regulations pertaining to security and to safeguarding classified information.

2. Implementation of this MOU will involve full industrial participation. Accordingly, the Governments will arrange to inform their respective procurement and requirements offices concerning the principles and objectives of this MOU. However, primary responsibility for finding business opportunities in areas of research and development and production shall rest with the industries in each nation.

Article IV

Security

To the extent that any items, plans, specifications or information furnished in connection with the specific implementation of this MOU are classified by either Government for security purposes, the other Government shall maintain a similar classification and employ all measures necessary to preserve such security equivalent to those measures employed by the classifying Government throughout the period during which the classifying Government may maintain such classifications.

Article V

Administration

1. The Netherlands-U.S. Committee for Procurement Cooperation, referred to in Article II above, will meet as agreed or at the request of either Government to review progress in implementing the MOU. They will discuss research and development, production and procurement needs of each nation and the likely areas of cooperation; agree to the basis of, and keep under review, the financial statement referred to below; and consider any other matters relevant to the MOU.

2. Each Government will designate points of contact at the Ministry of Defense level and in each purchasing service/agency under the Ministries of Defense.

3. An annual United States-Netherlands statement of the current balance, and long-term trends, of R&D cooperation and purchases between the two nations will be prepared on a basis to be mutually agreed. Such statement will take account of United States-Netherlands purchases of defense equipment and services and related offset agreements effected in the years from 1975 onwards and will be periodically reviewed.

Article VI

Annexes

Annexes negotiated by the responsible officials and approved by the appropriate Government authorities will be incorporated in this MOU.

Article VII

Duration

1. This MOU will remain in effect for a ten-year period and will be extended for successive five-year periods, unless the Governments mutually decide otherwise.

2. If, however, either Government considers it necessary for

compelling national reasons to terminate its participation under this MOU before the end of the ten-year period, or any extension thereof, written notification of its intention will be given to the other Government six months in advance of the effective date of termination. Such notification of intent shall become a matter of immediate consultation with the other Government to enable the Governments fully to evaluate the consequences of such termination and, in the spirit of cooperation, to take such actions as necessary to alleviate problems that may result from the termination. In this connection, although the MOU may be terminated by the Parties, any contract entered into consistent with the terms of this MOU shall continue in effect, unless the contract is terminated in accordance with its own terms.

3. The Parties hereto agree that, for the purposes of this MOU, references to the Kingdom of the Netherlands shall apply only to its territory in Europe.

Article VIII

Implementation

This MOU will come into effect on the date of the last signature.

For the Government of the Kingdom of the Netherlands The Minister of Defense	For the Government of the United States of America The Secretary of Defense
Date 24 Aug 1978	Date Jul 25 1978

Enclosure 2

Annexes to U.S.-Netherlands Memorandum of Understanding

Annex I

Memorandum of Understanding between the Government of the Kingdom of the Netherlands and the Government of the United States of America Concerning the Principles Governing Mutual Cooperation in the Research and Development, Production and Procurement of Defense Equipment, dated 24 August 1978.

Principles Governing Implementation

1. Introduction

On 24 August 1978, the Governments of the United States and the Kingdom of the Netherlands signed a Memorandum of Understanding (MoU) relating to the principles governing mutual cooperation in research and development, production and procurement of defense equipment. This document sets forth the agreed implementing procedures for carrying out the MoU.

2. Major Principles

A. The U.S. Department of Defense (DoD) and the Ministry of Defense of the Netherlands (MoD) will consider for their defense requirements qualified defense items and services developed or produced in the other country.

B. It will be the responsibility of government and/or industry representatives in each country to acquire information concerning the other country's proposed research, developments, and purchases and to respond to requests for proposals in accordance with the prescribed procurement procedures and regulations. However, the responsible government agencies in each country will assist sources in the other country to obtain information concerning, intended research and development, proposed purchases, necessary qualifications and appropriate documentation.

3. Action

DoD and MoD will review and, where considered necessary, revise, policies, procedures and regulations to ensure that the principles and objectives of this MoU, which are intended to be compatible with the broad aims of NATO Rationalization/Standardization, are taken into account. DoD and MoD agree that the following measures shall be taken, recognizing that among other factors, delivery date requirements for supplies, the interest of security and the timely conduct of the procurement process, are considerations related to insure free and full competition for the award of contracts:

A. Ensure that their respective requirements offices are familiar with the principles and objectives of this MoU.

B. Ensure that their respective research and development offices and institutes are familiar with the principles and objectives of this MoU.

C. Ensure that their respective procurements offices are familiar with the principles and objectives of this MoU.

D. Ensure wide dissemination of the basic understanding of this MoU to their respective industries producing and/or developing defense items and/or services.

E. Ensure that, consistent with national laws and regulations, offers of defense items produced in the other country will be evaluated without applying to such offers, either price differentials under buy-national laws and regulations, or the cost of import duties. Full consideration will be given to all qualified industrial and/or governmental sources in each other's country. Provisions will be made for duty-free entry certificates and related documentation to the extent that existing laws and regulations permit.

F. Assist industries in their respective countries to identify and advise the other government of their production capabilities and assist such industries in carrying out the supporting actions to maximize industrial participation.

G. Review defense items and requests for services submitted by the other country as candidates for respective requirements. Identify requirements and proposed purchases to the other country in a timely fashion to ensure that the industries of such country are afforded adequate time to be able to participate in the research and development production and procurement processes.

H. Use best efforts to assist in negotiating licenses, royalties, and technical information exchanges among their respective industries, and research and development institutes.

I. Ensure that those items and services excluded from consideration under this MoU for reasons of protecting national requirements, such as the maintenance of a defense mobilization base, (Appendix 3, Annex I), are limited to a small percentage of total annual procurement spending. It is intended that such defense items and services, as well as those items and services that must be excluded from consideration under this MoU because of legally imposed restrictions on procurement from non-national sources, be identified as soon as possible by the MoD and the DoD, and that such defense items and services be kept under review at this level.

J. Insure that the balance of reciprocal purchases takes into consideration the levels of technology involved, as well as the monetary value of purchases hereunder.

K. DoD and MoD will from time to time arrange visits in order to actively explore possibilities for cooperation on research and development, procurement, and logistical support.

4. Counting Procedures

The following purchases, to be identified jointly by DoD and MoD will be included in the counting procedures:

A. Purchases of items and services funded from appropriate funds of the U.S. Department of Defense or budgeted funds of the Netherlands Ministry of Defense and which, either/are:

(1) directly purchased by the MoD or DoD from one another; or

(2) directly purchased by the MoD from the industry of the other country; or

(3) purchased by the industry of one country from the Government or industry of the other country; or

(4) purchased as a result of jointly funded defense projects to which the United States and the Netherlands are the only contributors, to be credited in proportion to each other country's financial contribution to the project, and to work carried out in each country. The extent to which such purchases will be counted against the goals of the MoU will be agreed upon between MoD and DoD in each case;

(5) license fees, royalties and other associated income, when separately contracted, by industry and/or DoD or MoD with a licensor in the other country.

B. Purchases by the MoD or DoD from the industry of the other country, on behalf of other governmental departments and agencies.

C. Purchases by a third country government from the MoD or DoD or from industries of these two countries as direct result of the efforts of the government of the other country.

5. Administration

A. Each government will designate points of contact (procurement and logistics) at the Ministry of Defense level and in each purchasing service/agency and major acquisition activity.

B. Quality Assurance procedures outlined in STANAG 4107 and 4108 (subject to the USG reserve concerning reimbursement) will apply, unless other provisions are mutually agreed to on any specific contract. Reimbursement of services provided shall be afforded in accordance with the national laws and regulations of each country.

C. The terms of reference of the Netherlands/United States Committee of Procurement Cooperation is contained in Annex III.

For the Government of the   For the Government of the
United States of America   Netherlands

_____   _____

Date   21 Dec 1978   Date   21 Dec 1978

_____   _____

Appendices
1. Indicative Products List
2. Research and Development
3. DoD List of Restricted Defense Items

Appendix 1 to Annex 1

To: Memorandum of Understanding between the Government of The Netherlands and the Government of the United States of America concerning the Principles Governing Mutual Cooperation in the Research and Development, Production and Procurement of Defense Equipment, signed on the 24th of August 1978.

Indicative Products List (The Netherlands)

The product areas listed below are indicative of the Netherlands' industry capability.

The list shall not be considered limitative and is subject to up-dating from time to time as agreed.

In some cases the Netherlands' participation could take the form of production of components or sub-assemblies.

1. Aircraft/Aircraft systems

    a. Maritime/Fishery Patrol Aircraft
    b. Feeder line/Executive transport Aircraft
    c. Aircraft sub-assemblies
    d. Accessory Test-benches for aero-engines
    e. Test equipment (incl. depot) for avionic and electronic systems
    f. Laboratory test equipment
    g. Aerospace ground Equipment

2. Electronics

    a. Military and civil (automatic) telecommunications systems and equipment
    b. Automatic Air Traffic Control Systems
    c. Tactical display consoles
    d. Integrated command and fire control systems
    e. Radar-systems (e.g. navigation-, fire control-, 3D multi-tracking-, shipping control radar systems)
    f. Crypto systems
    g. Computers and data handling systems

169

h. Digital video processing systems
i. Electronic security systems
j. Navigation systems
k. Transponders
l. Paging systems
m. Self propelled air defense systems
n. Automatic message switching systems

3. Electro-optical equipment

a. (far) Infra-red equipment
b. Airborne passive IR day and night photo recce systems
c. Passive night vision goggles
d. Passive night viewing systems
e. Night vision systems (drivers and fire control) passive and thermal infra-red
f. Laser rangefinders

4. Vehicles

a. Military trucks and trailers
b. Aircraft and other Fuel tankers
c. Fire fighting vehicles — crash tenders
d. Truck-transportable containers/shelters
e. Tank transporting vehicles

5. Shipbuilding

a. Frigates
b. Mine countermeasure vessels (polyesther) ⎫
c. Submarines   ⎬ including depot
d. Pilot tenders   ⎪ and engineering
e. Hydrographic survey vessels   ⎭ services
g. Gearboxes
h. Ships propellers (fixed and variable pitch)
i. Generators
j. Electrical installations (incl. switch boards)

6. Ammunition and explosives

a. 0.50 ammunition
b. 25, 35 and 40 mm caliber ammunitions
c. 105 mm tank ammunition FS/APDS
d. 105 mm tank training rounds
e. 105 mm heat (improved)
f. 155 mm artillery ammunition
g. Proximity Fuses
h. Gunpowder
i. Smoke signals
j. Dummy ammunition
k. Ammunition boxes
l. Shackles for ammunition belts
m. NATO Seasparrow ancillaries (existing coproduction)
n. River Mines

7. Maintenance

a. Industry level maintenance of military and civil aircraft, aircraft systems and missile systems, including structural repair of aircraft
b. Depot and industry level repair and maintenance of aircraft engines
c. Depot maintenance on communication-radar-sonar and fire-control equipment
d. Industry and depot shipconstruction, repair and maintenance.

Appendix 2 to Annex 1

To: Memorandum of Understanding between the Government of The Netherlands and the Government of the United States of America concerning the Principles Governing Mutual Cooperation in the Research and Development, Production and Procurement of Defense Equipment, signed on the 24th of August 1978.

171

Research and Development

1. National Defense Research Organization (NDRO)-TNO

Address: 21 Koningin Marialaan, THE HAGUE.

Laboratories:
—Physics Laboratory, The Hague.
　Fields of work:　physics
　　　　　　　　　—radio communications;
　　　　　　　　　—signal processing;
　　　　　　　　　—microwaves;
　　　　　　　　　—datahandling;
　　　　　　　　　—digital computing techniques;
　　　　　　　　　—acoustics;
　　　　　　　　　—mine countermeasures;
　　　　　　　　　—mathematics/operations research.

—Laboratory for Electronic Developments of the Armed Forces,
　Oegstgeest.
　Fields of work:　electronic warfare and radar
　　　　　　　　　—signal processing;
　　　　　　　　　—microwave;
　　　　　　　　　—datahandling;
　　　　　　　　　—underwater detection;
　　　　　　　　　—systems control techniques.

—Prins Maurits Laboratory for Chemical and Technological
　Research, Rijswijk.
　Fields of work:　chemical research: determination of charac-
　　　　　　　　　teristics properties of toxic substances, in
　　　　　　　　　particular chemical warfare agents
　　　　　　　　　—study of mechanism of action of toxic sub-
　　　　　　　　　stances, in particular chemical warfare agents;
　　　　　　　　　—development of detection and alarming sys-
　　　　　　　　　tems for atmospheric contamination;
　　　　　　　　　—evaluation and development of means and
　　　　　　　　　equipment for protection to be used in a
　　　　　　　　　contaminated environment;

172

—desinfection and purification of material and equipment contaminated with toxic substances, in particular chemical warfare agents;

—research as regards chemical problems related to environmental hygiene.

Fields of work: technological research: investigations into the factors governing the decomposition processes of propellants in connection with the ballistic and chemical stability, in particular in view of the surveillance of military supplies

—study of the ignition sensitivity of propellants for fire-arms and rockets and the ignition capability of ignition systems;

—developments of pyrotechnic compositions;

—research on the physical and chemical properties of rocket propellants and on the functioning of rocket motors;

—study of detonations and of shock waves in air and water;

—research and development in the field of fuzes, shaped charges and ammunition;

—investigations into the explosion hazards of industrial products, during manufacturing, storage, transport and use.

2. *Civil laboratories of the Netherlands Organization for Applied Scientific Research TNO, performing defense (or defense-related) R&D:*

—Institute for Mechanical Constructions TNO, Delft,
   Fields of work: —tensions, vibrations, shock;
                   —manoeuvring, among others.
—Institute of Applied Physics TNO-TH, Delft.
   Fields of work: —sound, optics, among others.
—Metal Research Institute TNO, Apeldoorn.
—Paint Research Institute TNO, Delft.
—Plastics and Rubber Institute TNO, Delft.
—Central Institute for Nutrition and Food Research TNO, Zeist.
—Medical Biological Laboratory TNO, Rijswijk.

173

Fields of work: radiation damage in the human body;
                  —microbial infections;
                  —intoxication with chemical warfare agents.

3. *Institute of Maritime Research, performing defense and defense-related R&D*

—Netherlands Ship Model Basin (NSMB), Wageningen; (see attached table).
Fields of work: ship powering (depressurized towing tank for advanced research in hydrodynamics, among others);
                  —ocean engineering;
                  —ship handling (manoeuvring simulator, among others).

—Netherlands Maritime Institute (NMI), Rotterdam.
Fields of work: nautical, economic and social research in the field of shipping and shipbuilding.

4. *National Aerospace Laboratory (NLR), Amsterdam*

Fields of work: windtunnel testing, especially in transsonic flow;
                  —research on supercritical wings;
                  —research on coatings on aircraft engine components;
                  —operations research on air traffic control;
                  —operations evaluation of ground based air defense systems.

Central point of contact for defense research in the Netherlands:
                  Coordinator Defense Research
                  Ministry of Defense
                  4 Plein,
                  Room C-138
                  The Hague
                  Netherlands
                  tel. 070-721478.

Annex II

To: Memorandum of Understanding between the Government of the Netherlands and the Government of the United States of America concerning the Principles Governing Mutual Cooperation in the research and Development, Production, and Procurement of Defense Equipment, signed on the 24th of August 1978.

Principles Governing Logistic Support of Common Equipment

In implementing article I, para 13, of the MoU, the two Parties shall be governed by the following:

1. When developing or procuring defense equipment, both Parties will agree upon the basis for joint follow-on logistic support in areas such as configuration control, interchangeability of spare parts/components, maintenance, conversion, storage, and spare parts provisioning, etc.

2. Arrangements and procedures will be established concerning follow-on logistic support and other forms of logistic cooperation, e.g., joint utilization of facilities.

3. In the contracting procedure for logistic support, paragraph 9 of Article I of the MoU shall apply.

4. Both Parties will issue directives and guidelines to their respective armament and logistics agencies to achieve the described goals of this MoU.

For the Government of the United States of America	For the Government of the Netherlands
Date 21 Dec 1978	Date 21 Dec 1978

Annex III

To: Memorandum of Understanding between the Government of the Kingdom of the Netherlands and the Government of the United States of America Concerning the Principles Governing Mutual Cooperation in the Research and Development, Production and Procurement of Defense Equipment, dated 24 August 1978.

Terms of References

1. The Netherlands/U.S. Committee for Procurement Cooperation (hereafter to be called "the Committee") will serve, under the direct responsibility of the authorities, listed in Article II sub 2 and 3 of the MoU respectively, as the main body in charge of the adequate implementation of the MoU.

2. In particular, the Committee will be responsible for ensuring that the guiding principles of the MoU governing the mutual cooperation in research and development, production, procurement and logistic support of conventional defense equipment are being implemented to facilitate a mutual flow of defense equipment. To this end the Committee will meet as required, but not less than annually, to review progress in implementing the MoU. In this review:

A. They will discuss research, development, production, procurement and logistic support needs of such country and the likely areas of cooperation including joint activities in those fields.

B. They will exchange information as to the way the stipulations of the MoU have been carried out and, if need be, prepare proposals for amendments of the MoU and/or its annexes.

C. They will agree to the financial statement of the current balance, give guidance for its yearly preparation and formulate conclusions from it, such conclusions to include any long term trends which may be established.

D. They will consider any other matters relevant to the MoU.

E. They will report after each meeting and advise as appropriate.

F. The Committee will alternately meet in the United States and in the Netherlands. The country in which a particular meeting will take place will provide the Chairman and the secretariat for that meeting.

For the Government of the
United States of America

For the Government of the
Netherlands

Date   21 Dec 1979

Date   21 Dec 1979

Notice of Potential Foreign Source Competition

Bids or proposals for this procurement are being solicited from sources in the Netherlands. Furthermore, U.S. bidders may propose end items of the Netherland manufacture.

It has been determined by the Secretary of Defense that the restrictions of section 2 of title III of the Act of March 3, 1933 (47 Stat. 1520; 41 U.S.C. §10a; Buy American Act) shall not apply to items of Defense equipment described in this solicitation when produced or manufactured by the Netherland sources.

Determination and Findings Exception to the Buy American Act

I hereby make, as department head, the following findings and determination regarding the application of the restrictions of the Buy American Act, 41 U.S.C. Section 10a (1970) to the items of defense equipment described below.

Findings

1. Section 814(a) of the Department of Defense Appropriation Authorization Act, 1976, Pub. L. No. 94-106, 89 Stat. 544 (1975), as amended by section 802 of the Department of Defense appropriation Authorization Act, 1977, Pub. L. No. 94-361, 90 Stat. 930 (1976), provides that "it is the policy of the United States that equipment procured for the use of personnel of the Armed Forces of the United States stationed in Europe under the terms of the North Atlantic Treaty should be standardized or at least interoperable with equipment of other members of the North Atlantic Treaty Organization." The Act provides that ". . . the Secretary of Defense shall, to the maximum feasible extent, initiate and carry out procurement procedures. . ." to carry out that policy. The Act further provides that "whenever the Secretary of Defense determines that it is necessary, in order to carry out this policy . . . to procure equipment manufactured outside the United States, he is authorized to determine, for the purpose of section 2 of title III of the Act of March 3, 1933 (47 Stat. 1520; 41 U.S.C. 10a), that the acquisition of such equipment manufactured in the United States is inconsistent with the public interest."

2. The United States Government (U.S.) and the Government of the Kingdom of the Netherlands are seeking to achieve greater

cooperation in research, development, production and procurement of defense equipment in order to make the most rational use of their respective industrial, economic and technological resources, to achieve the greatest attainable military capability at the lowest possible cost, and to achieve greater standardization and interoperability of their weapons systems. In order to further these aims, the U.S. and the Government of the Kingdom of the Netherlands entered into a Memorandum of Understanding (MOU) relating to mutual cooperation in the research and development, production and procurement of defense equipment.

3. In furtherance of the MOU, the U.S. and the Government of the Kingdom of the Netherlands each have established policies for increasing cooperation in research, development, and production and procurement of military systems. In keeping with these policies and in the interest of enhancing their mutual security obligations, the U.S. and the Government of the Kingdom of the Netherlands intend to cooperate in all respects practicable, to the end that defense equipment production and procurement efforts of the two countries by administered so as to facilitate a mutual flow of defense procurement, at mutually determined levels.

4. In order to facilitate the objectives of agreement, the U.S. and the Government of the Kingdom of the Netherlands have agreed that, consistent with national laws and regulations, each government will evaluate offers of defense equipment produced in the other country without applying price differentials under the "Buy National" laws and regulations.

5. This Determination and Findings covers all items of Netherlands produced or manufactured defense equipment other than: (a) those items that have been excluded from consideration under the MOU and annexes thereto for reasons of protecting national requirements, such as for the maintenance of a defense mobilization base; and (b) those items that are subject to restrictions imposed by law on procurement from non-national sources.

Determination

Pursuant to 41 U.S.C. §10a (1970), I hereby determine that it is inconsistent with the public interest to apply the restrictions of the Buy American Act to the acquisition of those items of Netherlands produced or manufactured defense equipment that are covered by this Determination and Findings.

Date   10 April 1979

DoD List of Restricted Defense Items Under MOU for Reciprocal Defense Procurement

Section I – Items Procured Pursuant to ASPR 3-216

Navy

Fuzes, Safe and Arm Devices, and Similar Items

MK-13 Safe and Arm Device
MK-13 Triggering Device
MK-17 Safe and Arm Device
MK-33 Safe and Arm Device
MK-330 Fuze
MK-404 Fuze
MK-407 Fuze
FMU-109 Fuze

Missiles and Missile Components

AIM-7F Sparrow Missile
   Guidance and Controls Section
   MK-58 Rocket Motors
   MK-71 Warhead Metal Parts

AIM-9L Sidewinder Missile
   Guidance and Control Section
   MK-36 Rocket Motors
   DSU-15 Target Detector
   AN/WDU-17 Warhead

Trident I (C-4) Missile System
   Guidance and Control System
   MK-5 Electronic Assemblies (EA)

182

MK-5 Inertial Measurement Unit Electronics (IMUE)
Backfit of Poseidon (C-3) SSBNs

Flares

MK-46 Flares, Infrared Decoy

Sonobuoys and Components

AN/SSQ-36
AN/SSQ-41E
AN/SSQ-47B
AN/SSQ-53A
AN/SSQ-57A
AN/SSQ-62

Military Sealift Cargo

Ocean Transportation and Services

Air Force

MAC Commercial Airlift
GAU-8/A and 30 mm Ammo

Defense Logistics Agency

Textiles — Worsted

Army

L.A.P., Manufacturing & testing of projectiles (5.56 mm through 8 inch), mines, despensers, sockets, pyrotechoic devices, grenades, demolition charges, small arms ammunition and components, fuzes and components containing mech. timing devices

TOW Missile and Launcher
2.75 Rocket Items

LAP Motor   Igniter
Fin & Nozzle Assy   Motor Tube
Stabilizer Rod   Seal Rings
Felt Washer   Disc Charge Support
Ring Charge Support   Spacer Charge Support
O Ring   Lockwire
Metal Spacer   Launcher
Intervelometer   Fin Blades
Projectile Metal Parts for Cartridge 105 mm (Beehive)
Projectile M406, M107 – 155 mm
Projectile M509 – 8″
155 mm Cannister, XM625, XM626:
    Projectile Metal Parts for Cartridge 90 mm
Cartridge Case M118, M14B4
Fuze Time M84A1
Fuze Grenade M213, M219E1, M42/M46
Fuze Bomb Nose M904E3, M19
Fuze Rocket M423, M565, M564
Fuze M494/M571
Head Assy M525 Fuze
Casing Burster Warhead, M156
Fin Assy M158, M170
Adapter Booster – M147, M148
Body Assy and Base Plug, M404
Bomb, M117A1E1
Launcher Rocket 2AU 68A/A
Warhead Flechets WDU 4A/A
M18 Mine Programme
    Blasting Cap, Firing Device, Metal Parts, Test Sets
Laser Range Finder VVG-2 and XM21 for Solid State Balistic
    Computer for M60 Series Tank
Limited Light Sight
MX-9644 Image Intensifier Tube 25 mm
MX-7845 Image Intensifier Tube (1st generation)
MX-8501 Image Intensifier Tube (1st generation)
BA-4386 Battery
AN/PVS-4 Night Vision Sights
AN/PVS-5 Night Vision Goggles
AN/PVS-5A Night Vision Goggles

184

AN/VVS-2 Viewer
AN/VVS-3 Searchlight
Common Module Programme (thermal Imaging System)
   Tactical night vision systems —
     AN/TAS-4   AN/TAS-6
     AN/TAS-5   GLLD/TAS-4
Maintenance of idle portions of 21 GOCO facilities
Consolidated Facilities Scranton AAP

Section II Items Procured Pursuant to referenced
ASPR requirement

ASPR 1-2207.2 — Jewel Bearings & Related Items
ASPR 1-2207.3 — Miniature & Instrument Ball Bearings
ASPR 1-2207.4 — Precision Components for Mechanical Time
                  Devices

Appendix F*

NATO Standardization and Interoperability

Handbook of Lessons Learned

by William B. Williams, Virginia W. Perry, Harold F. Candy

December 1978

Information and data contained in this document are based on input available at time of preparation. Because the results may be subject to change, this document should not be construed to represent the official position of the U.S. Army Material Development and Readiness Command.

Approved for Public Release; Distribution Unlimited

U.S. ARMY PROCUREMENT RESEARCH OFFICE
U.S. Army Logistics Management Center
Fort Lee, Virginia 23801

Chapter 2

Lessons Learned

A. *Orientation*: This chapter presents the results of study team analysis of specific RSI projects involving the U.S. military services and one or more of the European NATO nations. The study results are formulated as lessons learned and encapsulate both objective information and subjective judgments.

B. *Categorization of Lessons Learned*: The lessons learned have been classified into 13 major subject categories so that readers with a particular interest only in certain areas can readily locate the covers the lessons learned in transferring U.S. technology to European members of NATO. The 13 categories are as follows:

*In Appendix F, the illustration is Chapter II of two chapters of the *Handbook of Lessons Learned* and gives a summation of the detailed findings.

RSI policy, then progressing through programme initiation, project management, the legal agreements, the technological and engineering considerations and the logistic support. All but the last category concern projects where the United States has purchased foreign technology and/or hardware. The last category, Coproduction, covers the lessons learned in transferring U.S. technology to European members of NATO. The 13 categories are as follows:

—Public Policy Related to RSI
—Programme Initiation
—Programme Management
—Memoranda of Understanding (MOUs)
—Licensing
—Contracts
—Technical Considerations
—Technology Transfer
—Configuration Management
—Quality Assurance
—Test and Evaluation
—Logistics
—Coproduction

C. *Format of Presentation of Lessons Learned*: Within each of the major subject categories, a number of lessons learned have been developed. These have been ordered within each category according to importance and degree of generalization or specialization. The catalog of lessons learned by category is presented in paragraph D below. Detailed narrative expanding on each lesson learned follows the last catalog entry. The catalog references the page where the detailed narrative of the particular lesson learned may be found. The abbreviation "LL" has been selected for "Lessons Learned" and is used in identifying the narrative descriptions.

D. *Catalog of Lessons Learned and Detailed Narratives.*

Category	Lessons Learned
Public Policy Related to RSI	1 — The President and the Congress Have Strongly Indorsed NATO RSI
	2 — Current Legislation Still Must Be Interpreted as Impeding NATO RSI
	3 — Proposed Legislation Will Enhance NATO RSI

188

Category	Lessons Learned
Public Policy Related to RSI (Continued)	4 — Congressional Resistance to U.S. Purchases of Foreign Systems Can Be Expected on a Case-By-Case Basis
Programme Initiation	1 — Consideration of NATO Systems to Meet U.S. Needs Must Begin Early
	2 — An RSI Plan Is Required on Cooperative R&D Programmes
	3 — The RSI Plan Should Be a Comprehensive Assessment of the Potential for Cooperation
	4 — Cost Estimation on Cooperative R&D Programmes Does Not Fit the Normal U.S. Pattern
Programme Management	1 — The U.S. Organization for an RSI Programme Depends on Programme Type and Size
	2 — A Strong and Effective Programme Management Office Is Needed for a Cooperative R&D Programme
	3 — Personnel Skills within a Project Office Should be Tailored to Meet the Need
	4 — Project Managers Should Become Familiar with the DOD and Army Staff Elements Which Deal Directly with RSI Management
	5 — An Understanding of the NATO Organizations with Primary Responsibilities for RSI Should Prove Useful to Programme Management Personnel
Memoranda of Understanding	1 — A Memorandum of Understanding (MOU) Is Usually Negotiated for Every RSI Programme
	2 — The Format for an MOU Covering a Cooperative Research and Development Programme is Well-Established
	3 — The Content of a Direct Purchase MOU Depends on the Foreign Government Role
Licensing	1 — The Project Manager Should Insure that Licensing Agreements Are Consistent with RSI Objectives of the Programme

Category	Lessons Learned
Licensing (Continued)	2 — Certain Terms and Conditions Are Common to All Licensing Agreements
	3 — Certain NATO Publications May Be Useful in Drafting Licensing Agreements
	4 — A Well-Negotiated Licensing Agreement Is a Key Feature of an RSI Programme
	5 — Licensing Agreements Must Be Approved by Higher Authority
Contracts	1 — Procurement Planning Is Essential to Programme Success
	2 — A Government to Government Contract Is Accomplished by a Letter of Offer and Acceptance (LOA)
	3 — Contract and RFP Procedures for an RSI Programme Differ from Those of a Normal U.S. Programme
	4 — The Uniform Contract Format Provides an Excellent Structure for the RFP and the Contract
	5 — U.S. Contract Provisions May Either Be Inappropriate or Require Tailoring on Foreign Contracts
Technical Considerations	1 — European Design and Production Philosophies Differ from Those of the U.S.
	2 — Engineering Practices in Europe Vary Widely From Those in the U.S.
	3 — NATO Standardization Agreements (STANAGS), Allied Publications (APs) and Data Exchange Agreements (DEAs) Support NATO Standardization and Interoperability
Technology Transfer	1 — Successful Technology Transfer Requires a Formal Process for Data Conversion
	2 — Parts Selections for the U.S.-Produced System Is a Key Factor in Technology Transfer
Configuration Management	1 — Configuration Management Is a Prerequisite for Achievement of NATO Standardization and Interoperability

190

Category	Lessons Learned
Configuration Management (Continued)	2 — Configuration Control Is Required on Cooperative R&D Programmes at Both International and National Levels 3 — A Tailored CM Plan Is Required for a Direct Purchase Programme on Which U.S. Production Is Anticipated
Quality Assurance	1 — Procedures for Procurement Quality Assurance are Covered by NATO Agreements 2 — Quality Assurance Plans for Foreign Purchases Must be Developed and Implemented
Test and Evaluation	1 — Competitive Testing Has Been Upheld by the Controller General as a Legitimate Method of Selecting a System 2 — Fair and Objective Testing Is Essential When Systems of Several Countries Are Competing 3 — Duplicate and Redundant Testing Must Be Avoided 4 — A Joint Test Programme Is Recommended for Cooperative R&D with Technology Transfer
Logistics	1 — There Must Be Common Understanding of Terms 2 — The Achievement of RSI May Increase U.S. Logistics Support Requirements 3 — Weapon System Standardization Leading to a Joint Logistic Support System Is Unlikely 4 — Logistic Interchangeability of Components May Be Difficult to Achieve 5 — International Interchangeability (I^2) of Components Would Make Feasible a Cooperative Logistic Support System (CLSS) 6 — Deterrents Exist to U.S. Army Participation in a Cooperative Logistic Support System 7 — The NATO Maintenance and Supply Agency (NAMSA) Is the Most Likely

191

Category	Lessons Learned
Logistics (Continued)	Route for Implementing a Cooperative Logistic Support System
	8 — The Weapon System Development Process Differs between the U.S. and the Other NATO Nations
	9 — Logistic Support Concepts Differ between the U.S. and the Other NATO Nations
	10 — Availability/Applicability of Logistic Support Information of Foreign Systems Is Questionable
	11 — Integrated Logistic Support (ILS) Planning for a Foreign System may be More Difficult than for a U.S.-Developed System
	12 — U.S. Purchase of an "Off-the-Shelf" Foreign System Raises Special Logistic Support Considerations
	13 — NATO Stock Numbers Will Facilitate Supply Support
Coproduction	1 — Prerequisites for Successful Coproduction Are System Maturity, Strong Programme Management and Multinational Empathy
	2 — The Consortium Method of Management Has Inefficiencies
	3 — Extended Negotiations Must Be Expected in Reaching Coproduction Agreements
	4 — Coproduction Requires Workload Apportionment and Careful Scheduling to European Industrial Plants
	5 — Configuration Management and Technology Transfer Responsibilities Must Be Defined for Each Participant
	6 — A Configuration Management Plan Is Essential to Maintain the Integrity of the Technical Data Package

Appendix G

Modes of Collaboration and an Assessment

a. The Specialization Mode

Assignment of a weapon or weapons, components or equipment to a lead nation/industry based on agreed specialized ability and capability. Part of a Family of Weapons mode to be described later, or as a mode in itself.

b. The Merger Mode

Merging technical industries of the same family of weapons or specialization and the assignment of weapons, components or equipment to the merged structure. Merger can be within a nation or encompass a group of nations and their industries.

c. The Institutional Mode

Fully-planned, coordinated and NATO-sponsored institutional structures (government and industry), designed from top down (to only about the second major echelon of production — namely, policy and major components), sufficiently to carry out the fullest collaboration in the shortest timeframe (Multinational Enterprises).

d. The Permissive Mode

A mode used primarily for project type or more small group enterprises which normally are not "NATO-sponsored" but take place initially outside the NATO framework (but never *entirely*). These are usually ad hoc, *not* necessarily minor, and bear a similarity in their national and industrial structures to carry them out,

193

as is evidenced by past successful efforts. This mode should be encouraged and expanded in use. It works well in an Alliance milieu.

e. The Functional Cooperation Mode

A mode which would require member nations to pursue NATO programmes and projects over all others, either on a permissive or institutional basis. An effort to prioritize all NATO-type projects and programme willingly.

f. The Pooled Production Mode

A kind of either permissive or institutional mode which would employ joint authorities and industries of all the pooled member nations on an equal footing.

g. The Integrated Project Mode

An overall, single organization set up to cover several projects of either codevelopment or coproduction to serve as the common policy/top management agency. The savings would result from avoiding the overhead of each project as at present.

h. A Technological/Production Common Community Mode

A community agreement by all the members to set up technological cooperative structures to handle both R&D and Production. Such community programmes to be led by the heaviest spenders but participated in fully and fairly by the lesser spenders.

There are other modes, of course, but these should suffice to provide a selection upon which to offer institutional recommendations. In retrospect, if they were to be rearranged by difficulty and/or timing, it is clear that (c) and (d) and (f) have been used in part in the past and could continue as they have or become the bases of a far more effective arrangement built upon (a) and (b) with a whole new Institutional Mode (c) composed of the suggested organization and agreements which follow in the next section.

194

Time required should be rigorously set at four to five years at most. Mode (e) could well fit into the new Mode (c) as part of the binding agreement. Also, Modes (g) and (h) could be incorporated into a total Mode (c), or at worst, be pursued by themselves. However, it would appear that if (c) and (h) were to be realized, the potentialities would be enormous for more complete IMS. It must be added that, despite a large number of models, each cooperative programme has its peculiar diversities.

It should be apparent that the author has avoided recommendations built around a strictly European mode (or threat) or an American mode (or threat). Neither "Europeanization" nor "Americanization" can do the job alone. It is our total resources, economic, technological and military which are necessary to match the Soviet threat. Every balance sheet of power acknowledges this fact. It must be all, not an insufficiency, to be credible and defensible. Deviciveness is the handmaiden of Europeanization *or* Americanization. If Europe feels they can go it alone, the result is obvious failure. So too, if Americans feel that Europe will defend it (America) or that a conflict would not eventually come to U.S. soil, the result will be disastrous. Clearly, an Atlantic Alliance must be built that permits the best combinations of all the *international* modes.

Another useful, but different, approach illustrating the diverse means of carrying out cooperative programmes is this group of examples from an article by John B. Walsh, Assistant Secretary General for Defense Support, NATO:

TABLE 1. DIVERSE EXAMPLES OF COOPERATIVE PROGRAMMES[1]

Joint Development and Combined* Production	TORNADO Multi-Role Combat Aircraft (Germany, Italy, U.K.)
Licensed Partial Production	LEOPARD I Tank (Italy)
Licensed Complete Production	ROLAND Surface-to-Air Missile (U.S.)

1. Walsh, John B., "Armaments Cooperation in NATO." *NATO's Fifteen Nations*, December 1979 — January 1980, No. 6, p. 8.
*Each country builds part of the final product.

Licensed Combines Production	F-16 Aircraft (Belgium, Denmark, Netherlands, Norway)
Direct Sales	MIRAGE, LEOPARD I, M-113 Armoured Personnel Carrier, etc.
Coordinated Development-Production	WEAPON FAMILIES
Interface Specifications	EUROCOM Communications — Specifications NATO Standardization — Agreements (STANAGS)

Bibliography

Articles and Periodicals

Abrahamson, James A. "F-16 — NATO's Military and Economic Cornerstone." *Defense Systems Management Review* (Summer 1977): 18-23.

"Airborne Early Warning and Control System." *NATO Review*, Vol. 27, No. 1 (February 1979): 6.

Anderson, David K. "The Counter-Mobility Potential in the NATO Context." *Strategic Review* 7 (Winter 1979): 67-75.

Anderson, Frederic M. "Weapons Procurement Collaboration: A New Era for NATO?" *Orbis* (Winter 1977): 965-990.

"An Industrial View of Armament Export and Collaboration." *NATO's Fifteen Nations*, Vol. 23, No. 5 (October-November 1978): 70-71.

Antonov, A. and Ziborov, G. "NATO: Escalating the Arms Race." *International Affairs* (August 1978): 67-73.

Appleyard, James C., et al. "U.S. Arms Transfer to NATO: Past, Present, Future . . ." *NATO's Fifteen Nations* 22 (December 1977-January 1978): 70-71, 74-77.

Bacon, Kenneth H. and Otten, Alan L. "Allies' Arsenal: NATO Seeks to Bolster Coordination of Arms Development and Production for Efficiency." *Current News* Pt. I (February 5, 1979): 7-8. Original in *Wall Street Journal* 5 February 1979, p. 1.

Bagley, Worth H. "Sea Power: Neglected Key to a Revitalized NATO Strategy." *International Defense Review* 11 (No. 4/1978): 509-514.

Baroni, T. "In NATO Communications RSI-NICS Concept at all Levels." *Signal* 33 (September 1978): 19-20, 22.

Bartlett, Dewey F. and Polk, James H. "NATO Arms Standardization — Two Views." *AEI Defense Review* (No. 6/1977).

— "Standardizing Military Excellence: The Key to NATO's Survival." *AEI Defense Review* (No. 6/1977): 2-13.

Basil, Robert A. "NATO Must Standardize." *National Defense* 62 (November-December 1977): 208-211.

Beard, Robin. "U.S. NATO Policy: The Challenge and the Opportunity." *U.S. Naval Institute Proceedings* 104 (November 1978): 52-61.

Behuncik, John G. "Neutron Weapons and the Credibility of NATO Defense." *Journal of Social and Political Issues* 3 (Spring 1978): 3-16.

Berry, Clifton, Jr. and Schemmer, Benjamin F. "How Europe Sells." *Armed Forces Journal International* (August 1977): 17-18.

"A Better Bad Deal: Jimmy Carter Learns the Limits on Limiting Strategic Arms, Tough on NATO." *The Economist* 265 (October 22, 1977): 14-15.

Birrenbach, Kurt. "European Security: NATO, SALT and Equilibrium." *Orbis* (Summer 1978): 297-308.

Blanchard, George D. "Language Interoperability – A Key for Increased Effectiveness in NATO." *Military Review* 58 (October 1978): 58-63.

– "CENTAG/USAREUR Interoperability: A Total Programme from the Bottom Up." *Strategic Review* (Winter 1977): 7-13.

Boileau, O. C. "Some Current Trends Toward Weapons Standardization." *NATO's Fifteen Nations* 22 (June-July 1977): 70-71.

Bolton, David. "European Defense – the Challenge to NATO." *RUSI, Journal of the Royal United Services Institute for Defense Studies* (September 1975): 38-43.

Borklund, C. W. "NATO RSI and Arms Sales Abroad: Why the Dichotomy Won't Work." *Government Executive* 10 (December 1978): 43, 45, 48.

– "Perry's NATO Triad: How Pentagon Thinks Armament 'Co-DP' Will Work." *Government Executive* (March 1979): 16-28.

Borawaki, John. "Mutual Force Reductions in Europe from a Soviet Perspective." *Orbis* 22 (Winter 1979): 845-873.

Bowman, Richard C. "NATO: Standardization for Improved Combat Capability." *Commanders Digest* (September 8, 1976): 1-8.

– "The Two-Way Street and NATO Standardization – a clarification of the U.S. position." *International Defense Review*, No. 1 (1978): 35-40.

Boyes, Jon L. "The Role of National Communications Systems in NICS (NATO Integrated Communication System)." *Signal* (January-February 1973): 41-48.

– "NATO at the Crossroads." *Signal* 32 (January 1978): 49-53.

– "Editorial." *Signal* (April 1979): 7.

Boyle, R. D. "Naval Communications in NATO – Still Some Gaps." *International Defense Review* 4 (1978): 515-519.

Brayton, Abbot A. "NATO's Unused Resources." *Infantry* 68 (January-February 1978): 23-24.

Brezhnev, Leonid. "NATO & Eastern Europe: Disarmament." *Vital Speeches of the Day* 44 (June 15, 1978): 517-519.

Brookhiser, Richard. "Operation Forge: Watch on the Ruhr." *National Review* 30 (October 27, 1978): 1333-1336.

Brown, David A. "NATO Facing Challenges in Warsaw Pact, Finances." *Aviation Week & Space Technology* 108 (March 13, 1978): 41+.

– "NATO's New Challenge: Western Alliance Seeks to Update Nuclear Capability." *Aviation Week & Space Technology* 107 (August 1, 1977): 12-15.

Brown, George S. "The Strategic Importance of 7 Vital International Areas." *Commanders Digest* 20 (March 17, 1977): Entire issue.

Brown, Harold. "Inter-Allied Goals for a Strong NATO Defense." *Command Magazine* 1 (December 1978): 2+.

— "Our National Security Position: Training, Material Readiness and Mobility." *Vital Speeches of the Day* 45 (October 15, 1978): 27-30.

— "Today's National Security Policy." *Air Force Policy Letter for Commanders* (November 1977): 14-20.

— "World Freedom and the Promise of NATO." *Commanders Digest* 20 (October 6, 1977) 3, 5-23.

Buckley, Christopher. "Saving the West with General Haig." *Current News* Pt II (September 14, 1978): 1-F to 4-F.

Bulban, Erwin J. "General Support Rocket System to Become Cooperative Effort." *Aviation Week & Space Technology* 23 (January 1978): 20-21.

Burke, Gerard K. "Fighting the Unthinkable: Nuclear War in the 1980s." *Military Review* 58 (June 1978): 9-19.

Burrows, Bernard. "The Defense of Western Europe — Prospects for Further Collaboration." *Royal Air Force Quarterly* (December 1978): 328-343.

"Buying NATO's Arms: Can Europe Agree to Show America How?" *The Economist* (August 3, 1974): 32-33.

Callaghan, T. A., Jr. "NATO Standardization: Buzz Word or Necessity?" *Military Electronics/Counter Measures* (August 1977): 40-42.

— "No Two-Way Traffic Without A Two-Way Street." *NATO Review*, No. 5 (October 1977): 22-27.

— "Standardization — A Plan for U.S./European Cooperation." *NATO Review*, No. 4 (August 1975): 11.

Campobasso, Thomas A. "Market Imperatives of NATO Cooperation." *Signal* (April 1969): 37-39.

Canby, Steven L. "European Mobilization: U.S. and NATO Reserves." *Armed Forces and Society* 4 (Winter 1978): 227-244.

Canby, Steven L. "NATO: Reassessing the Conventional Wisdoms." *Survival* 19 (July-August 1977): 164-168.

"Carter Continues NATO Buildup: Navy Plans Slowed." *Congressional Quarterly Weekly Report* 36 (January 28, 1978): 167, 170-172.

Carter, Jimmy. "The NATO Parley: A Defensive Alliance." *Vital Speeches of the Day* 44 (June 15, 1978): 521-523.

"Carter's Goal: More Sharing of the NATO Load." *Business Week* (August 8, 1977): 78-79.

"Carter Rallies NATO." *Newsweek* (October 22, 1979): 59.

Center for Strategic and International Studies. "Allied Interdependence Newsletter No. 9." *Current News* (March 15, 1979): Entire issue. Critique of House Armed Services Committee on NATO Standardization, Interoperability, and Readiness.

Chandler, Robert W. "NATO's Cohesion: Europe's Future." *Air University Review* 29 (May-June 1978): 8-21.

Clarke, John L. "NATO Standardization: Panacea or Plague?" *Military Review* (April 1979): 59-65.

"Close-Up: It's a Born-Again NATO." *U.S. News & World Report* 84 (June 12, 1978): 31-32.

Cohen, Eliot. "NATO Standardization: The Perils of Common Sense." *Foreign Policy* (Summer 1978): 72-90.

Coleman, Herbert J. "Defense Chief Focuses on NATO Needs." *Aviation Week & Space Technology* 108 (February 13, 1978): 16-17.

— "Eurogroup Chief Hits Standardization Lag." *Aviation Week & Space Technology* (December 16, 1974): 14-15.

— "Standardization within NATO Urged." *Aviation Week & Space Technology* 108 (February 6, 1978): 25-26.

Cooling, Benjamin F. and Hixson, John A. "Interoperability of Allied Forces in Europe: Some Historical Peacetime Realities, Part I." *Military Review* 58 (August 1978): 63-73.

— "Interoperability of Allied Forces in Europe, Part II." *Military Review* 58 (September 1978): 67-74.

— "Lessons of Interoperability: Portent for the Future?" *Military Review* (June 1979): 38-47.

Corcoran, Edward A. "Support Troops in Combat Operations in Europe." *Army Logistician* 10 (January-February 1978): 18-23.

Corddry, Charles. "New Focus on NATO." *Guardsman* 32 (March 1978): 2-5.

Cormack, A. J. R. "NATO Small Arms — Trials or Not?" *Defense* 9 (January 1978): 18-19, 21.

— "The NATO Small Arms Trials." *International Defense Review* 11 (No. 7/1978): 1043-1048.

Cornell, Alexander H. "International Codevelopment and Coproduction of Weapons: Some Conclusions and Future Prospects." *U.S. Naval War College Review* (December 1970): 64-75.

Cornford, Clifford. "European Equipment Cooperation." *RUSI, Journal of the Royal United Services Institute for Defense Studies*, Vol. 124, No. 1 (March 1979): 46-49.

Coughlin, Eugene F. "A Twenty-One Jewel Watch: Mutual Logistic Support in NATO." *Defense Transportation Journal* (April 1976): 12-18.

Creech, W. L. "NATO Posture." *Air Force Policy Letter for Commanders* (May 1978): 9-18.

Criscimagna, Ned H. "The Yesterday, Today, and Tomorrow of Integrated Logistics Support." *Defense Management Journal* 13 (October 1977): 59-63.

Critchley, Julian. "A Community Policy for Armaments." *NATO Review*, No. 1 (February 1979): 10-14.

Cuffe, Donald S. "Cooperative Logistics Programmes Strengthen NATO Forces, Increased Effort Needed." *Defense Management Journal* (October 1973): 20-24.

Daley, Edmund K. "Standardization or Bankruptcy for NATO." *U.S. Naval Institute Proceedings* 104 (November 1978): 79-87.

Daniels, John K. "NATO Standardization — the Other Side of the Coin." *National Defense* (January-February 1977): 301-304.

Davidson, C. J. "NATO Standardization — A New Approach." *Journal of the Royal United Services RUSI* 122 (September 1977): 77-79.

Davis, Jacquelyn K. "Soviet Doctrine Implications for NATO." *National Defense* 63 (January-February 1979): 28-31, 56.

— "End of the Strategic Triad." *Strategic Review* 6 (Winter 1978): 36-44.

— "SALT and the Balance of Superpower Strategic Forces." *NATO's Fifteen Nations* 23 (February-March 1978): 56-61.

Dean, Robert W. "The Future of Collaborative Weapons Acquisition." *Survival*, The International Institute for Strategic Studies (July-August 1979): 155-163.

Débats: De La Standardization à l'Interoperabilité, *Aviastro* (Janvier 1976): 32-35.

"Defense Communications: Why 'Most Everything Now' Will be Interconnected." *Government Executive* (June 1978): 15-21.

DeWeerd, Harvey A. "Is U.S. Again Preparing for the Wrong War?" *Army* 28 (February 1978): 26-30.

Dodd, Norman L. "Standardization in NATO." *National Defense* (November-December 1975): 210-213.

"Defense Department Sustains Effort to Aid NATO Standardization." *Aviation Week & Space Technology* (April 25, 1977): 32.

DelPech, Jean Laurens. "La Standardization des Armaments." *Defense Nationale* (Mai 1976): 19-36.

Dodd, Norman L. "Britain and NATO Standardization." *Defense* (May 1975): 242-246.

"The Duel Over Arms for NATO." *Business Week* (June 5, 1978): 102-103.

Dunn, Keith A. "Soviet Perceptions of NATO." *Parameters* 8 (September 1978): 58-69.

Ebel, Wilfred L. "Raw Materials: The Difference Between Winning and Losing." *Army Logistician* 10 (March-April 1978): 8-11.

Edgington, Walter R. "NATO Standardization and the European Defense Industry — An American View." *Defense* 9 (October 1978): 745+.

Ehrhardt, Carl A. "Lessons of the Brussels NATO Summit." *Aussenpolitik* (English Edition), No. 3 (1975): 270-282.

Eiland, Michael D. "The Two-Way Street in NATO Procurement." *Strategic Review* (Summer 1977): 60-70.

Eliot, Chris. "The Rescue of Air Crew." *NATO's Fifteen Nations* (October-November 1977): 98-102, 105-106.

— "Two NATO Exercises." *NATO's Fifteen Nations* (December 1977-January 1978): 114-121.

Elliot, John D. "Interdependence — The Impact on U.S. Security." *Defense Systems Management Review* (Summer 1977): 32-42.

Ellsworth, Robert. "New Imperatives for the Old Alliance." *International Security* 2 (Spring 1978): 132-148.

Emery, Davis F. "The Soviet Naval Threat to NATO Europe." *Strategic Review* 6 (Fall 1978): 53-61.

"European NATO Members Discuss Position on SALT." *Aviation Week & Space Technology* 108 (May 22, 1978): 26.

Even-Tov, Ori. "The NATO Conventional Defense: Back to Reality." *Orbis* (Spring 1979): 35-49.

Ezell, Edward C. "The Squad Automatic Weapon — A New Element in the NATO Infantry Arms Debate." *International Defense Review*, No. 1 (1978): 81-85.

Ford, John J. "NATO Standardization and Interoperability — A Time for Involvement." *National Defense* 63 (January-February 1979): 44-46, 74.

"Foreword." *AEI Defense Review* (American Enterprise Institute for Defense), No. 6, Public Policy Research, Washington, D.C. (1977): 1.

Fouquet, David. "The Atlantic Arms 'Race'." *European Community* (August-September 1976): 26-29. Also in *Military Review* (April 1977): 37-42.

Freedman, Lawrence. "British Foreign Policy to 1985: I Britains Contribution to NATO." *International Affairs* (January 1978): 30-47.

— "European Security: The Prospect of Change." *RUSI Journal for Defense Studies* 123 (March 1978): 20-26.

Fullerton, John. "Small Arms: Biting the Bullet." *Defense & Foreign Affairs* (January 1979): 29-31.

— "Southern Theaters: Is the Warsaw Pact Outflanking NATO's Southern Flank?" *Defense & Foreign Affairs* (#2/1979): 36-38.

Furlong, R. D. M. "Can NATO Afford AWACS?" *International Defense Review* (October 1975): 667-676.

Galen, Justin. "NATO's Lost Decade: How the U.S. Gave the Warsaw Pact a Surprise Attack Capability." *Armed Forces Journal International* 115 (June 1978): 19-20+.

— "NATO's Lost Decade — Part II: Restoring the NATO-Warsaw Pact Balance — The Art of the Impossible." *Armed Forces Journal International* 116 (September 1978): 32-34, 37-38, 40-46.

— "NATO's Theater Nuclear Dilemma: A New Set of Crucial Choices." *Armed Forces Journal International* (January 1979): 16-23.

"Gen. Haig Urges NATO to Adjust Strategy for Third World Threats." *Review* (March 1979): 10-16.

Gerhardt, Wolfgang. "What About Multinational Corps in NATO." *Military Review* (March 1979): 10-16.

Gessert, Robert A. "NATO Standardization." *National Defense* 61 (March-April 1977): 366-367.

— "United States Arms Export Policy and Weapons Cooperation." *NATO's Fifteen Nations* (December 1977-January 1978): 56-68.

Gilbert, John. "Procurement and Standardization Within NATO." *AFL-CIO Free Trade Union News* 33 (September 1978): 3.

Godsell, Geoffrey. "The Soviet Threat: NATO Lives." *Current News* Pt II (September 29, 1978): 1F.

Goodby, James E. "Standardization of NATO Equipment Discussed by Department." *The Department of State Bulletin* (April 26, 1976): 556-558.
— "The Puzzle of European Defense: The Issue of Arms Procurement." *Survey* (Summer/Autumn 1976): 218-232. Also in *The Atlantic Community Quarterly* (Winter 1976-1977): 473-487.
Gray, Colin S. "NATO Strategy and the Neutron Bomb." *Policy Review* 7 (Winter 1979): 7-26.
— "Nuclear Weapons in NATO Strategy." *NATO's Fifteen Nations* 23 (February-March 1978): 82-83+.
Greenwood, Allen. "International Industrial Cooperation." *NATO's Fifteen Nations*, Vol. 23, No. 2 (April-May 1978): 96-98.
Gundersen, H. F. Zeiner. "The Alliances Strategic Concept." *NATO Review* 26 (February 1978): 11-14.
— "NATO — A Military Appraisal." *For Your File* (February 10, 1978): 5-8.
— "The Balance of Forces and Economic Problems." *NATO Review*, Vol. 27. No. 5 (October 1979); 3-7.
Hadley, Arthur T. "Our Underequipped, Unprepared NATO Forces: The Surprising Soviet Lead in Technology and Tactics." *Current News* Pt II (June 5, 1978): 1F to 5F.
Hagelin, Bjorn. "One for All or Four for the Fifth: Standardization and the F-16 in Europe." *Cooperation and Conflict* (3/1978): 133-146.
Haig, Alexander, Jr. "The Challenge for the West in a Changing Strategic Environment." *NATO Review*, No. 3 (June 1976): 10-13.
— "Europe's New Balance of Power — A Warning from the NATO Chief." *U.S. News & World Report* 84 (June 5, 1978): 20-22.
— "NATO and the Security of the West." *NATO Review* 26 (August 1978): 8-11.
— "What NATO Faces Today." *The Atlantic Community Quaterly* 16 (Winter 1978-1979): 425-431.
"Haig Hits U.S. On NATO Leadership." *Aviation Week & Space Technology* (March 5, 1979): 15.
Harvey, David. "NATO and the U.S. Budget." *Defense and Foreign Affairs Digest* (2/1979): 34-35.
Heiser, Joseph M. "NATO Principles of Logistics and U.S. Readiness: A Changing Environment." *Defense Management Journal* 14 (March 1978): 18-23.
Hessman, James D. and Bottiny, Ellen D. "FY 1980 Budget Report, and the NATO Scenario Continues." *Seapower* (February 1979): 18-27.
Hillenbrand, Martin. "NATO and Western Security in an Era of Transition." *International Security*, Vol. 2, No. 2 (Fall 1977): 3-24.
Hill-Norton, Sir Peter. "NATO in 1975: The Military Issues at Stake." *Military Review* (September 1975): 50-55.
— "An Interview with the Chairman of the NATO Military Committee on Standardization and the Two-Way Street." *For Your File*, NATO Bulletin for Commanders and Public Information Officers, NATO, No. 14 (March 5, 1976): 1-4.

"House Panel Skeptical of Arms Cooperation Policy with NATO Allies." *Congressional Quarterly Weekly Report* (February 24, 1979): 323-325.

Howe, Russell W. "NATO: The Uncoordinated Giant." *Saturday Review* (April 29, 1978): 8.

"Instability and Change on NATO's Southern Flank." *International Security* 3 (Winter 1978/1979): 150-177.

"Interoperable Helicopter Force Being Developed." *Aviation Week & Space Technology* (July 17, 1978): 60.

"Jaguar and Tornado Aircraft Integral to NATO." *Signal* (April 1979): 87.

Jefferson, George R. "Making Standardization Work." *Aviation Week & Space Technology* (April 24, 1978): 11.

Jobe, Morris B. "Industry Aid for NATO." *National Defense* 61 (March-April 1977): 363-365.

Johnsen, Katherine. "Management: NATO Standardization Efforts Increase." *Aviation Week & Space Technology* 109 (October 30, 1978): 64.

Kennedy, Robert. "Precision ATGMs and NATO Defense." *Orbis* 22 (Winter 1979): 897-927.

Kidd, Isaac C. "The Defense of the Atlantic." *NATO's Fifteen Nations* 23 (October-November 1978): 28-34.

— "NATO's Double Dependence on the Atlantic." *NATO Review* 26 (October 1978): 3-8.

Kielmansegg, J. A. Graf. "Europe's Heightened Role in Global Strategy." *Strategic Review* (Winter 1979): 49-55.

Komer, Robert W. "Defense Adviser for NATO Affairs." *National Defense* 63 January-February 1979): 5+.

— "Coalition Warfare." *Army* 26 (September 1976): 28-32.

— "Ten Suggestions for Rationalizing NATO." *The Atlantic Community Quarterly* 15 (Summer 1977): 192-200.

Korkegi, Robert H. "AGARD's Role in NATO." *NATO Review*, No. 3 (June 1979): 25-26.

Kozicharow, Eugene. "NATO Standardization Advances." *Aviation Week & Space Technology* (December 1977): 8-10.

— "European Defense Unity Pushed." *Aviation Week & Space Technology* (March 5, 1979): 12-14.

— "NATO Leaders Optimistic Despite Major Problems." *Aviation Week & Space Technology* (March 12, 1979): 55-58.

— "Standardization Effort at Pivotal Stage." *Aviation Week & Space Technology* (June 6, 1977): 105-111.

Krukin, Jeffrey A. "NATO Sea Sparrow." *National Defense* 63 (January-February 1979): 38-40.

LaBerge, Walter B. "Cooperation Improvement of NATO Communications." *Signal* (February 1977): 8-11.

— "Standardization and Interoperability: Another Perspective." *NATO Review* 24 (December 1976): 13-15.

— "Improving NATO Through Armaments Collaboration." *Signal* (April (1979): 43-47.

LaBerge, Walter B. "A Concept of a Two-Way Street." *Defense Systems Management Review* (Summer 1977): 3-8.
— "Chanson de Roland." *NATO Review*, No. 3 (June 1977) 10-15.
Leonard, Major General William C. "Ensuring Collective Defense Forces Can Operate Together — A Challenge for the Allies." *NATO Review*, No. 4 (August 1975).
Lidy, A. Martin. "NATO Standardization — An Alternative Approach." *Defense Systems Management Review* 1 (Summer 1977): 43-62.
Lindsey, George R. "The Place of Maritime Strength in the Strategy of Deterrence." *Naval War College Review* 30 (Spring 1978): 26-33.
Loureiro Dos Santos, Jose Alberto. "Portugal's Role in Western Defense." *NATO Review* 26 (December 1978): 9-13.
Luciolli, Mario. "The Atlantic Alliance in a Changed World." *NATO Review*, Vol. 27, No. 5 (October 1979): 12-15.
Lugvigsen, Eric C. "Huskier NATO Heads '79 Defense Priorities." *Army* 28 (March 1978): 14-19.
Luns, Joseph M. A. H. "Thirty Years Later, Aims of the Alliance Still Valid." *NATO Review*, No. 2 (April 1979): 3-8.
— "NATO: The Next Ten Years." *RUSI* 122 (December 1977): 3-7.
Lunsford, Richard J. "Defense Planning: A Time for Breadth." *Parameters* 8 (March 1978): 15-25.
Malone, Daniel K. "The French 75." *National Defense*, Journal of the American Defense Preparedness Association (March-April 1979): 40-46.
Marriot. "Fire Power of the (NATO) Striking Fleet." *NATO's Fifteen Nations* 23 (April-May 1978): 44-46+.
Mason, Kathleen. "Federal Signals: NATO Study Prompts DOD Change" and "House Report Rips NATO." *Signal* (April 1979): 8.
McClane, Joseph L. "The Specialized Character of NATO." *U.S. Naval Institute Proceedings* 103 (April 1977): 19-23.
McLucas, John L. "The Air Combat Fighter: Progress for Standardization." *NATO Review*, Vol. 23, No. 6 (December 1975): 3-6.
Medeiros, Raymond R. "NATO Common Infrastructure." *The Military Engineer* 69 (November-December 1977): 392-395.
Meller, Rudi. "Pentagon Endorses Family of Weapons Concept." *International Defense Review*, Vol. 12, No. 5 (1979): 702-703.
Middleton, Drew. "Major Issues at Guadeloupe: U.S. Stand on NATO Defense." *Current News* Pt II (January 5, 1979): 1-F.
Miley, Henry A., Jr. "Weapon Standardization." *National Defense* (November-December 1977): 212-213.
Milsom, J. F. "Think Again NATO: An Unconventional Approach to the Defense of Western Europe." *Defense* 9 (May 1978): 296-298.
Milton, Theodore R. "The Back Door to NATO Standardization." *Air Force Magazine* (May 1977): 168.
— "NATO's Year of Decision." *Air Force Magazine* 60 (August 1977) 49-53.
— "Rationalization — A NATO Solution." *National Defense* 62 (January-February 1978): 324-326.

Milton, Theodore R. "NATO's 30th Anniversary." *The Retired Officer* (April 1979): 15-18.

Moller, Orla. "The Eurogroup: The May Ministerial Meeting and Beyond." *NATO Review*, No. 4 (August 1977): 3-5.

Morse, John H. "New Weapons Technologies: Implications for NATO." *Orbis* (Summer 1975): 497-513.

Mulley, Fred. "Britain's Role In NATO: Increasing Commitment." *Defense & Foreign Affairs Digest* 6 (#10/1978): 6-9.

Mumford, Bill. "NATO's Long Term Defense Programme — Forward: NATO Defense at the Summit." *NATO Review*, No. 3 (June 1978): 3-5.

Mumford, W. F. "1977/78: Vintage Years for NATO Defense Planning." *NATO Review* 25 (December 1977): 3-5.

Neff, Richard. "NATO Political Consultation, Fact or Myth?" *NATO Review* (1975): 7-9.

"North Atlantic Alliance Summit: Text of Remarks on NATO Defense Policy." *Weekly Compilation of Presidential Documents* 14 (June 5, 1978): 1020-1022.

"NATO Duplication: 14 Nations Have 232 Different Weapons in 5 Categories." *Armed Forces Journal International* (July 1975): 24.

"NATO Initiatives (Underway)." *Armed Forces Journal International* (April 1978): 17.

"NATO Missile Standardization Pushed." *Aviation Week & Space Technology* (June 2, 1975): 61-71.

"NATO Officials Endorse AWACS; French Consider Participation." *Aviation Week & Space Technology* (May 29, 1978): 20-21.

"NATO: Our Unlimited Commitment." *Defense Monitor* 7 (June 1978): 2-8.

"NATO and the Neutron Bomb — and Conventional War in Europe?" *Defense Monitor* 7 (June 1978): Entire issue.

"NATO and Theater Nuclear Forces: Continued Tokenism, Inadequacy, and Indecision." *Armed Forces Journal* (March 1979): 29-33.

"NATO Arms Standardization: Two Views." *AEI Defense Review* #6 (1977).

"NATO C³." *Signal* (February 1977): Entire issue.

"NATO Chief Seeks New Kind of Leadership by U.S." *U.S. News & World Report* (February 26, 1979): 39-42.

"NATO Plans Future Defense: Airlift Refuelling Emphasized." *Aviation Week & Space Technology* 108 (April 23, 1978): 61-62, 65.

"NATO's Navies: Alliance at Sea." *NATO's Fifteen Nations* 23 (Special Issue 1978): Entire issue.

"NATO's Allied Command Atlantic: Some Words on History and Structure." *NATO's Fifteen Nations* 23 (October-November 1978): 35-36.

"New Directions for NATO." *Aviation Week & Space Technology* (July 3, 1978): 14-20.

Norton, Augustus R. "NATO and Metaphors: The Nuclear Threshold." *Naval War College Review* 30 (Fall 1977): 60-75.

"Not Invented Here." *Armed Forces Journal International* (August 1973): 25.

Nunn, Sam. "Deterring War in Europe: Some Basic Assumptions Need Revising." *NATO Review* 25 (February 1977): 4-7.

Nunn, Sam and Bartlett, Dewey. "NATO and the New Soviet Threat." *NATO's Fifteen Nations* 22 (April-May 1977): 36-42+.

Osborn, Palmer and Bowen, William. "How to Defend Western Europe." *Fortune* 98 (October 9, 1978): 150-162.

Ozdas, M. N. "Twenty Years of Scientific Cooperation: An Assessment and Some Prospects." *NATO Review* 26 (August 1978): 16-21.

Pedersen, Jimmie L. "Interoperability of US-NATO Communications." *Signal* 32 (April 1978): 31-34.

Perry, William J. "NATO Two-Way Street Called Essential." *Aviation Week & Space Technology* 110 (February 12, 1979): 49-51.

— "New Directions for NATO." *Defense Systems Management Review* 1 (Autumn 1978): 66-73.

— "The Role of Technology in Strengthening NATO." *NATO's Fifteen Nations* 23 (February-March 1978): 52-55.

"Perspectives on the Military Budget." *The Defense Monitor*, Vol. VIII, No. 6 (May 1979): 2-8.

Pigaty, Leo J. "Practicing Interoperability." *Army Logistician* 9 (September-October 1977): 8-11.

Polk, James H. "Military Standardization Within NATO, How Far Should We Go?" *AEI Defense Review*: 14-24.

— "The New Short War Strategy." *Strategic Review* 3 (Summer 1975): 52-56.

Prina, L. Edgar. "A New Look at NATO." *Military Review* (July 1977): 25-33.

— "NATO's Still Smoldering Southern Flank." *Sea Power* 20 (November 1977): 13-17.

Radi, Luciano. "A European Initiative in the Armaments Field." *NATO Review*, No. 3 (June 1977): 8-10.

Ragano, Frank P. "U.S. Roland — A Giant Step Toward Weapon Commonality." *Defense Systems Management Review* (Summer 1977): 9-12.

— "U.S. Roland: A Milestone in Technology Tranfer." *Defense Management Journal* (May 1978): 3-10.

"Rationalization/Standardization/Interoperability." *Defense Systems Management Review* (Summer 1977): Entire issue.

Ratliff, Walter. "NATO Needs: A Challenge to Industries." *Air Force Policy Letter for Commanders* (February 1979): 16-26.

"Remarks of President Jimmy Carter at NATO Ministerial Meeting." Lancaster House, England, Tuesday, May 10, 1977. *Defense Systems Management Review*, Vol. 1, No. 3 (Summer 1977): v-viii.

"Reservations Aired on Programme to Push NATO Standardization." *Aviation Week & Space Technology* 109 (October 23, 1978): 26-27.

Reynolds, Roger D. "NATO Host-Nation Logistics Support." *Army Logistician* 9 (May-June 1977): 14-16.

Richardson, John H. "Roland, A Technology Transfer Programme." *Defense Systems Management Review* (Summer 1977): 13-17.

Rockefeller, Nelson A. "Assessment of NATO and the Defense of the Free World." *The Atlantic Community Quarterly* 16 (Winter 1978-1979): 403-408.

Robinson, Clarence A., Jr. "Conventional Force Buildup Emphasized." *Aviation Week & Space Technology* (August 15, 1977): 45-51.

– "Force Management Key To Effectiveness." *Aviation Week & Space Technology* (August 29, 1977): 36-47.

– "Hurdles Confront Standardization." *"Aviation Week & Space Technology* (June 21, 1976): 14-17.

– "NATO Agrees on Air Warfare Doctrine." *Aviation Week & Space Technology* (July 5, 1976): 17-19.

– "NATO Research Cooperation Stressed." *Aviation Week & Space Technology* (August 8, 1977): 20-22.

– "NATO's New Challenge: Strength Sought at Least Cost." *Aviation Week & Space Technology* (August 8, 1977): 36-47.

– "NATO's New Challenge: U.S. Funds Major Standardization Drive." *Aviation Week & Space Technology* (September 12, 1977): 52-53, 56-59, 62-65.

– "U.S. Mulls NATO Standardization Moves." *Aviation Week & Space Technology* (June 28, 1976): 21-23.

"Roland: Army's Leading 'Case-in-Point'." *Government Executive* (March 1978): 23.

"Roland: Exchange of Expertise." *National Defense* (May-June 1978): 549-550.

Rose, Francois de. "Scientific and Technological Progress: Problems for the West." *NATO Review* 26 (October 1978): 16-20.

Schemmer, Benjamin F. "AFJ Interview' Improving NATO's Efficiency and Getting the Alliance More Resources." *Armed Forces Journal International* 116 (September 1978): 26-27, 28.

– "AFJ Interview: It's Easier to Turn this Building Around . . . Than it is to Turn Around 14 NATO Allies . . ." *Armed Forces Journal International* 116 (September 1978): 47-52.

– "Bloody Battle Over U.S. Commitment to NATO for 3% Real Budget Increase." *Armed Forces Journal International* 116 (November 1978): 8-14.

– "Carter's FY80 Defense Budget Meets NATO's 3% Real Growth Commitment." *Armed Forces Journal International* (February 1979): 18.

– "Pentagon Reevaluates Carter Arms Transfer Policy. NATO Standardization Jeopardized." *Armed Forces Journal International* (August 1977): 12-14.

– "Soviet Sub Threat Is Now 10 Times Germany's When World War II Broke Out." *Armed Forces Journal International* (July 1975): 24.

Scott, John F. "The Neutron Weapon and NATO Strategy." *Parameters* 7 (No. 3/1977): 33-38.

Seignious, George M. "SALT II: The Centre Piece of East-West Relations." *NATO Review*, Vol. 27, No. 5 (October 1979): 8-11.

Shear, Harold E. "The Southern Flank of NATO." *NATO's Fifteen Nations* (December 1978-January 1979): 17-20.

Simmons, Henry T. "NATO Equipment Standardization and Commonality — — U.S. Opinions and Proposals." *International Defense Review* (April 1975): 156-157.

Simpson, John and Gregory, Frank. "West European Collaboration in Weapons Procurement." *Orbis* (Summer 1972): No. 2.

Sismore, E. B. "Ground Environment for the Future: The Air Defense of Allied Command Europe." *Royal Air Force Quarterly* (December 1978): 345-352.

"Six NATO Countries Study PATRIOT Buy." *Armed Forces Journal International* (April 1979): 20.

Smith, Daniel M. "Logistics Impact of the Division Restructuring Study — Arms, Fuel, and Maintain Forward." *Army Logistician* 10 (March-April 1978): 2-7.

"Splitting up NATO's Arms Trade." *Business Week* (International Edition) (October 23, 1978): 111-114.

Stachurski, Richard J. "The Nunn-Bartlett Report: A Realistic Prescription for NATO." *Air University Review* 29 (July-August 1978): 21-25.

"Standardization within NATO." *Defense Systems Management Review* (Summer 1977): iii-62. This entire issue is devoted to articles or governmental documents on the subject of NATO standardization. Each article is listed separately in this bibliography.

Stevens, Phil. "NATO and the Warsaw Pact — An Assessment." *Military Review* 58 (September 1978): 34-42.

Stoehrmann, Kenneth C. "Toward a Common European Armaments Effort." *Air University Review* (January-February 1974): 22-31.

Stone, John. "Equipment Standardization and Cooperation." *NATO Review*, Vol. 22, No. 4 (1974): 26-28.

Stoney, William E. "The Process of Standardization, An Overview." *Defense Systems Management Review* (Summer 1977): 1-2.

— "Achieving NATO's Standardization Objectives." *Signal* (August 1978): 78-80.

Taber, Richard D. "NATO's Amphibious Trump Card." *National Defense* 62 (May-June 1978): 534-535+.

"Tactical Nuclear Weapons — The European Predicament." *Bulletin for Peace Proposals* (#4 1978): 378-386.

Taylor, Peter P. W. "NATO's Dispersal Capability — A Fatal Flaw?" *Royal Air Forces Quarterly* 18 (Spring 1978): 11-17.

"The Standard Frigate." *NATO's Fifteen Nations*, Vol. 34, No. 1 (February-March 1979): 95-104.

"13 NATO EW Initiatives." *Armed Forces Journal International* (April 1979): 35.

Thomer, Egbert. "One Step Toward Standardization?" *NATO's Fifteen Nations* 22 (October-November 1977): 43, 45-51.

Towell, Pat. "Arms Standardization: Priority Issue for Carter." *Congressional Quarterly Weekly Report* (December 4, 1976): 3271-3275.

Tucker, Gardiner L. "Standardization and Defense in NATO." *RUSI, Journal of the Royal United Services Institute for Defense* (March 1976): 7-14.

— "Standardization and the Joint Defense." *NATO Review* (January 1975): 10-14.

"Two Opposing Views: Should NATO Standardize?" *Armed Forces Journal International* 116 (March 1978): 16.

"The Two-Way Street and NATO Standardization — A Clarification of the U.S. Position." *International Defense Review* 11 (#1/1978): 35-40.

Ulsamer, Edgar. "NATO: On the Road Toward a Coalition Warfare Posture." *Air Force Magazine* 61 (January 1978): 50-56.

— "NATO's New Cautious Optimism." *Air Force Magazine* 61 (June 1978): 37-42.

van Eekelen, W. F. "Equipment Procurement — Need for Longer Term NATO Planning." *NATO Review*, No. 3 (June 1979): 6-9.

Vaern, Grethe. "The Atlantic Alliance and European Integration." *NATO Review*, Vol. 26, No. 2 (April-May 1978): 23-29.

Vest, George S. "NATO On Turning Thirty." *Signal* (April 1979): 21-22.

Vigor, P. H. "The Soviet Union and the Northern Flank of NATO." *NATO's Fifteen Nations* 23 (April-May 1978): 58-60.

Waddell, D. W. "Commonality — Or, What's in a Word?" *Defense Systems Management Review* (Summer 1977): 24-31.

Wall, Patrick. "NATO Must Standardize." *Naval International* (May 1976): 6-7. Also in *Military Review* (December 1976): 58-63 (and) *The Atlantic Community Quarterly* (Spring 1977): 50-56.

— "Can Standardization Succeed?" *Defense*, Vol. 7, No. 12 (December 1976).

Walsh, John B. "Initiatives in Standardization/Interoperability." *NATO Review* 26 (October 1978): 8-11.

"What DARCOM Is Doing About NATO Interoperability." *Government Executive* (March 1978): 22-25.

Whitely, Peter. "The Importance of the Northern Flank to NATO." *NATO's Fifteen Nations* 23 (April-May 1978): 18-20, 23-25.

Wilczynski, Josef. "Technology and the NATO-Warsaw Pact Strategic Balance." *Australian Outlook* (December 1973): 286-306.

Wilson, Teck A. "European Industry's Outlook." (November-December 1977): 214-215, 259.

Windsor, Philip. "A Watershed for NATO." *World Today* 33 (November 1977): 409-416.

Wolf, Charles and Leibaert, Derek. "Trade Liberalization as a Path to Standardization in NATO." *International Security* (Winter 1978): 136-159.

Woodcock, Michael J. "NATO Standardization." *Military Review* (October 1975): 39-48.

Worner, Manfred. "NATO Defenses and Tactical Nuclear Weapons." *Atlantic Community Quarterly* 16 (Spring 1978): 22-32.

Wright, Gerald. "NATO in the New International Order." *Behind the Headlines* 36 (#4/1978): Entire issue.

Yakheim, Dov. S. "Improving NATO Defenses: The Institutional Dimension." *Military Review* (October 1977): 43-55.

Books

Ashcroft, Geoffrey. *Military Logistics Systems in NATO: The Goal of Integration. Part I, Economic Aspects; Part II, Military Aspects.* London: International Institute for Strategic Studies, Adelphi Papers, Nos. 62 and 68, 1969.

Atlantic Community in Crisis: A Redefinition of the Transatlantic Relationship. Edited by Walter F. Hahn and Robert F. Pfaltzgraff. New York: Pergamon Press, 1979.

Bartlett, Dewey E. *NATO Arms Standardization: Two Views.* Washington, D.C.: American Enterprise Institute for Public Policy Research, 1977.

Callaghan, Thomas A., Jr., *U.S./European Cooperation in Military and Civil Technology.* Revised Edition. Washington, D.C.: Center for Strategic and International Studies, September 1975.

Calmann, John. *European Cooperation in Defense Technology: The Political Aspect.* London: The Institute for Strategic Studies, April 1967.

Conrad, David M. *Implementation of NATO Guidelines on Intellectual Property Rights (IPR) for Armaments Standardization.* Washington, D.C.: Logistics Management Institute, January 1979.

Cornell, Alexander H. *An Analysis of International Collaboration in the Organization and Management of Weapons Coproduction.* National Technical Information Service, U.S. Department of Commerce, Springfield, Virginia, August 1971.

Davis, Jacquelyn K. *Soviet Theater Strategy: Implications for NATO.* Washington, D.C.: United States Strategic Institute, 1978.

Foch, Rene. Europe and Technology: *A Political View.* The Atlantic Paper -70/2. Paris: The Atlantic Institute for International Affairs, 1970.

Gessert, Robert A. *The Economics of NATO Standardization.* McLean, Virginia: General Research Corporation, 1977.

— *Improving NATO's Theater Nuclear Posture: A Reassessment and a Proposal.* Washington, D.C.: Center for Strategic and International Studies, 1977.

Gessert, Robert A.; Heverly, J. Ross; and Pettijohn, William C. *NATO Standardization and Technology Transfer.* General Research Corporation CR-196. McLean, Virginia: General Research Corporation, August 1977.

Gessert, Robert A. et al. *NATO Standardization and Licensing Policy — Exploratory Phase.* McLean, Virginia: General Research Corporation, November 1976.

— *DARCOM OIRD's Role in NATO Rationalization/Standardization/Interoperability.* McLean, Virginia: General Research Corporation, February 1978.

211

Gessert, Robert A. *U.S. Arms Export Policy and Weapons Cooperation.*
McLean, Virginia. General Research Corporation, 1977.

Goodman, Elliot R. *Detente and the Defense of Europe.* In D. W. Sheldon,
Ed., Dimensions of Detente, Praiger, New York, 1978, pp. 172-195.

– *The Fate of the Atlantic Community.* Published for the Atlantic
Council of the United States, Praeger Publishers, New York, 1975,
p. 583.

Gordon, Colin. *The Atlantic Alliance – A Bibliography.* Frances Pinter Ltd.,
London, Nichols Publishing Company, New York, 1978.

Harlow, C. J. E. *The European Armaments Base: A Survey. Part 1: Economic
Aspects of Defense Procurement; Part 2: National Procurement Policies.*
London: The Institute for Strategic Studies, June 1967.

Hill-Norton, Peter. *No Soft Options: The Politico-Military Realities of NATO.*
Montreal: McGill-Queen's University Press, 1978.

International Military Exercises. Aspects of NATO. NATO Information
Service, 1110 Brussels, September 1978.

James, Robert Rhodes. *Standardization and Common Production of Weapons
in NATO.* London: The Institute for Strategic Studies, July 1967.

Jordan, Robert S. *Political Leadership in NATO: A Study in Multinational
Diplomacy.* Boulder, Colorado: Westview Press, 1979.

Kaldor, Mary. *European Defense Industries – National and International
Implications.* Monograph, Brighton Institute for the Study of International
Organizations, 1972. (1S10 Mono.)

Kramish, Arnold. *Atlantic Technological Imbalance: An American Perspective.*
London: The Institute for Strategic Studies, August 1967.

Mendershausen, Horst. *Outlook on Western Solidarity: Political Relations in
the Atlantic Alliance System.* (R-1572-PR) Santa Monica, California:
Rand Corporation, June 1976.

North Atlantic Treaty Organization. *NATO Handbook.* NATO Information
Service, Brussels, May 1979, p. 94.

NATO Working on Industrial Property. *Military Equipment and Industrial
Property Legislation.* Volume I. Brussels, November 1976.

NATO Information Service. *Eurogroup.* 2nd Edition. Brussels, 1975.

NATO Information Service. *NATO Facts and Figures.* Brussels, 1978.

Ritchie, Ronald S. *NATO, The Economics of An Alliance.* The Ryerson Press,
Toronto, 1956. (Done under the auspices of the Canadian Institute of
International Affairs.)

Sloss, Leon. *NATO Reform: Prospects and Priorities.* Beverly Hills, California:
Sage Publications, 1975.

Standardization in NATO. R.V.S.I. and Brassey's Defense Yearbook, 1975/76.
London: Brasseys, 1975, pp. 390-395. (v 10 N 2 1975/76.)

The Military Balance 1978-1979. The International Institute for Strategic
Studies, London, 1978.

Tucker, Gardiner L. *Towards Rationalizing Allied Weapons Production.*
Paris: The Atlantic Institute for International Affairs, 1976.

Udis, Bernard. *From Guns to Butter: Technology Organizations and Reduced*

Military Spending in Western Europe. Cambridge, Massachusetts: Ballinger Publishing Company, 1978.

Van Deventer, Brigadier General Elliot, Jr., (USAF Ret.). *International Logistics; Interallied Collaboration in Weapons Production.* Industrial College of the Armed Forces, Washington, D.C., 1967.

Wall, Patrick, *Standardization — The Need for a Two-Way Street. R.V.S.I. and Brassey's Defense Yearbook 1977/78.* Boulder, Colorado, Westview Press, 1977, pp. 171-186.

Wolf, Joseph J. *The Growing Dimensions of Security: The Atlantic Council's Working Group on Security.* Washington: Atlantic Council of the United States, 1977.

Contract Studies/Reports/Papers

Allied Partnership on Armaments. Report on Transatlantic Seminar, Co-Chaired by U.S. Senator Sam Nunn and Congressman Charles E. Bennett, CSIS Report, Center for Strategic and International Studies, Georgetown University, Washington, D.C., March 1977.

American Defense Preparedness Association. Meeting Report. *Executive Symposium on NATO Standardization and Interoperability.* August 4, 1977 at the National War College, Fort Lesley J. McNair. Washington, D.C.: American Defense Preparedness Association, 1977.

American Defense Preparedness Association. Meeting Report. *International Synposium on NATO Standardization and Interoperability.* March 8-9, 1978. Washington, D.C.: American Defense Preparedness Association, 1978.

Ashcroft, Geoffrey. *Military Logistic Systems in NATO: The Goal of Integration, Part I: Economic Aspects.* Adelphi Papers No. 62. London: The International Institute for Strategic Studies, December 1969.

— *Military Logistic System in NATO: The Goal of Integration, Part II: Military Aspects.* Adelphi Papers No. 68. London: The International Institute for Strategic Studies, June 1970.

Behrman, Jack N. *Multinational Production Consortia: Lessons from NATO Experience.* A Report Prepared Under Contract for the U.S. Department of State, August 1971.

Bray, Frank T. J. and Moodie, Michael. *Defense Technology and the Atlantic Alliance: Competition or Collaboration?* Cambridge, Massachusetts, Institute for Foreign Policy Analysis, 1977, p. 42.

Callaghan, Thomas A., Jr. *Allied Interdependence NEWSLETTER No. 10.* The Center for Strategic and International Studies, Georgetown University, Washington, D.C., April 2, 1979.

— *Allied Interdependence NEWSLETTER No. 11.* The Center for Strategic and International Studies, Georgetown University, Washington, D.C., May 3, 1979.

Callaghan, Thomas A., Jr. *Allied Interdependence NEWSLETTER No. 12.* The Center for Strategic and International Studies, Georgetown University, Washington, D.C., May 31, 1979.

— *Allied Interdependence NEWSLETTER No. 13.* The Center for Strategic and International Studies, Georgetown University, Washington, D.C., June 21, 1979.

— *Allied Interdependence NEWSLETTER No. 14.* The Center for Strategic and International Studies, Georgetown University, Washington, D.C., August 1, 1979, pp. 1-13.

— *Standardization: Lessening the Danger of Nuclear War.* Washington, D.C.: Center for Strategic and International Studies, July 21, 1977.

Canby, Steven. *The Alliance and Europe: Part IV. Military Doctrine and Technology.* Adelphi Papers No. 109. London: The International Institute for Strategic Studies, Winter 1974.

Curriculum Study, NATO RSI. Final Report of the Study Group on NATO RSI, FY 1979, National Defense University, Washington, D.C., 1979.

Currie, Malcolm R. *The Department of Defense: International Cooperative Research and Development.* A statement by the U.S. Department of Defense Director of Research and Engineering before the Research and Development Subcommittee, Armed Services Committee of the United States Senate, 94th Congress, First Session, April 21, 1975, p. 10.

— *The Department of Defense Programme of Research, Development, Test and Evaluation, FY 1977.* An overview statement before the Armed Services Committee of the United States House of Representatives, 94th Congress, Second Session, February 10, 1976.

Dean, Robert W. *Future of Collaborative Weapons Acquisition.* (P-6199) Santa Monica, California: Rand Corporation, September 1978.

Defense Science Board, *Achieving Improved NATO Effectiveness Through Armaments Collaboration.* 1978 Summer Study, Newport, Rhode Island: Naval War College, July 31-August 11, 1978.

Facer, Roger. *The Alliance and Europe: Part III. Weapons Procurement in Europe: Capabilities and Choices.* Adelphi Papers No. 108. London: The International Institute for Strategic Studies, 1975.

Green, Hugh. "Prospects for European Arms Cooperation," *The Defense of Western Europe.* No. 5 of papers presented at the National Defense College, Latimer, September 1972. Edited by John C. Gornett, St. Martin's Press, New York, 1974.

Greenwood, David. *Methodology to Quantify the Potential Net Economic Consequences of Increased NATO Commonality, Standardization and Specialization.* Potomac, Maryland: C & L Associates, Inc. (Prepared for International Economic Affairs Directorate, Office of the Secretary of Defense) August 1978.

Heyhoe, D. C. R. *The Alliance and Europe: Part VI: The European Programme Group.* Adelphi Papers No. 129. London: The International Institute for Strategic Studies, Winter 1976-1977.

Hoad, Malcolm W. *Strengthening NATO Capabilities: A Hi-Lo Ground Force Mix for Area Defense.* (R-2038-AF) Santa Monica, California: Rand Corporation, 1977.

Hoehn, W. E., Jr. et al. *Strategic Mobility Alternatives for the 1980's.* Santa Monica, California: Rand Corporation, March 1977.

James, Robert Rhodes. *Standardization and Common Production of Weapons in NATO.* The Institute for Strategic Studies, No. 3 on Defense Technology and the Western Alliance.

Komer, Robert W. *Needed: Preparation for Coalition War.* (P-5707) Santa Monica, California: Rand Corporation, August 1976.

NATO Defense Planning Workshop. *8th NATO Defense Planning Workshop, Rome, Italy, April 1972: Proceedings.*

NATO, North Atlantic Assembly, Military Committee. *Report of the Sub-Committee on Defense Cooperation.* Presented by Mr. A. Hamilton McDonald, Rapporteur, International Secretariat, October 1979.

Pettijohn, William C. and Druse, William C. *Defense Appropriations Act Speciality Metals Clause and NATO Standardization.* McLean, Virginia: Vertex Corporation (Prepared for Assistant Secretary of Defense, International Security Affairs) April 1977.

"Standardization Policy of the United States." Section 814 (a) of the Department of Defense Appropriation Act, 1976. Relating to Standardization. Section 802, 803, reproduced in *Defense Systems Management Review,* Summer 1977, pp. 61-62.

– *Towards Rationalizing Allied Weapons Production.* Atlantic Papers 1/1976. Paris, Atlantic Institute for International Affairs, 1976, p. 54.

Western European Union. Assembly. *European and Atlantic Cooperation in the Field of Armaments.* Doc. 689. Paris: Western European Union, 1975.

Western European Union. Assembly. Committee on Defense Questions and Armaments. *A European Armaments Policy Symposium: Paris, March 3-4, 1977.* Paris: Western European Union.

Wolf, Charles, Jr. et al. *"Offset" for NATO Procurement of the Airborne Warning and Control System: Opportunities and Implications.* (R-1875-1-PR) Santa Monica, California: Rand Corporation, February 1976.

– *"Offsets" Standardization and Trade Liberalization in NATO.* (P-5779) Santa Monica, California: Rand Corporation, 1976.

Lectures

Callaghan, Thomas A., Jr. "The Conventional Force Balance CAN be Redressed." An address to the American Institute of Aeronautics and Astronautics. Conference on the International Aerospace Market Outlook. Los Angeles, California, August 22, 1978. *The Center for Strategic and International Studies,* Georgetown University, Washington, D.C.

Luns, Joseph M. "Speech by the Secretary General to the Air League," London, October 25, 1974.

Nunn, Sam. "Tactical Nuclear Posture in NATO, A Reassessment." Admiral Raymond A. Spruance lecture given at the U.S. Naval War College, Newport, Rhode Island, June 9, 1979. (Senator from Georgia, member of Senate Armed Forces Committee).

Newspaper Items

Good, Stephen. "F-16's Rolling Off Production Lines." *The Providence Sunday Journal*, October 15, 1978, p. C-8:1-3.

Mathewson, William. "Closing Ranks? Selections of Future NATO Tank Will Give Clue To Success of Alliance's Standardization Plan." *The Wall Street Journal*, January 27, 1976, p. 38:1-5.

Morgan, Dan. "U.S. Seeks to Rebut Show Rapping F16." *The Washington Post*, Friday, March 16, 1979, p. A-4:1-4.

"NATO Ponders New Missile Based in Central Europe." *The New York Times*, reproduced in *The Providence* (RI) *Journal*, July 16, 1979, p. A-2.

Paul, Bill. "Defending Europe: As Soviet Forces Grow, NATO Strives to Lift Its Combat Readiness." *The Wall Street Journal*, 30 June, 1978, p. 1:1, 25:1-2.

Sibera, George. "France Nuzzles to NATO, Fears Soviet Arms Threat." *Newport Daily News*, (Paris, UPI), May 13, 1972, p. 14:1-2.

"Soviet Navy Too Big for Defense is Claim." *Newport Daily News*, (RI) Tuesday, August 14, 1979, p. 9, 1:2 (London, UPI).

Public Documents

NATO Long-Term Defense Programme Reports

NATO. *Decisions of the Defense Planning Committee in Ministerial Session on 18 and 19 May 1978.* Note by the Chairman, Joseph M. A. H. Luns, with Annexes A-J. Brussels: SHAPE, May 24, 1978.

NATO Task Force One. *Long-Term Defense Programme on Readiness.* Final Report 1240/20/S002/78. Brussels: SHAPE, March 1, 1978.

NATO Task Force Two. *Long-Term Defense Programme on Reinforcement.* Report TF2(79)-1. Brussels: SHAPE, February 22, 1978.

NATO Task Force Three. *Long-Term Defense Programme on Reserve Mobilization.* Brussels: SHAPE, March 1, 1978.

NATO Task Force Four. *Long-Term Defense Programme on Maritime Posture.* Brussels: SHAPE, February 21, 1978.

NATO Task Force Five. *Long-Term Defense Programme on Air Defense.* Final Report 1250.05.06/29-5-0/S027/78. Brussels: SHAPE, March 1, 1978.

NATO Task Force Five. *Long-Term Defense Programme on Air Defense.* Enclosure 1, Air Defense Weapons Objective. 1250.05.06/29-5-0/S028/78 Enclosure 2, Surveillance, Command, Control, and Communications Objective. 1250.05.06/29-5-0/S029/78.

Enclosure 3, Identification Objective. 1250.05.06/29-5-0/S030/78
Enclosure 4, Land-Maritime Interface Objective. 1250.05.06/29-5-0/78
NATO Task Force Six. *Long-Term Defense Programme on Communications, Command, and Control.* Final Report 2309.2/1-10/S001/78. Brussels: SHAPE, March 1, 1978.
NATO Task Force Seven. *Long-Term Defense Programme on Electronic Warfare.* Final Report CHEL 3240/12 POL. Brussels: SHAPE, March 6, 1978.
NATO Task Force Eight. *Long-Term Defense Programme on Rationalization.* Final Report LTDP/TF8. Brussels: SHAPE, March 7, 1978.
NATO Task Force Nine. *Long-Term Defense Programme on Consumer Logistics,* Volumes I and II. Final Report LTDP/TF9. Brussels: SHAPE, February 27, 1978.

U.S. Government Congressional Budget Office

U.S. Congressional Budget Office. *Assessing the NATO/Warsaw Pact Military Balance.* Washington: U.S. Government Printing Office, 1977.
U.S. Congressional Budget Office. *Planning U.S. General Purpose Forces: Overview.* Washington: U.S. Government Printing Office, 1977.
U.S. Congressional Budget Office. *Planning U.S. General Purpose Forces: The Tactical Air Forces.* Washington: U.S. Government Printing Office, 1977.
U.S. Congressional Budget Office. *Planning U.S. General Purpose Forces: The Theater Nuclear Forces.* Washington: U.S. Government Printing Office, 1977.
U.S. Congressional Budget Office, *Strengthening NATO: POMCUS and Other Approaches.* Washington: U.S. Government Printing Office, 1979.
U.S. Congressional Budget Office. *U.S. Air and Ground Conventional Forces for NATO: Air Defense Issues.* Washington: U.S. Government Printing Office, 1978.
U.S. Congressional Budget Office. *U.S. Air and Ground Conventional Forces for NATO: Firepower Issues.* Washington: U.S. Government Printing Office, 1978.
U.S. Congressional Budget Office. *U.S. Air and Ground Conventional Forces for NATO: Mobility and Logistics Issues.* Washington: U.S. Government Printing Office, 1978.
U.S. Congressional Budget Office. *U.S. Air and Ground Conventional Forces for NATO: Overview.* Washington: U.S. Government Printing Office, 1978.

U.S. Government Congressional Documents

U.S. Congress. House. Committee on Armed Services. *Hearings on Military Posture and H.R. 10929.* 95th Congress, 2nd Session. Part 1 pp. 1039-1320; Part 3, Book 2, pp. 1383-1527, 1807-1870.

217

U.S. Congress. House. Committee on Armed Services. Special Subcommittee on NATO Commitments. *Report of the Ad Hoc Subcommittee on U.S. Military Commitments to Europe.* House Report 93-978. 93rd Congress, 2nd Session. April 9, 1974.

U.S. Congress. House. Committee on Armed Services. Report of the Committee Delegation to NATO. *NATO and U.S. Security.* 95th Congress, 1st Session. May 25, 1977.

U.S. Congress. House. Committee on Armed Services. *Hearings on NATO Standardization, Interoperability and Readiness and H.R. 11607 and H.R. 12837.* 95th Congress, 2nd Session. March 14, 1978.

U.S. Congress. House. Committee on Armed Services. *NATO Standardization, Interoperability and Readiness,* Print. 95th Congress, 2nd Session.

U.S. Congress. House. Committee on Government Operations. Legislation and National Security Subcommittee. *Hearings on Problems in the Standardization and Interoperability of NATO Military Equipment.* July 21, 1977 and November 10, 1977.

U.S. Congress. House. Committee on Government Operations. *Interim Report on the Standardization and Interoperability of NATO Military Equipment.* House Report 95-806. November 3, 1977.

U.S. Congress. House. Committee on International Relations. *Export Licensing of Advanced Technology: A Review.* Hearings before the Subcommittee on International Trade and Commerce. 94th Congress, 2nd Session, 1976.

U.S. Congress. House. Committee on International Relations. Subcommitee on Legislation and National Security. *Problems in the Standardization and Interoperability of NATO Military Equipment,* Hearing. Washington: U.S. Government Printing Office, 1977. 2 Pts. (Y4. G7417: N81/Pt. 1 & Pt. 2.)

U.S. Congress. House. Committee on International Relations. *NATO Standardization: Political, Economic, and Military Issues for Congress,* Report. Washington: U.S. Government Printing Office, 1977. p. 58 (Y4. 1N8/16: N81/3).

U.S. Congress. House. Committee on International Relations. *Sale of AWACS to NATO.* 94th Congress, 2nd Session.

U.S. Congress. House. Committee on International Relations. Subcommittee on Europe and the Middle East. *Hearings on Western Europe in 1977: Security, Economic, and Political Issues.* 95th Congress, 1st Session. June 14, 28; July 20, 27; October 3-4, 1977.

U.S. Congress. Senate. Committee on Armed Services. Report of Senators Sam Nunn and Dewey F. Bartlett. *NATO and the New Soviet Threat.* January 1977.

U.S. Congress. Senate. Committee on Armed Services. Subcommittee on Manpower and Personnel. *Hearing on NATO Posture and Initiatives.* August 3, 1977.

U.S. Congress, Senate, Committee on Armed Services. *European Defense Cooperation.* Hearings before the Subcommittee on Research and Development, and Manpower and Personnel. 94th Congress, 2nd Session, 1976.

U.S. Congress. Senate. Committee on Foreign Relations. *U.S. Foreign Econ-*

omic Policy Issues: The United Kingdom, France and West Germany. 94th Congress, 1st Session. 1977.

U.S. Congressional Research Service. Library of Congress. *NATO Standardization: Political, Economic and Military Issues for Congress.* Prepared for Congress. House Committee on International Relations. 95th Congress, 1st Session. March, 1977.

U.S. Congressional Research Service. Library of Congress. *NATO Standardization and Defense Procurements Statutes.* January 26, 1978.

U.S. Government Department of Defense Directives and Instructions

DOD 2000.9   International Coproduction Projects and Agreements Between the U.S. and Other Countries or International Organizations.

DOD 2020.4   U.S. Participation in Certain NATO Groups Relating to Research. Development, Production and Logistic Support Within NATO.

DOD 2010.5   DOD Participation in NATO Infrastructure Programme.

DOD 2010.6   Standardization and Interoperability of Weapon Systems and Equipment Within NATO.

DOD 2010.7   Policy on Rationalization of NATO/NATO Member Telecommunication Facilities (C^3I).

DOD 2010.8   Department of Defense Policy for NATO Logistics.

DOD 2015.4   Mutual Weapons Development Data Exchange Programme (MWDDEP) and Defense Development Exchange Programme (DDEP).

DOD 2050.1   Delegated Approval Authority to Negotiate and Conclude International Agreements.

DOD 2140.2   Recoupment of Non-recurring Costs on Sales of U.S. Government Products and Technology.

DOD 3100.3   Cooperation with Allies in R&D of Defense Equipment.

DOD 4120.3   DOD Standardization Programme.

DOD 4155.19   NATO Quality Assurance.

DOD 5000.1   Major Systems Acquisition.

DOD 5000.2   Major Systems Acquisition Process.

DOD 5100.55   United States Security Authority for NATO and CENTO Affairs.

DOD 5010.12   Management of Technical Data.

DOD 5010.19   Configuration Management.

DOD 5100.53   U.S. Participation in Certain NATO Groups Relating to Research Development. Production and Logistic Support of Military Equipment.

DOD 5105.20   Defense Representation, United States Mission to the North Atlantic Treaty Organization and Europe.

DOD 5230.11   Disclosure of Classified Information to Foreign Governments and International Organizations.

DOD 5530.3   International Agreements.

U.S. Government Department of Defense Reports and Memorandums

Bucy, J. Fred et al. *An Analysis of Export Control of U.S. Technology – A DOD Perspective.* Defense Science Board Task Force on Export of U.S. Technology. Washington: Office of the Director of Defense Research and Engineering. February 1976.

U.S. Department of Defense. Office of the Secretary of Defense. *A Report to the Congress on the Standardization of Military Equipment in NATO.* (First Report to the Congress by the Secretary of Defense.) 1975.

U.S. Department of Defense. Office of the Secretary of Defense. *Rationalization/Standardization Within NATO.* (Second Report to the Congress by the Secretary of Defense.) 1976.

U.S. Department of Defense. Office of the Secretary of Defense. *Rationalization/Standardization Within NATO.* (Third Report to the Congress by the Secretary of Defense.) 1977.

U.S. Department of Defense. Office of the Secretary of Defense. *Rationalization/Standardization Within NATO.* (Fourth Report to the Congress by the Secretary of Defense.) 1978.

U.S. Department of Defense. Office of the Secretary of Defense. *Rationalization/Standardization Within NATO.* (Fifth Report to the Congress by the Secretary of Defense.) 1979.

U.S. Department of Defense. Office of the Secretary of Defense. *Department of Defense Annual Report,* Fiscal Year 1980. January 25, 1979.

U.S. Department of the Navy. Chief of Naval Operations. *Analysis of U.S. Navy Possible Purchases of NATO European Equipment to Enhance Standardization and Interoperability.* 1977.

U.S. Department of State and Department of Defense. *Implications for U.S. Foreign Policy and Industry of Standardizing Military Equipment for NATO.* Proceedings of State-Defense Colloquium. March 9, 1975.

U.S. Joint Chiefs of Staff Memo to the Director of Defense Research and Evaluation, September 12, 1977, Subject: *High Priority Categories for NATO Standardization or Interoperability.*

U.S. Military Traffic Management Command. Transportation Engineering Agency. *An Analysis of MTMC Participation in the REFORGER 76 Exercise.* Newport News, Virginia: The Command, 1977.

U.S. Military Traffic Management Command. Transportation Engineering Agency. *An Analysis of MTMC Participation in the REFORGER 77 Exercise.* Newport News, Virginia: The Command, 1978.

U.S. Military Traffic Management Command. Transportation Engineering Agency. *An Analysis of MTMC Participation in the REFORGER 78 Exercise.* Newport News, Virginia: The Command, 1979.

U.S. Government General Accounting Office

U.S. General Accounting Office. *Analysis of the Joint Chiefs Study on Strategic Mobility: Further Study Recommendations* (PSAD-78-126, B-163058). Washington: U.S. General Accounting Office, August 1978.

U.S. General Accounting Office. *Benefits and Drawbacks of U.S. Participation in Military Cooperative Research and Development Programmes with Allied Countries* (PSAD-74-42). Washington: U.S. General Accounting Office, June 4, 1974.

U.S. General Accounting Office. *Planning Host Nation Support for U.S. Troops in Europe* (LCD-78-402). Washington: U.S. General Accounting Office, August 9, 1978.

U.S. General Accounting Office. *Problems in Supporting Weapons Systems Produced by Other Countries* (LSD 76-450). Washington: U.S. General Accounting Office, January 4, 1977.

U.S. General Accounting Office. *Relationships Between U.S. and NATO Military Command Structures — Need for Closer Integration* (LCD-77-447). Washington: U.S. General Accounting Office, October 1977.

U.S. General Accounting Office. *Transatlantic Cooperation in Developing Weapon Systems for NATO — A European Perspective* (PSAD-79-26). Washington: U.S. General Accounting Office, March 21, 1979.

U.S. General Accounting Office. *Sharing the Defense Burden: The Multinational F-16 Aircraft Programme* (PSAD-77-40). Washington: U.S. General Accounting Office, August 15, 1977.

U.S. General Accounting Office. *Standardization in NATO: Improving the Effectiveness and Economy of Mutual Defense Efforts* (PSAD-78-2). Washington: U.S. General Accounting Office, January 19, 1978.

U.S. General Accounting Office. *Status of the F-16 Aircraft Programme* (B-163058). Washington: U.S. General Accounting Office, April 1, 1977.

U.S. General Accounting Office. *U.S. Military Equipment Prepositioned in Europe — Significant Improvements Made but Some Problems Remain.* (LCD-78-431A). Washington: U.S. General Accounting Office, December 5, 1978.

U.S. General Accounting Office. *Continuing Problems with U.S. Military Equipment Prepositioned in Europe* (LCD-76-441). Washington: U.S. General Accounting Office, July 12, 1976. (Secret.)

U.S. Government Military Services and Institutions

Bartlett, Robert R. et al. *Centralized C^3 in NATO: Force Multiplier or Short Circuit.* Maxwell Air Force Base, AL: Air War College, 1978.

Burns, William F. *Cohesion and Competition in the Atlantic Community: Implications for Security.* Carlisle Barracks. PA: U.S. Army War College, 1976.

Carver, Charles F., III. *An Examination and Evaluation of the NATO Maintenance and Supply Organization.* Wright-Patterson Air Force Base, OH: School of Systems and Logistics, Air Force Institute of Technology, 1976.

Cooling, Benjamin. *Lessons of Allied Interoperability: A Portent for the Future.* Carlisle Barracks, PA: U.S. Army War College, 1978.

Deutsch, Harold C. *A New American Defensive Doctrine for Europe?* Carlisle Barracks, PA: U.S. Army War College, 1976.

Dickerson, I. W. *Preparing for Nuclear War.* Maxwell Air Force Base, AL: Air Command and Staff College, 1978.

Francis, George F. *NATO Infrastructure: Is There a Better Way?* Maxwell Air Force Base, AL: Air War College, 1976.

Gentry, Jerauld R. *Evolution of the F-16 Multinational Fighter.* Washington, D.C.: Industrial College of the Armed Forces, 1976.

Grassman, James W. *Standardized Operational Flying Training: Does NATO Need It Now?* Maxwell Air Base, AL: Air War College, 1978.

King, Patrick. *Major U.S. Troop Withdrawal From Europe and Subsequent European Defense Options.* Maxwell Air Force Base, AL: Air War College, 1975.

Madison, John H., Jr. et al. *NATO Rationalization and the U.S. Army.* Carlisle Barracks, PA: U.S. Army War College, 1977.

Munger, Murl. D. et al. *NATO Warning Times — Validity and Implications for Reserve Component Deployment.* Carlisle Barracks, PA: U.S. Army War College, 1977.

NATO Defense Posture in an Environment of Strategic Parity and Precision Weaponry. Carlisle Barrracks, PA: U.S. Army War College, 1976.

Paul, Herbert D. et al. *NATO Logistics: Factors Affecting Theater Air Warfare with an Outline of a Unified Commander's Basic Logistic Plan.* Maxwell Air Force Base, AL: Air War College, 1977.

Rasmussen, Robert D. *The A-10 in Central Europe: A Concept of Deployment-Employment.* Maxwell Air Force Base, AL: Air War College, 1978.

Steadmar, Kenneth A. *NATO Strategy for the Future: A Concept.* Fort Leavenworth, KS: U.S. Army Command and General Staff College, 1976.

Stratton, Jerry R. *Military Unionization: Has it Crippled NATO?* Maxwell Air Force Base, AL: Air War College, 1978.

Szyliowicz, Joseph S. and O'Neill, Bard E. *Petropolitics and Atlantic Alliance.* Washington, D.C.: National War College, 1976.

Taylor, Peter P. W. *NATO's Dispersal Capability: A Fatal Flaw?* Maxwell Air Force Base, AL: Air War College, 1977.

Teichmann, Axel B. *Central Region Air Force Command and Control Structure: Past-Present-Future.* Maxwell Air Force Base, AL: Air War College, 1977.

Thamasett, Otto J. *The Army and the Two-Way Street — Foreign Systems Acquisition.* Fort Belvoir, VA: Defense Systems Management College, 1977.

Winters, George R. *NATO Standardization Versus U.S. Data Releasability: An Approach to Resolving the Conflict.* Fort Belvoir, VA: Defense Systems Management College, 1977.

Wissinger, Kenneth L. *Creek Swing/Ready Switch — A Challenge Met.* Maxwell Air Force Base, AL: Air War College, 1978.

U.S. Government Office of Management and Budget

U.S. Office of Management and Budget. *1976 International Conference on Procurement and Grants Management.* July 1976.

Index

responsibilities, 103-110
— permanent, enfranchised organizations, non-NATO and NATO, 104
— institutionalize top level arrangements, 104
— strengthen the IEPG, 104
— stronger offices at ministerial levels, 104
— International Staff (IS) as coordinating chair, 105
— strengthen and enlarge IS authority and responsibilities, 105
— create a NATO Weapons Development/Production/Management Council, 106
— create Weapons Family Managers, 107
— create a NATO Weapons Procurement Agency (NWPA), 108
— continue and enlarge NAMSO, 109
— continue MAS, ASI, AGARD, 110
EXOCET — Naval Surface-to-Surface Missile, 37

Facer, Roger, *The Alliance and Europe: Part III Weapons Procurement in Europe — Capabilities and Choices*, 86
Facey, David, Director of Air Defense Systems, NATO, 21, 23
Fairey, 29
Family of Weapons (FoW), 52, 56, 62, 74, 85, 106, 107, 108
See also Weapons Family Managers (WFM's)
F-16 A High Performance Fighter Aircraft, 10, 16, 26-30, 38
F-16 Air Combat Fighter Aircraft, 10, 12, 17, 26, 33, 38, 62, 76, 85
F-16 A High-Performance Fighter Aircraft, 26-30

— background, 27
— purpose and participants, 27
— cost and offsets, 28
— organization and management, 28, 29
— problems, 29, 30
— summary and postscript, 30
F-104 G Starfighter, 1, 10, 13, 16, 27, 32, 38, 40, 54, 57
first hypothesis, 11
— findings, 11
Fokker, 29
Force Goals, 146
Force Proposal, 145
Fouquet, David, "To Compete and/or Cooperate? The Atlantic Arms 'Race'," *Military Review*, 72
Four Power Group, 104
FINABEL — France, Italy, the Netherlands, Germany, Belgium, Luxembourg, and the United Kingdom, 62, 63, 104
Franco-German Roland, 22
French Ministry of Aeronautics, 12

General Dynamics Corp., 29
General Memoranda of Understanding (GMOUS), 60, 63, 74
United States agreements with Canada, the U.K., Germany, France, Italy, the Netherlands, Norway, Portugal, Greece, Turkey, Denmark and Belgium, 63 and Appendix E
General Support Rocket/Missile System, 38
Germany (also FRG), 21, 22
Goodman, Elliot, 71
"The Puzzle of European Defense: The Issue of Arms Procurement," *The Atlantic Community Quarterly*, 71, 72
groups of experts, 14

Haig, General Alexander, 8
Half-truths, myths and certain

226

vs. deterrence, 98
— "go it alone", 98
— European industrial base fragmented, 98
— burden sharing unresolved, 98
— lack of structure for cooperation, 98
— untouchables, out-of-phase projects, 98
— reluctance to face the magnitude of the problem, 98

Jaguar — Ground Attack Aircraft, 16, 27, 28, 39, 58
Joint Tactical Information Distribution System (JTIDS), 46
juste retour, 103

Komer, Robert W., "Origins and Objectives of NATO Long-Term Defence Programme", 66
Kormoran — Air-to-Ship Missile, 39

LaBerge Walter, Assistant Secretary General for Defence Support, 26
Lanchester's equation, 83
Lance — Tactical Ballistics Missile, 39, 54
Light Anti-Tank Weapon, M72, 40
Long-Term Defence Programme (LTDP), 10, 21, 56, 148, and Appendix D, 135-150
Luns, Secretary General Joseph M., 7, 35

Main Battle Tank, 45
Major Commanders, 147
Mallard, 45
management orphans of NATO, 90, 93-94
managerial principles — 1969, 15
Mark 44 torpedo, 10, 40, 43, 57
See also NATO Mark 44 torpedo
Mark 46 torpedo, 40, 43, 57
Marshall plan, 14
Martel — Air-to-Surface Anti-Radar

and TV-Guided Missile, 39
Memorandum of Agreement, 18
Messerschmitt-Boelkow-Blohm (Euromissile), 23
Milan — Anti-Tank Wire-Guided Missile, 40, 51
Miley, General Henry, Jr., "Weapon Standardization," *National Defense*, 72
Military/Strategic/Doctrinal Arguments, 87
Military Dependence vs. Independence, 87
The Military Need for More Voice in New Weapons, 88
Military Communications/Command and Control, 89
The Military/Industrial/Governmental Complex, 89
Mirage, 27
Mobile Acoustic Communications Study, 46
Modes of Collaboration and an Assessment, Appendix G, 193-196
— The Specialization Mode, 193
— The Merger Mode, 193
— The Institutional Mode, 193
— The Permissive Mode, 193
— The Functional Cooperation Mode, 194
— The Pooled Production Mode, 194
— The Integrated Project Mode, 194
— A Technological/Production Common Community Mode, 194-95
— Diverse Examples of Cooperative Programmes, 195-96
Moss, 19
Multinational Configuration Control Board, 29
Multinational Memorandum of Understanding (MMOU or MOU), 18, 25, 27, 28
Multinational Program Management

228

231

233

About the Author

Dr. Alexander H. Cornell, currently professor in the Department of Economics and Management, Rhode Island College, Providence, R.I., carried out the research for and writing of this work as a NATO Fellow for 1979–1980. He has studied, taught and practiced in such varied fields as Business Administration, Systems Analysis, Personnel Management, Public Administration, History, Logistics and Naval Science.

COLOPHON

letter: baskerville 11/13 and 9/11
setter: H. Charlesworth, England
printer: Samson Sijthoff Grafische Bedrijven, Alphen aan den Rijn
binder: Callenbach, Nijkerk